Violence Inevitable

Violence Inevitable

The Play of Force and Respect in Derrida, Nietzsche, Hobbes, and Berlin

Rick Parrish

LEXINGTON BOOKS

A division of
ROWMAN & LITTLEFIELD PUBLISHERS, INC.
Lanham • Boulder • New York • Toronto • Plymouth, UK

LEXINGTON BOOKS

A division of Rowman & Littlefield Publishers, Inc.
A wholly owned subsidiary of The Rowman & Littlefield Publishing Group, Inc.
4501 Forbes Boulevard, Suite 200
Lanham, MD 20706

Estover Road
Plymouth PL6 7PY
United Kingdom

British Library Cataloguing in Publication Information Available

Library of Congress Cataloging-in-Publication Data

Parrish, Rick, 1975–
Violence inevitable : the play of force and respect in Derrida, Nietzsche, Hobbes, and Berlin / Rick Parrish.
p. cm.
Includes bibliographical references and index.
ISBN-13: 978-0-7391-1212-0 (cloth : alk. paper)
ISBN-10: 0-7391-1212-0 (cloth : alk. paper)
1. Violence. 2. Violence—Social aspects. 3. Justice. I. Title.
B105.V5P37 2006
179.7—dc22 2006023223

Printed in the United States of America

™ The paper used in this publication meets the minimum requirements of American National Standard for Information Sciences—Permanence of Paper for Printed Library Materials, ANSI/NISO Z39.48–1992.

For Frank Gagliardi

Contents

Acknowledgments

Foremost among those I wish to thank are Howard Schweber and Eric Gorham. I am supremely grateful for their years of tireless guidance. I would also like to offer my special thanks to Richard Boyd, Patrick Riley, Lester Hunt, and Don Downs, and also to Gary Herbert, Bernie Yack, and Marion Smiley, who have all provided important comments and critiques that helped me make this project better than I thought it could be. Melissa Parrish (my sister), Meredith Clark, and Tricia Louque also helped me improve this project in ways I would not otherwise have conceived. I would also like to thank Jeff Johnson, John Evans, and Dan Kapust; the various participants of the UW-Madison Political Theory Colloquium; from Taiwan: Steve, Eric, and Donna; DBZ; from RXS: David, Abbey, Ryan, Katie, John, Chad, Erik, and X; from BSECKF: Fu Leung, Dana Daniels, Tim, Andrea, Dan, and Ben; from CPT: Sarah, Meghan, Jacob (i.e. "Skippy"), Rick, Rob, and Tanya; Sarah Fell from Lexington Books; my late dog, Hobbes; and my parents—all of whom, whether they knew it or not (and whether they wanted to or not), contributed in some important way to this work. Finally, I would like to offer my thanks to the several detractors I encountered at conferences, whose skepticism proved Nietzsche's point that our best enemies can be our best friends.

Introduction

A beginning is a very delicate time, as much for a book as for a proposition or a revolution. This is especially so because in each case the beginning is written after the fact. One simply does not know what one has until one has finished it, and although no book is ever really finished, just as no law ever ceases conserving itself and no revolution ever ceases justifying itself, at some point one must put down one's pen or one's sword, take a deep breath, and craft a beginning to the story. Written by the author or the victor, this anterior, *post-hoc* beginning produces "proper interpretative models to read in return, to give sense, necessity and above all legitimacy"[1] to the work, which was itself without a justificatory narrative until it was evaluated and its beginning was crafted. As endings, beginnings are thus not only summaries—they are in some sense exercises in *post hoc* self-legitimation. If they fail, the revolution was always just a crime, the proposition was always simply a reiteration, and the book was never anything more than the sum of ink, paper, time, sweat, and seclusion.

The ink, paper, time, sweat, and seclusion traced by this paper are unified into a book by the one question that motivated it and the several themes that, woven together, constitute the main thrust of its narrative. I had the good fortune to be reading Derrida and Nietzsche at the same time, when I realized that, although they both agreed that humans are the creators, rather than the discoverers, of meaning and value in the world, they used this common premise to carry their thought in completely different directions. Thus, the original question that, in retrospect, was the foundational inquiry of *Violence Inevitable*, was this: If humans are the creators of meaning and value, rather than the subjects of some higher or prior authority, how must we act in order to be true to this principle? It is usually assumed that if humans are the creators, rather than the discoverers, of meaning and value in the world, we would do justice to them by voluntarily circumscribing our own creations of meaning so as to allow others to exist as the independent creators that they are by nature. But if humans are value creators it is also possible to argue that the most just person is she who promotes her own meanings and values as strenuously as possible, both in order to do justice to her own creative human nature, as well as to give others what is due them as creators, i.e., another meaning against which to struggle. Considered in the most banal terms, the issue is this: We often argue more vehemently with those we respect than we do with those we do not respect. Although it may appear counterintuitive, the case may be that justice for beings that are fundamentally creators, rather than discoverers, involves the attempt to overcome others' creativity and convince them of the merits of our own positions. On the other hand, those we consider beneath us receive the injustice of being ignored, and hence allowed to continue their own creations unmolested. Nothing about the nature of persons as creators of meaning and value necessarily clashes with this violent interpretation of justice.

In chapter one I examine the logic of these two possible paths to justice for meaning creators by discussing Derrida and Nietzsche, the representatives of these two paths through which I originally accessed this dilemma or aporia.

Jacques Derrida has championed the more common, perhaps more peaceful, approach by advocating deconstruction as a technique to bring silenced voices into ongoing human discourse. He contends that we approach justice as we come to respect the other's unique creative voice and let, as much as possible, that other maintain the independence of his creative nature. Friedrich Nietzsche, on the other hand, is well known for arguing that the healthiest and liveliest persons are those who struggle for discursive dominance. He suggests that justice is done when we embrace our creative natures by trying to overcome the creativity of others and impose our own systems of meaning and value upon them. By Nietzsche's account, this contest for creative supremacy constitutes justice for ourselves because we do not voluntarily stifle our own creativity, as well as justice for others because, by struggling against them, we tacitly accept them as equal creative entities who are worthy to engage in a contest for creative dominance.

Although Derrida's and Nietzsche's positions appear diametrically opposed, I argue that they actually contaminate, infringe upon, or breach each other's boundaries, demonstrating what Derrida calls an "economy of violence." This constitutes the first major theme of *Violence Inevitable*—the contention that some level of violence is indeed inevitable to any politics or any intersubjective situation. Derrida's arguably more peaceful justice and Nietzsche's potentially more violent justice each contain elements of violence and peacefulness, as each author in fact recognizes. This economy of violence shows that, whether we pursue justice as either a letting-be of the other or as an aggression against the independence of the other, violence is inevitable for persons as creators. We are destined (doomed, some would say) to the political process of trading violences among each other as we all struggle to impose our own meanings and values upon the world, to the detriment of the meanings and values proposed by others. We may act out this violence with more or less vigor, but it remains an inevitable and indispensable part of the human condition.

Pursuant to this argument, I elaborate a definition of violence that has caused concern among some colleagues. Following Derrida, I suggest that violence is fundamentally a lack of respect for the personhood of an other. Persons are the creators of meaning and value in the world, so any act is violent to the extent that it rejects an other's status as an independent source of meaning. This definition has caused concern because some feel it is overbroad: any act is violent to the extent that it rejects the creative personhood of the other. Thus, murder is supremely violent because it destroys any possibility that the other can be a creative entity at any point in the future, but a verbal argument also contains an element of violence because it is an attempt to overcome the independent creativity of the other and convince the other of one's own position. It is obviously not my intention to suggest that an argument is as violent as a murder. Rather, I intend to show that there is a basic affinity among many otherwise extremely dissimilar acts. Much of what persons do is premised upon a rejection of the independent creativity of the other in favor of our own dominance. Although we may not often recognize it, some level of violence among persons is inevitable.

The mutual contamination of violence and justice that is necessitated by the economy of violence is also reflected in the often infuriating paradoxes within and among justice, violence, law, and freedom. These paradoxes and infringements are ubiquitous, necessary, and inevitable. For instance, justice is paradoxical because it requires both freedom and law—it demands the liberty to choose as well as a standard that must be met. The terms and boundaries of these paradoxes (rather too complex to elaborate upon in a brief introduction) are laid out in chapters one and two, and are explored in depth throughout this entire work. These paradoxes at the base of our human creations serve the important function of arresting mechanistic calculability; they guarantee our existential freedom. If the fundamental bases of intersubjectivity were without these paradoxes, there would be no room at the core of our existence for creation, interpretation, or freedom—there would be only the simple mechanistic unfolding of a calculable process.

As the ongoing human discursive project through which these inevitable violences and paradoxes are played out as we continually attempt to reach final, unassailable answers to questions of violence and justice, politics is also protected by the aporetic structures at the base of our humanity. The constant political struggle to create and promulgate answers to the fundamental questions of human existence—which is at the core of all politics—is itself part of the nature of discursive intersubjectivity. In his State of Nature, Thomas Hobbes shows us politics is its rawest form. Because in the natural condition of total discursive freedom individuals create different sets of meanings and values, they are unable to communicate or coordinate. Without these abilities they are resigned to constant, pseudo-Nietzschean, battles to determine whose created system will be iterated over all others. Only when one person, who Hobbes calls the Leviathan, dominates all signification by forcing his personhood upon all others, can we finally have peace. But this violent peace, accomplished by the imposition of one set of meanings and values upon all others, is degrading to the creative personality of the subjects. Isaiah Berlin sees this and all such enforcement of one value system as a positive libertarian destruction of the negative liberty that constitutes the essence of our creative human nature. Thus Berlin and Derrida tend to present economically peaceful answers to the question of justice, preferring to maximize the sphere of negative liberty in which individual persons are left free to realize their capacities as independent creators. Nietzsche and Hobbes, on the other hand, tend to argue for the imposition of one system of meanings and values upon others. Whereas Hobbes contends that this is the only way to ensure the felicitous living that makes the enjoyment of our vestigial liberty possible, Nietzsche argues that we show the greatest respect to both ourselves and others when we joyfully live out our natures as meaning creators, striving for discursive dominance and giving others a worthy opponent against which to fight.

But as I assert at the end of chapter three, any final answer to the questions of justice and violence—whether it be a relatively peaceful Derridean or Berlinian answer, or a more violent Nietzschean or Hobbesian response—would mean the end of politics. As the end of that distinctly human process of constantly creating and contesting new meanings and values in the world, final answers to questions of violence and justice would mark the end of our humanity and the beginning of our existence as merely phenomenal entities, devoid of any remainder or excess beyond the programmatic enforcement and enactment of determined responses.

This leads me chapter four, in which I operationalize the aporias at the core of human existence by examining the ambiguities in the pursuit of public safety in an unpredictable contemporary world. As the state's disciplinary technologies and the ubiquity of legalism (as the mechanistic, rule-oriented aspect of our human nature) continue to grow in the worthy name of public safety, we may also be in danger of losing the unpredictability or incalculability (our freedom-oriented aspect) that is necessary to our humanity. As I discuss throughout this work, and which has been brought into high relief after 9/11, it is a natural part of the structure of discursive intersubjectivity for persons, groups, and states to try to remove the danger represented by both incalculability and by others' abilities to reject one's own promulgated positions. But that undecidability and creative potential is not only the possibility of danger, it is also the opportunity for freedom, which is the opportunity for humanity. Although some level of violence is both necessary for safety and inevitable as part of discursive intersubjectivity, too much violence in the name of security would end freedom and politics, and thus destroy our humanity. In our ongoing post-9/11 debates about increased security measures, we must concern ourselves not only with restrictions on our movement and the privacy of our personal information—we must also consider that increasing levels of security and legalism may finally overcome our uniquely human undecidability/unknowability. This would render us impervious to attack, but it would also destroy our humanity.

It is a near-truism that Plato started the philosophical project of systematically investigating the universally objective Truths of the universe. Although his conception of persons as the discoverers of meaning and value continues to dominate even today, during the twentieth century it became a more common idea that humans are the creators of value and meaning in the world. According to this idea that persons are creators, meanings and values are not exogenously pre-given, as with Platonic Forms, natural law, the clear and distinct light of reason, or objective biological data, and subsequently discovered by philosophical investigation. They are created by persons thinking and acting within a world that has no meanings or values outside of those imposed upon it by creative persons.

It is well beyond the scope of this work to offer a history of the premise that persons are creators, so it must suffice for me to note that this concept—perhaps one of the great paths not taken by Western Philosophy—is not simply the angst-ridden, late twentieth century invention it is often taken to be. In fact, the idea that persons create meaning and value within a world devoid of exogenous truth is at least as old as the pre-Socratic Protagoras, who claimed that "of all things, the measure is man."[2] As I discuss in chapter two, no less an Enlightenment figure than Thomas Hobbes made the strong claim that "to *know truth*, is the same thing as to *remember* that it was made by ourselves."[3] For Hobbes, who occasionally quotes Protagoras, the creative nature of persons leads to the brutality of the state of nature and necessitates a sovereign that will make and enforce specific meanings and values. Among other pre-contemporary figures, Friedrich Nietzsche is well-known for his belief that "*there are altogether no moral facts*."[4] He therefore argues that "men gave themselves all their good and evil. Verily, they did not take it, they did not find it, nor did it come to them as a voice form heaven."[5]

The twentieth century witnessed existentialists like Martin Heidegger and Jean-Paul Sartre, who are widely recognized to claim that persons create meaning and value within a world devoid of objective truth. Sartre himself says that "I apprehend myself at once as totally free and as not being able to derive the meaning of the world except as coming from myself,"[6] a clear formulation of the existentialist idea that, because existence precedes essence, persons imbue both themselves and all other objects with meaning and value. As I demonstrate in chapter three, Isaiah Berlin has brought this concept into the realm of liberal theory. For Berlin, "the desire of men not to have their personalities set at too low a value, assumed to be incapable of autonomous, original 'authentic' behaviour, even if such behaviour is"[7] both one of the main reasons to pursue a system of negative liberty, and a primary motivation for national liberation movements that strive for the recognition of their members as persons.

In chapter one, I argue that Jacques Derrida agrees with this proposition that persons are the creators, rather than the discoverers, of meaning and value in the world. In fact, one of this book's most unique contributions is this identification of the common premise—that persons are the creators of meaning and value in the world—within the work of four such diverse figures as Derrida, Nietzsche, Hobbes, and Berlin. By reading these four major figures together and entwining their different but complementary investigations of the nature and implications of human creativity, I hope to render a more complete account of my themes than if I explored only one of these authors. It is not my intention to unnecessarily blur the lines among their distinct contributions, or to gloss over the disagreements among them. Rather, the very divergence of their approaches and answers to questions of violence and justice for creative humanity is itself an important aspect of my project. Even so, as I hope to show throughout this book, their disagreements tend to be more complementary than we might usually expect. This is an important goal, since political theorists too often erect elaborate barriers between modernists and postmodernists, between liberals and non-liberals, and between Nietzsche and nearly everyone else. When we focus on the similarities of these distinctive figures, how they use different approaches to yield different answers to similar questions, we may gain a more robust and well-rounded insight into justice and violence, two of the more important concepts in political theory.

It is customary to begin any work that explores Derrida by rehearsing the well-trodden history of structuralism, existentialism, postmodernity in general, and poststructuralism in particular. The author then generally mounts a practiced defense of Derrida's overall project, and critiques his major critics as flippant, mean-spirited, provincial, or basically obtuse. The list of books devoted to the basics of postmodernism and the important ongoing debates about Derrida is long but distinguished, so I do not feel it necessary to restate these arguments again.[8] Throughout this book I have done my best to define Derrida's (and others') sometimes arcane terms, and to carefully elaborate all the connections I make among my primary sources' ideas. Given this effort, I expect that my intended audience will find my work readable and interesting, even if their primary interest does not lie in seeking clarity within the more abstruse texts of recent political theory.

Notes

1 Derrida, Jacques, "Force of Law: The 'Mystical Foundation of Authority,'" *Cardozo Law Review* 11, Nov., 1990, p. 993.

2 DK80b1.

3 Hobbes, Thomas, *Philosophical Rudiments Concerning Government and Society* (1650), XVIII.4.

4 Nietzsche, Friedrich, *Twilight of the Idols*, in Kaufmann, Walter, trans., *The Portable Nietzsche*, New York: Penguin Books, 1982, p. 501.

5 Nietzsche, *Thus Spoke Zarathustra*, 171.

6 Sarte, Jean-Paul, *Being and Nothingness*, Translated by Hazel E. Barnes, New York: Washington Square Press, 1992, 78.

7 Isaiah Berlin, "Two Concepts of Liberty," in *Liberty: Incorporating Four Essays on Liberty*, Ed. Henry Hardy, Oxford: Oxford UP, 2002, 206.

8 Those who are just beginning their investigation into the rise of postmodernism may want to begin with Lawrence Cahoone's anthology of primary source material from the seventeenth century to the present, entitled *From Modernism to Postmodernism.* One of the more rigorous and interesting commentaries on postmodernity in general is *The Postmodern Turn* by Kellner and Best, in which they explore the rise of several manifestations of postmodernist thought from Kierkegaard and Nietzsche to the present. *The Condition of Postmodernity: An Enquiry into the Origins of Cultural Change*, by David Harvey, is another excellent examination of postmodernism that does this job far better than I could here. Jonathan Culler's *On Deconstruction* is another fascinating work: as Culler traces the development of poststructuralism's historical growth he simultaneously explains the inevitability of its often infuriatingly paradoxical methods and conclusions. Readers who would like even-handed, readable introductions to Derrida would do well to study *Deconstruction*, by Christopher Norris, as well as the non-academic but very useful (and well-illustrated) *Derrida for Beginners*, by Jim Powell. For a deeper but still accessible explanation of deconstruction, read *Deconstruction in a Nutshell: A Conversation with Jacques Derrida*, by John D. Caputo.

Chapter One
The Aporia of Justice and the Economy of Violence

I. Person as Face

In a moment of uncharacteristic brevity, Derrida writes that "all value is first constituted by a theoretical subject."[1] The presence of this theoretical subject, this person, is announced primarily by the face, "the nonmetaphorical unity of body, glance, speech, and thought,"[2] that "exchanges its glance"[3] with another face. A mere visage, the form of a face without the face's intersubjective essence, becomes a face only when it is both seeing and seen, and only other faces see. Therefore, the existence of this face, of this "inaugural unity of a naked glance and of a right to speech"[4] is a fundamentally intersubjective event, requiring the presence of faces against which to "face off." Without an interlocutor, the visage or format of a potential face can never become an actual face.

Approaching the same point from another direction, as he often does, in order to arrest the reification of one word or angle of attack, Derrida explains that this intersubjectivity is necessary for the existence of a face because "the ear of the other says me to me and constitutes the *autos* of my autobiography."[5] The voice of one face is not properly speech until it is received as such by an other, when "the other will have perceived with a keen-enough ear what I will have addressed or destined to him or her."[6] Language requires both a speaker and a listener who is an other to the speaker—in fact, this "structure 'inside-outside' . . . is language itself"[7]—so the speaking face can only be such when juxtaposed to another face that, rather than merely listening passively, is constituting the speaking other intersubjectively through its own reception of the message.

When encountering the face of the other, one necessarily cognizes that face "*as other*, that is, as that which does not reveal itself, as that which cannot be made thematic."[8] The face is not perfectly knowable or classifiable, it is neither the allegorical re-presentation of some absent person or merely "a visage which may be the surface of things or animal faces, aspects, or species"[9]—the face is that which is not *I*, that which exceeds one's grasp and manipulation of the merely phenomenal. The face is understood as the "presence, *ousia*"[10] of a person because it is this "glance-speech,"[11] manifested in the physical presence of the organs of the face that constitutes the fundamental fact of personhood. An object is a theoretical subject, a person, only if it has this ability to interact with others through sense and the promulgation of meaning through language. Because this use of language is not merely a phenomenal addition to a preconstituted subject, but is rather fundamental to the existence of the intersubjective subject itself, thought "already must be speech, but above all the body must also remain a language."[12] Persons therefore are primarily discursive entities that occur as language, existing face-to-face as the creators of meaning as they operate as language within the world.

This special relationship among faces is itself characterized by a "maintain[-ance of] distance"[13] because the presence of the other as face is irreducible to a mere phenomenal object. "Through its freedom of speech," its innate existence as sovereign communicator and user of language in order to assert its otherness to all others and transcendence of imposed categories or identities, the face interrupts all the "historical totalities"[14] that would seek to reduce it to mere objectiveness. In this invocation of the freedom of speech we have already come upon the politics inherent in all intersubjectivity. Although the freedom of speech appealed to here is on one level simply a *capability* of speech, it also conjures the core of an inseparable political project. Intersubjectivity is not necessarily a given—it is a political accomplishment achieved and sustained by the mutual recognition of faces through a continuing acknowledgment of each other's freedom of speech. More than the simple capability to communicate, the freedom of this speech is simultaneously the human existential freedom that comes from being more than a mere phenomenal object, as well as the political right to be heard and hence recognized by others.

The basic connection of this face-to-face relationship, "this being-together as separation," is an intersubjective relationship among faces who recognize each other as such, entities that are essentially other to each other but capable of existence towards each other through language. This face-to-face relationship of related othernesses "precedes . . . society, collectivity, community"[15] or any other corporate identity. These secondary discursive accomplishments all require both the fundamental recognition of the otherness of other faces as persons, rather than as mere phenomenal objects, as well as the basic understanding that, as faces, they are mutually constituting and hence related. Again we see the politics at the heart of intersubjectivity. Unless the face maintains its discursive distance from other faces, the face ceases to exist; unless a person or a people continually enforces its freedom of speech, its right to independent personhood, it devolves into mere visage, mere animal phenomenality.

Thus the intersubjectivity of mutually constituting others is a primary relationship that makes possible all community, but does not constitute it. Inasmuch as faces are irreducible to mere objects for each other, and are able to relate discursively because as face-glance they are constituted as language, all subsequent relationships are built upon this fundamental association of faces that are others. It is the discursive nature of the basic face-to-face relationship that renders possible community, society, and all other subsequent forms of interpersonal relationship. As interaction among individual persons whose nature it is to constitute value in the world, this face-to-face relationship "marks the limit of all power, of all violence, and the origin of the ethical."[16]

"A mortal [who] can only start from here,"[17] from the place of his own perspectival face, must interact with other faces, all of which manifest an "idiomatic hereness"[18] as presences in the world, but which also exceed the world of simple phenomenality. When that face meets other perspectival faces, the ensuing relationship among others is ethical primarily because of that fundamental otherness. Ethics itself, as a concept that applies among different persons, begins with the face-to-face relationship of these perspectival glance-speech unities. As the beginning of ethics (as well as politics), this intersubjective moment that opens relations among persons inaugurates the possibilities of respect for and violence towards others.

II. Violence

Although the term 'violence' is often taken to refer primarily to physical acts that harm the body of oneself or another, we also commonly speak of psychological, emotional, and other types of violence. Our common usages of violence are perhaps best captured by Giuliano Pontara, who formulated a careful multipart definition of violence that avoids drawing some of the harsh distinctions common in the work of some analytical philosophers.[19] Pontara writes that "for violence to occur the following condition is necessary: there is at least a human being who (passively or actively) causes another human being's (physical or psychological) death or who (by doing or omitting to do certain actions) inflicts (physical or mental) suffering upon another human being or who (by doing or omitting to do certain actions) disables him (physically or psychologically)."[20] Although this and other related definitions of violence are practical and simple, and much embraced by social science, they refer only to forms of violence that are derivative of what Derrida calls arché-violence, the most fundamental and primordial form of violence. Within Derrida's writings one can trace a very useful archeology of violence that yields this basic arché-violence that is inherent to all manifestations of violence. Derrida does not necessarily disagree with definitions like Pontara's; he claims to get behind them to their most essential structure, to their most basic and irreducible form. He traces this kernel that constitutes the core structure of violence through such common daily events as physical assault and other inflictions of suffering, down to the fundamentally discursive nature of all interpersonal relations.

This basically discursive violence, "is tied" not to our use of language to, as Pontara puts it, cause a person's psychological death or disability, but to the very "possibility of language"[21] itself that Derrida says structures our relationships with other persons. Of course we are used to speaking of the violences of the use of language, the most paradigmatic of which is perhaps the magical incantation. Jean-Jacques LeCercle discusses magical incantations, the most blunt form of violent language, in which "hardly has the magic formula escaped my lips when my foe collapses."[22] Although such magic is fictitious, a belief in it gives real power to this language: among people who believe in the language-violence of magic, for example, the declaration that someone is a witch is an "annunciation [that] works like an illicit performative, one with retroactive effect"[23] on the labeled person. Even though "there are no witches in reality . . . there are witches in speech,"[24] and using that term against someone can lead to dire consequences—as evidenced, for example, by the late seventeenth century witch trials of Salem, Massachusetts. By simply declaring a specific individual to be a criminal, bills of attainder act in a similar fashion. When a legislative body passes a bill of attainder, it bypasses the judicial process to redefine a specific person as a criminal who must be punished.

In both of these examples, the physical violence invoked by language is the result of an ontologically prior violence of labeling that is inherent in the nature of signification itself. It is this prior, more basic violence that Derrida looks behind. Although it is clear that language can incite physical violence, language is also one of the primary weapons used to inflict emotional and psychological violence. Perhaps the most common way of doing this is by claiming that a person is signified by some noun that has negative connotations, as with insults. Because they are based upon a pejorative, limiting, or otherwise negative labeling, the violences of insult are derivative of the more fundamental violence of all significations and appellations in general—the violence that is itself the very structure of discourse.

The fundamental, pre-ethical, arché-violence described by Derrida is the basis and format for these common types of linguistic violence, as well as physical violence. Violence can only be perpetrated by a person (a face). According to Derrida "there is no natural or [merely] physical violence,"[25] for acts of nature do not give rise to a judgment. Although we may speak figuratively of the natural violence of a storm or natural disaster such entities are not blamed, are not brought "before some instrument of justice"[26] and held accountable for the injuries they have caused. Inscribed within the concept of violence is the possibility of a judgment by the entity who commits the act, and because the actor has freely chosen to do violence it can be critiqued for having done so. As only persons are capable of free choice and judgment, only persons can choose to do violence.

On this point Derrida remains squarely within an ethical tradition at least as old as Aristotle. In his *Nichomachean Ethics*, Aristotle argues that actions "receive praise or blame [only] when they are voluntary."[27] Even more specifically, actions are only praised or blamed if they are based upon a decision. Although both persons and animals have volition, only persons are possessed of the capacity for decision-making.[28] It is this decision-making ability that allows for the possibility of justice and injustice, of praising or blaming, for "someone does injustice or does justice whenever he does them willingly."[29]

Kant also "trace[s] the determinate concept of morality back to the Idea of freedom."[30] The essence of free will, which belongs to all rational beings (all faces, all persons) consists in, according to Kant, "acting on no maxim other than one which can have for its object itself as at the same time a universal law."[31] This is, of course, one of the formulations of the categorical imperative itself, which leads Kant to argue that morality and a free will are indissolubly linked. A being who was "directed from outside in regard to its judgements,"[32] rather than being free to choose how it acts, would therefore be unfree and non-moral. It would be just another natural phenomenon that is not called upon to account for itself.

An unfree being could not, according to both Kant and Derrida, justifiably be brought before any instrument of justice. If a lawbreaker's transgressions were the result of "a motive of the senses, the deed could not have been committed by the criminal as a free being, and he could not consequently be held responsible for it."[33] In fact, for Kant the criminal as free agent must be punished simply because he *chose* to break the law, not for any such utilitarian ends as future deterrence or the emotional satisfaction of the victims. Punishment for utilitarian ends is a violence to the personhood of the lawbreaker, who as a person "can never be manipulated just as a means of realizing someone else's intentions."[34] Such would constitute treating the criminal as a mere phenomenal object, denying that he is a person who specifically chose to promulgate a new value in the world that was nevertheless at odds with the laws of the state. It would instead consider him a broken machine that would be repaired through incarceration.

More recently formulated and widely used definitions of justice also recognize the necessity of free will for the existence of violence. In his influential article on the nature of violence, Robert Audi argues that "a frenzied lunatic" who swings "fists in the air and scream[s] inarticulately into the night" would not be doing violence because his mental state renders him not responsible for his actions, although his behavior "can be analyzed in terms of its similarity to, and the potential it implies for, the doing of violence."[35] That is, the lunatic's demonstrated physical ability to swing his fists and scream insults at passersby might provide to an onlooker some clue as to his ability to conduct violence, but his current mental situation renders him incapable of the choice required for violence to occur. Similarly, John Harris writes that "*an act of violence occurs when injury or suffering is inflicted upon a person or persons by an agent who knows (or ought reasonably to have known), that his actions would result in the harm in question.*"[36]

But each of these arguments already approach or represent the more common, derivative conceptions of violence. According to Derrida, before any common ethical violence, there already exists within an "irreducible zone of factuality, an original, transcendental violence, previous to every ethical choice, even supposed by ethical nonviolence."[37] This arché-violence, as Derrida calls it, "is tied to phenomenality itself, and to the possibility of language."[38]

As usual, Derrida exploits a related double-meaning: *Arché* translates as both "beginning" and "sovereignty,"[39] an intentional dual-invocation that itself contains at least three implications. First, arché-violence is the first form of violence, and as such it governs all subsequent forms. That is, it institutes and defines the genre "violence" and thus functions as the template by which other potential violences are identified. Second, arché-violence is the violence of a sovereign, of one who has the power to institute and define, be it the sovereign face of discursive ethics or the political sovereign. In this second invocation, arché-violence is the act of establishing and promulgating one's own claims within a discursive environment crowded with other sovereigns with similar abilities. It is this sense of arché-violence that I explore in chapter two through my discussion of how Hobbes' sovereign creates peace by creating and enforcing definitions.

Third (foreshadowing Derrida's deconstruction of Benjamin's distinction between foundational and conservative violence), a sovereign is a conservative entity that maintains his domain against forces that would destroy it and establish a new regime. But because conservation contains within itself an element of continual re-foundation, just as foundation includes the idea of conserving that which has been founded, the foundational aspect of arché-violence as "beginning-violence" and its conservative facet as "sovereign-violence" are not mutually exclusive. Viewing the same situation from a different angle, the two invocations of arché-violence fold into each other. Inasmuch as arché-violence as the first violence founds the genre of "violence," it acts as the instituting sovereign of its second invocation. But it can only act as the sovereign by virtue of its primary place in the order of violence.

In all its invocations, this most primordial violence "appears with *articulation*,"[40] with the institution, which is simultaneously an ossification, of the definitive, finite and hence limited and limiting, positions that are opened by the discourse that originally constitutes the relationship among faces. This discursive arché-violence, "the violence of difference, of classification, and of the system of appellations"[41] is inescapable because articulation requires a positioning by those within discourse. The articulation of specific positions by persons to others is the very essence of discourse. "A speech produced without the least violence," without the least articulation, "would determine nothing," not even self-identity. It "would say nothing"[42] because such speech would not take a position or make a determination, and would hence be outside of discourse. It may be an unarticulated contemplation or other such positionless meditative chant, perhaps of the sort sometimes uttered by those who seek to shed their selfhood (their specific and articulated positionality), but it would not be speech at all.

But this original and irreducible relationship among persons as faces is characterized by speech, by discursive positioning. "Through [their] freedom of speech"[43] faces assert their own discreet, independent identities beginning at the moment of face-to-face encounter. This assertion of identity, of difference, is a speech, a determinate, meaningful communication issued by one face and received as such by an other. The other is of course necessary for this most basic discursive positioning because as a relationship this positioning requires the identification of an other capable of relations (i.e., a face). Speech itself, as above, "becomes effective—performed and performing—not at the moment it apparently takes place, but only later, when ears will have managed to receive the message."[44] No face can exist without an other against which to identify itself, and this identification takes place as language, which itself also requires the existence of an other. Self-assertion, identity, language, and violence thus arise simultaneously as facets of a single event.

The "transcendental origin of an irreducible violence" in this situation is constituted in "the necessity of speaking of the other as other, or to the other as other, on the basis of its appearing-for-me-as-what-it-is: the other,"[45] the additional. Because "the absolute form of experience"[46] is egoity—a perspectival finitude that, to use a banal philosophical analogy that nonetheless plays well with the terminology of this discourse, is best thought in terms of the limited perspective afforded by the sight organs embedded within the human face—one can only conceive of the other from a position of one's egoity, one's finite perspective. As irreducibly perspectival, one's conception of the other (at the original moment of encounter between faces) is as an-other-to-oneself, as an entity constituted primarily vis-à-vis oneself, such that oneself is the ontologically primary term of the dyad. Thus Derrida writes that this "reduction of the other to a *real* moment of *my* life, its reduction to the state of empirical alter-ego, is an empirical possibility, or rather eventuality, which is called violence."[47]

By this necessary move, the other as face, which "always behind its signs and its works, always within its secret interior, and forever discreet, interrupting all historical totalities through its freedom of speech . . . is not 'of this world'"[48] of bare cause and effect, is reduced to mere phenomenality. As a phenomenal object, the other is outside the ethical face-to-face relationship—it is simply an object, to be used, altered, discarded, or ignored as one sees fit. Deploying the language of traditional metaphysics, Derrida accesses this matter by arguing that because Being as a concept does not exist "before the Existent . . . it begins by hiding itself beneath its determination."[49] Being has no existence independent of its determinations, those things that themselves are said to exist. "Being, since it is always, in fact, determined as an existent and is nothing outside the existent, is always dissimulated"[50] and unknowable for the face that, grounded in its own perspective, can only perceive the phenomenality of the face of the other in reference to itself. The person as face is therefore "incapable of respecting" the other's "Being"[51] in itself, instead reducing it to determinateness and "to intra-wordliness," which "is the origin and very meaning of what is called violence, making possible all [conceptual and physical] straitjackets."[52]

Approaching this same issue from the perspective of grammar, Derrida writes that "the dative or vocative dimension which opens the original direction of language, cannot lend itself to inclusion in and modification by the accusative or attributive dimension of the object without violence."[53] Language that attempts to respect the other as value-creating "ego, the origin of the world" (and here I already preview justice) rather than doing violence to it by conceiving of it as merely phenomenal, as "entirely in the world,"[54] would occur in the dative or vocative. The other would be addressed as the recipient of an action. For example, one could speak of an other by saying "I bought a book for Ben," putting

Ben in the dative case as the indirect object of an action. Ben is the intended recipient of the direct object and merely phenomenal item. One could also speak to Ben directly, saying "Here is your book, Ben." Here Ben is spoken to in the vocative case as a person capable of both comprehending that he is being offered a phenomenal object and of accepting ownership of it. In this situation, the other is considered as more than merely phenomenal—it is conceived of as a face, a subject, an alter-*ego* that is to be addressed and called to through language, and is capable of a response. The other is understood to be an indirect object of any action, such that he or she is the personal recipient of an address or an action. Even if I give Ben something harmful, such as poison, he is still the indirect object of the action and is therefore still respected as a person (although certainly not as much as if I gave him a book out of friendship).[55]

But because of the face's necessarily egoistic, perspectival nature that can not help but conceive of others as phenomenal objects, this peaceful vocative is always tarnished by the accusative or attributive. In the attributive, the other is conceived of as fundamentally *my* other, as an attribute of oneself, as an adjective attached to one's own proper noun. For example, someone who says "Ben is my friend," certainly recognizes that Ben is a person, but structures this thought such that Ben is an attribute of oneself rather than a fully other entity. In the accusative dimension one conceives of the other as properly a direct object of one's own actions, so that things are said or done to the other as an object, rather than given or presented to the other as a Face. In the sentence "I like Ben," Ben is the direct object of an action by the speaker. Ben is an object of the same class as bunnies or chess—simple phenomenal objects that are mentioned in a direct relationship of subordination to myself. Although the speaker of this sentence likes Ben, and probably considers Ben a person, the structure of the phrase depicts Ben as a sense-object that is spoken of, rather than to. Even in the relatively peaceful sentence "I bought a book for Ben," Ben is inevitably categorized and hypostasized into the phenomenal object that has the characteristic of having received a book. The sentence is incapable of accounting for the fullness of Ben's personhood, although it does contain an at least tacit acceptance of it.

As usual, Derrida's attempts to weave his arguments into a web that defies narrow linearity have been successful, and I have again gotten ahead of myself. I must return hence to the point that discursive positioning is required for articulation. This necessity of position for articulation that is the root of arché-violence in turn implies the iterability of that position, which is the key to why discourse is itself violent for Derrida. He writes that "position is already iterability, a call for self-conserving repetition"[56] because any claim—any discursive position—is a universal claim that in order to be universal must continually re-found itself. Any position, even the position that universal positions are impossible, is a universal claim and is therefore considered iterable universally. This universal iterability denies in its structure the legitimacy of counter-claims made by others, thus denying that others are really faces, independent sources of meaning that are capable of their own independent speech.

In its iterations every claim, every discursive position, must go through an Ordeal of the Undecidable—otherwise the statement is mere inhuman mechanistic calculation. If a person is responsible for his or her decisions, if a person is capable of doing violence, if a visage is actually a face and not merely a direct object (as with the accusative dimension of language), then that person's decisions must not be "protect[ed] . . . by some theoretical assurance, or by the certainty of being right, of being on the side of science, of consciousness or of reason."[57] If they were, then these decisions would be the mere "deployment of a program . . . technical application of a rule or a norm, or . . . subsumption of a determined 'case.'"[58] If a person is simply a set of determinate "attributes or predicates . . . and if the decision is simply the consequence or what follows from this set of possibilities, then it's not a decision"[59]—it is merely the necessary effect of a set of causes, as with the mechanistic physics of simple phenomenal objects. But the person as face exceeds mere phenomenality—it is the meaning-creating, value-instituting "origin of the world"[60] that intersubjectively creates discursive positionality. Discourse is characterized by the creation of meaning and value, rather than by mere mechanistic calculation.

Putting it differently, Derrida argues that, "a decision that didn't go through the ordeal of the undecidable would not be a free decision,"[61] it would only be the mechanistic application of a general rule. If a position is a pure mechanistic re-statement the re-stater denies oneself as a source of meaning independent of a general rule which is structurally its own claim to universal iteration, but a human discursive act is inscribed with a position of meaning-creation. A person who did violence to himself—who denied himself as a source of meaning—would simply fall silent and be without positionality, but one who does function within discourse re-decides independently whether or not to apply a rule or repeat a claim. Independent perspective and meaning creation are the essences of individuality; personhood *is* positionality.

So position itself includes the claim of universal iteration, that is, conservation of itself. But thanks to the ordeal of the undecidable, each new iteration, each moment of conservation within discourse, is an independent refounding that re-decides anew a previously-given position as though it had not previously existed. Therefore each outcome of the ordeal of the undecidable is both conservative and institutive of a rule or claim. The ordeal of the undecidable is hence the paradox inherent in any claim or counter-claim: An iteration of any previous position is both foundational in itself, re-decided anew from scratch in an act of meaning-creation, and therefore includes its own new claim to universal iteration, and is also conservative in that it is an iteration of a previous claim. This paradox also applies to a new discursive position, which as a foundation constitutes a new claim against the universal iteration of some opposing claim, but which also contains within itself its own claim to universal iteration—a concept which it simultaneously stands against as it challenges the iteration of the opposing claim.

The point, as Richard Beardsworth (one of Derrida's most noteworthy commentators) explains, is that "a decision is always needed because there is no natural status to language, and that given this irreducibility of a decision, there are different kinds of decisions—those that recognize their legislative and executive force and those which hide it under some claim to naturality *qua* 'theory' or 'objective science.'"[62] In the first case the person recognizes and embraces its status as a creator of meaning, but in the second case (and as a preview of my discussion of Nietzsche) the person more closely resembles Nietzsche's scientific ascetic who, while still a person and thus a creator, denies his nature and instead claims to discover pure objective fact. But in either event, a person "is always . . . a legislator and policeman,"[63] a creator and subsequent enforcer of her creations of meaning and value. Some of us simply embrace this creative nature and recognize that we are "form-giving forces that give new interpretations and directions"[64] to the world, but others reject this fact in spite of its inevitability, and continue to claim that they are discoverers and spectators rather than creators. In a more Derridean idiom, any discursive positioning is the outcome of an ordeal of the undecidable that is itself necessary because there is no objective, transparently discoverable truth. Rather, persons exist as the choosers, the creators, of discursive positionality (meaning; value).

This paradoxical stance of any positioning points to Derrida's claim that discourse "is *economy*: violence against violence, light against light."[65] The term "economy" is used to invoke two complementary ideas. By one sense of the term, to behave with economy is to use or have something only to the degree necessary or practicable. But an economy is also a system of trade and distribution, in which the objects of the economy are passed around from person to person. According to Derrida, discourse is always violent to some extent because in making a universally iterable claim one always does violence to another by denying that other as a source of meaning. Yet because "like pure violence, pure nonviolence is a contradictory concept"[66] discourse can never be completely violent or nonviolent; it is always an economy of violence. Derrida makes this claim because "pure violence, a relationship between beings without face, is not yet violence, is pure nonviolence. And inversely: pure nonviolence, the nonrelation of the same to the other . . . is pure violence."[67] Both meanings of economy are deployed here: Because both total violence and total peacefulness are impossible, they can only exist economically, meaning partially, mixed with each other to varying degrees. Discourse is also economical because it consists of persons, each of whom acts with economic (that is, partial, impure) amounts of violence and nonviolence, trading these economic levels of peace and violence back and forth as they conduct discourse with each other. Discourse is in this way an economic system in which the commodities are violence and nonviolence.

Violence as the denial of the other as a source of meaning can never be a pure violence because that would require the complete denial of the other's similarity to oneself as a being capable of creating meaning. "A horizon is always a horizon of the same," and pure violence would constitute the obliteration of this horizon, such that, "the elementary unity"[68] between the two faces would cease. This would constitute the complete denial that the other has a face, the capability of perspective and position. In this situation one would have no relation to the faceless other, who would not even be recognized as a person against whom violence could be perpetrated. The complete violence against the other, the complete effacement of the other, would be nonviolent—not peaceful, but outside of or at a right angle to violence—because no discursive relationship between the two would be possible.

As another way of understanding how a relationship with the wholly other is impossible, Derrida discusses death. Because death "concerns the impossibility of existence itself, and not merely the impossibility of this or that,"[69] one can not *be* dead. "The impossibility of being dead, the impossibility of living or rather 'existing' one's death"[70] renders death a completely foreign other to life. There is no way one can be in relation to the very impossibility of any being at all. It is inaccessible at even the most basic level of understanding, which always requires thinking of being dead as somehow *being* dead, existing in a state of deadness. The complete and utter otherness of death is an impossible thought, so no relation with it is possible.

On the other hand, the complete recognition of the other as a source of meaning would necessitate the complete recognition of the similarity between oneself and the other as fundamentally sources of meaning. In this situation one would identify with "the other immediately and originally, silently, in communion with the other's own experience" to the extent that the other "would cease to be the other."[71] A complete unity would deny the possibility of calling to or addressing the other just as much as it would reject the possibility of doing violence in the accusative or attributive. Inasmuch as one thing can not simultaneously hold conflicting attributes, this denial of the difference between oneself and other would thereby do violence to the possibility of differing positions. This self-identical dyad could not maintain a discursive relationship because pure identity would deny the independent positionality of the two. It would completely bind one to the fullness of the other's being, denying oneself as an independent person and necessitating the total acceptance of the other's promulgations.

III. . . . And Introducing Justice

Therefore all persons necessarily practice arché-violence through the pre-ethical structure of the discursive face-to-face relationship, but they practice it economically. To the extent that in one's discursive practices one "*let[s]* be [the] other in their truth," in their independence as sovereign sources of meaning, as faces, one comes "as close as possible to nonviolence."[72] The full achievement of nonviolence, while impossible due to the paradox presented above, would "gain access to the egoity of the alter ego as if to its alterity itself,"[73] fully respecting its nature as a face, calling to it purely in the vocative as an independent ego rather than objectifying it in the attributive, actively living with it in the dative without imposition, instead of acting upon it in the accusative.

This impossible full recognition of all as meaning-creating faces is, as the opposite of violence, the essence of justice for Derrida. Discourse is increasingly violent to the extent that it "*reduces* the other" to a mere object or attribute of one's own life, "when it *leads* the other, whether through psychology, demagogy, or even pedagogy which is not instruction."[74] Leading the other through psychology, demagogy, or forceful pedagogies reduces a person to an attribute of one's life because in these ways one tries to remake the other in his own image, subtly forcing the other's own creations of meaning and value to comply with one's own. Respecting the personhood of the other, calling to him in the dative or vocative and seeking discussion on some point of disagreement would entail a moment of undecidability in which one suspends one's own position and becomes open to the creations of the other as a full partner in the dialogue. The subtle violences Derrida refers to above are the product of varying degrees of rejection of the other's personhood as one seeks to influence him through rhetoric or other trickery.

Although politics (and life in general) are replete with examples of this quiet violence, one of the clearest and most useful examples is that of political campaign advertisements. A candidate does not simply state his positions—he uses verbal and visual cues as systematically as possible in order to do the most convincing possible in such a short period of time. Lyndon Johnson's famous "Daisy Girl" spot, in which a young girl picking flowers becomes the image of a nuclear explosion, is not only an image of violence; it is also a violent image in that it gains its power not from calling to the other's personhood but from its psychological impact upon the other as a direct object. Even so, this ad still calls to the personhood of the other by offering the structure of a choice, no matter how violently it imposes one decision on the audience. Both because choices are not offered to pure phenomenal objects and because objects can not be rhetorically forced to choose as the advertisers intended, the "Daisy Girl" spot still retains a kernel of recognition of the personhood of its audience. If the audience did not consist of persons, the ad would be either unnecessary or futile. By attempting a violent imposition on its audience, this ad both tacitly recognizes the personhood of its audience and tries to infringe upon it.

Campaign advertisements are a good median example of discursive violence because they call to the personhood of the other through their structure of a choice while simultaneously trying to violently impose the decision upon their audience through the use of discursive force, but they also serve as good examples because they are part of the apparatus a person uses to construct his or her own political power. As I will discuss in chapter two, a major aspect of one's political power is successfully forcing others to define terms as one wishes. Campaign ads are more or less delicate are attempts to perform this violence of imposition, even as they affirm the choice of those upon whom they are trying to force definitions.

A less violent example may be that of the relationship between a dissertation advisor and her student. The very essence of the advisor's relationship to the advisee is as a senior to a junior colleague, with the explicit recognition that the advisee is a person who, although consciously constructing a contribution to the ongoing discourse of a field of knowledge (or creation), requires some assistance due to his relative inexperience. With some unfortunately notable exceptions, dissertation advisors tend to recognize that their main task is to provide structure and guidance, rather than enforced mandates, to a person who is trying to complete his first book. The advisor recognizes the personhood of the student in the structure of the job itself because, just as the concept of law includes the possibility of its enforcement, the concept of advice-giving includes the possibility of that advice being considered and either accepted or rejected. As I will continue to stress throughout this work, law is that which specifically rejects the possibility of choice. Advice, on the other hand, is *given* (as in the dative or vocative) rather than imposed, and even if the advisor feels very strongly about some issue, she is likely to guide her student towards a conclusion rather than imposing it upon him. The relative peacefulness of the usual advisor-advisee relationship is further evidenced by the fact that many advisees request that their advisors impose deadlines and restrictions upon them to further structure their work environment.

The paradoxical nature of this example begins to demonstrate that the violence in intersubjective language is minimized to the extent that it is characterized by a "'letting-be' of an existent (other) as something existing outside"[75] of oneself as an independent, meaning-creating face. Justice, as the respect for the other as a creator of meaning, is manifested in a "*rectitude* of address"[76] towards the other "as other, irreducible to *my* ego, precisely because it is an ego,"[77] a sovereign face rather than a mere phenomenal object, such as a simple rock or vegetable. An address to a person exhibits rectitude—moral correctness, righteousness, correct judgment—when that address fully recognizes the personhood of the person being addressed by addressing him as a discursive entity that transcends simple phenomenality. The reduction of this rectitude of address to the point of a complete lack of address describes a continuum of relative justice through relative violence. This is perhaps best illustrated by the fact that persons are often more infuriated when they are ignored than when they are spoken to in an offensive or condescending manner. Even if someone is addressed in a negative way, the fact that she is being addressed in some capacity is a sign that she is conceived of as a person to some degree, rather than as a purely phenomenal object. For example, if a person offers a public lecture on ethics, she would be frustrated if everyone in the audience disagreed with all of her ideas, but she would likely be even more aggravated if someone wandered through the auditorium or perhaps laid down on the stage to take a nap, as though she were not speaking. Although the audience members disagree with her, at least they recognize her existence as a person, whereas the wandering person does not.

As another example, consider how parents often speak of their young children as though those children were out of earshot, even when they are immediately present. Of course, the personhood of the children is absent (that is, it is not yet developed). When a child develops sufficiently, he or she will begin reacting to being spoken of as an object, and will speak up to remind the adults that he or she is in fact capable of understanding and responding. At that point parents are forced to begin accepting the independent subjectivity of their children.

John Harris inadvertently presents a very interesting example of this violence of non-recognition when he considers what he calls the "obstetrical example"[78] of violence:

> In this example a doctor is faced with two possibilities: a pregnant woman in his care will die if she carries her child to term, when she is dead the child can

> be safely delivered alive by *post mortem* Caesarian section. Alternatively the life of the mother can be saved by the performance of an operation which crushes the skull of the foetus so that it can be extracted from the womb without danger to the mother.[79]

Harris uses this example to discuss the potential violences of each choice made by the doctor, who must choose between killing the mother or the fetus. As stated, this is a good example of how doing justice to one person (assuming the admittedly implausible position that the fetus is a person) often necessitates doing violence to another. But even though this example implies the personhood of the mother, Harris himself never actually speaks of the mother as a person. As this example is phrased, it is the doctor, not the mother or the two of them together, who is faced with an agonistic ethical and medical decision of which some violence will inevitably be a part. Both Harris and his doctor do a violence to the mother by ignoring her potential for her own positions and decisions on the matter of her own life and that of her child.[80]

Even though examples such as these are not rigorous philosophical justifications, I take them to be commonly recognized events to which many persons can relate. But some might disagree with these examples, arguing that violence requires the use of great force, such that "to neglect is not to commit an act of violence because neglecting cannot be done with great force."[81] Arguing in this way, Robert Audi claims that "a person might, with consummate nonviolence, destroy an automobile by disassembling it and dissolving its parts in aqua regia."[82] Yet the careful disassembling of a vehicle, or the clinical and methodical slander, oppression, or murder of a person begins with the same motivation as a more obviously forceful act, and yields similar results. No matter how it is operationalized, violence proceeds from the rejection of the other as a meaning and value creating entity, and has as its goal the silencing or subsumption of the other beneath one's own personhood. As my above examples show, and as I will discuss more fully in both chapters two and three, some more obviously forceful violences may actually be more respectful of the personhood of an other because forceful violences imply the actor's recognition that the other is a significant danger to his own personhood. The individual who curls up on stage for a nap during an ethics presentation does not even recognize the potential for recrimination or retribution by the speaker, whereas one who argues with the speaker in an attempt to iterate his own positionality over the speaker's at least recognizes that the speaker, as a person, is attempting to promulgate her own positionality. Similarly, my discussion of Thomas Hobbes will demonstrate that violence does not result from "a lack of clear awareness of other people's independent standing in the world; rather, it is a way in which the agent responds to the very real and very acute knowledge of the others as power centers representing a constant threat to him."[83]

In his disturbing 1934 painting *Le viol* [The Rape], Belgian Surrealist painter René Magritte presents a more complex example of the intricate play of violence and justice. In this oft-reproduced painting, Magritte, "who explored the connections between language and experience in ways that anticipated the employment of a semiotic understanding of art by post-modernists,"[84] depicts the format of a face surrounded by wavy brown hair, in which the eyes are breasts, the nose is a navel, and the mouth is a pubic triangle. Theodore Gracyk's interpretation, in which *Le viol* constitutes "one of the most graphic subordinations of a woman to an object," that is, a violence, because "it reduces her to genitalia,"[85] is perhaps the most obvious. By this common account of The Rape, which is also an account of violence as the reduction of the other from a person capable of creating meaning and value to a mere phenomenal object, a dehumanizing physical rape is epitomized by the defacing artistic rape of replacing a woman's face with a body. The image of a woman's personhood subsumed beneath her sexual physicality may encourage violence towards women,[86] but it also constitutes a primary violence in itself. By promoting the idea that a woman is simply a physical body without personhood, available for penetration and devoid of independent creative nature, this "image of mindless physicality justifies [physical] rape,"[87] but it is also a rape in itself. Thus, inasmuch as the female is depicted as a primarily physical entity by replacing her face, the perceived seat of her personhood, with merely phenomenal sex organs, *Le viol* can show how "the 'rape' of an attractive face encountered on a street occurs each time a man superimposes his own image of the woman's body, an obvious wish fulfillment, on the exposed face."[88]

By this account, *Le viol* also shows how a feminine "fear of the objectifying masculine gaze bereaves [her] of [her] own interiority."[89] So far there are two violences enacted by *The Rape*: the violence done to a woman by perceiving her as primarily physical and sexual, rather than as a person who leaps beyond the merely phenomenal, and the violence of physical rape that is arguably promoted by this reduction. This fear of the objectifying masculine gaze adds a third violence that comes into play when a woman understands that she is perceived as primarily physical, with limited or nonexistent personhood. At this point she begins to fear the physical violence of rape that this encourages, and she begins to conceive of herself as primarily physical, rather than as a person. The fear that she most fundamentally *is* a merely phenomenal body, available for penetration and without the independent ability to secure herself, overtakes her mind, and she reifies this aspect of her being.

But a more sophisticated interpretation is offered by Alan Soble, who concludes that "after Magritte welds together her face and body," the woman in *Le viol* "achieves a tangible union of body and mind, flesh and spirit"[90] that represents an *economical* violence, inhabited by a continued but certainly reduced level of respect for her personhood. Rather than focusing solely on the violent half of the story, in which the woman is defaced and sexualized, Soble shows that her merely phenomenal "sexual parts from the lower regions of the body have been . . . raised to and located on her face," thus transforming them "into a face" and imbuing them "with spirit."[91] Soble's interpretation of *Le viol* thus demonstrates the inevitable mutual contamination of violence and respect for the personhood of the other—the other consists of both phenomenal and transcendent, both mechanistic and undecidable, and by combining them both in this way Magritte shows how violence is always inhabited by some peacefulness of respect. First, if the rape had been total, the violence pure, the sex organs would not have been formatted as a face, since the total non-relation to the other would have precluded the recognition that a face is indeed present. By creating a face out of the sex organs, Magritte continues to recognize, or argues that one who commits such a violence continues to recognize, the assailed personhood of the victim. Indeed, such an act could not be a "rape" without at least tacit, minimal recognition that that act is in imposition upon an independent personhood. Second, *Le viol* shows that no relation to the other is a pure peacefulness without rape. Even during overtly peaceful intersubjective intercourse (in this case an intentional double *entendre*), one's perception of the other can not help but be inhabited by an egoistic violence that conceives of the other as "a body to penetrate [or envelop] and possess."[92] Under the gaze of the other, the transcendence of personhood announced by the face is always partially obscured by the phenomenality of the body; the fullness of the other's being is always violently limited, codified, and thematized by the other's gaze upon it.

This mention of the hidden mutual contamination of violence and respect points to a deep paradox within justice that, although irreducible, must (paradoxically) be overcome. Derrida writes that "to be just or unjust and to exercise justice, I must be free and responsible for my actions, my behavior, my thought, my decisions . . . but this freedom or this decision of the just, if it is one, must follow a law or a prescription, a rule."[93] In order for an act to be just it must be an act of independent meaning-creation on the part of the actor, for otherwise the act would not be the result of free decision. As Derrida puts it, the act "might be legal; it would not be just."[94] An unfree act, the mere mindless application of a rule or the perfectly calculable unfolding of some mechanistic process, can not be a just act. Although a period of light, steady rain after a drought or a shark attack on a despot might be considered fortuitous, the lack of free decision by the clouds or sharks means that their actions could not be considered just.

On the other hand, an action that does not adhere to a rule or law is not just, either. Because justice itself is the recognition of the other as a source of meaning, an individual act must conform to, must iterate, this rule in order to be called "just." Justice is "the only incarnated nonviolence in that it is . . . an immediate respect for the other himself"[95] as a source of meaning and value—this is its determinate content, its essence. Thus any act that does not conform to this ethical law can not be called just, but, as Derrida argues, justice always contains an element of the incalculable, such that "the decision between just and unjust is never insured by a rule."[96] If one respects the other as a meaning creator simply because that is the mandate of the universal ethical law, one reduces oneself to a merely legalistic, mechanistic device that is incapable of the incalculable freedom required for the free act of justice.

This is one point of access to the deep rift between the Platonic conception of persons as the discoverers of value and the idea of persons as creators, as manifested by an argument between Kant and Derrida that I shall mention briefly.[97] It is well known that for Kant, duty—which he defines as "the necessity to act out of reverence for the law"[98]—is the only moral reason for performing any act. To do "good, not from inclination, but from duty,"[99] is the result of the "consciousness of the *subordination* of [one's] will to a law."[100] When we attend "to the necessity with which reason prescribes"[101] this principle to us, we accept the "legislative form"[102]—the legalistic, prescriptive, rule-oriented nature—of the categorical imperative as justice that is discovered and universally objective, rather than created by persons. In fact, the very name of Kant's ethical principle communicates its place as the primary legal dictate in his system of thought. As a "categorical imperative," the ethical law is an inescapable dictate that demands obedience in all circumstances, without consideration of one's individual ends or desires (as with a hypothetical imperative).

Kant argues that unless an act is motivated by duty to this universal ethical law, that act is done out of inescapably self-interested concerns that strip it of its moral worth. For example, if a person helps the poor because he expects that others will then help him in return, or because it will help his reputation, or simply because it makes him feel better about himself, this otherwise laudable action is fundamentally selfish and hence morally bankrupt. The only way that helping others, telling the truth, or any other praiseworthy act is ethical is if it is done based on a subsumption of one's individual will to the universal legislation of the categorical imperative.

By Derrida's aporetic account of justice, Kant's ethic of reverence for the law is merely legalistic. Subordinating one's will to law is a rejection of one's personhood as a creator of meaning and value, as a being that exceeds the calculable and decides each act anew. If we reject our creativity, the very essence of our personhood, and subordinate it to a single objective ethical law, we reduce ourselves to simple empirical objects and place ourselves outside of the possibility of justice, which itself requires the freedom of decision not guaranteed by law. One who follows the law simply because it is The Law is no better than a billiard ball that rolls away when it is hit by a cue.

In his excellent study of the philosophical concept of violence, Piotr Hoffman agrees, arguing that "if the freedom that commits itself to follow its (self-imposed) law—the law of the categorical imperative—is to remain free . . . then it can never lose its capacity to *repudiate its own law* by becoming 'lawless.'"[103] When the freedom of personhood is replaced with absolute and unquestioned acceptance of the dictates of The Law, the morality of justice is reduced to the orderliness of legality. This necessary and ever-present possibility of repudiating The Law is of course the opening of a true decision that "exceeds my own being, my own possibility, my own potentiality"[104] as a simple phenomenal object and a passage into an ordeal of the undecidable. But inasmuch as the categorical imperative "means respect of fellow human beings and of oneself as a member of the human community," the *épokhal* suspension of this law that generates the real possibility of its repudiation makes possible "the repudiation by man of his bond of fellowship with other men and of his own status as a member of the human community."[105] This disrespect towards the personhood of others, although a necessary possibility if a person is to maintain the freedom of her humanity, "can be nothing other than an option for violence."[106] But although justice requires the possibility of the suspension of its rule, justice also has a definite content—the peaceful recognition of others as meaning and value creators. If a person chooses to act in such a way that she does not recognize the personhood of the other, she acts violently and unjustly. So again, justice is a paradoxical combination of legalistic adherence to a law, *and* a free act of independent meaning creation.

In discussing this paradox of justice, Derrida uses the example of a judge who "must not only follow a rule of law or a general law but must also assume it, approve it, confirm its value, by a reinstituting act of interpretation, as if ultimately nothing previously existed of the law, as if the judge himself invented the law in every case."[107] When a judge (or any person) makes a decision he or she can neither mindlessly apply general rules nor strike out on his or her own entirely, hence the paradox that justice is both conservative and foundational. This paradox that appears in the "justice system," as well as in any other act of justice, is exactly that paradox inherent in the basic structure of violence itself: the paradox of iterability which "requires the origin to repeat itself originarily, to alter itself so as to have the value of origin, that is, to conserve itself [which] inscribes conservation in the essential structure of foundation."[108]

There is also a temporal element to this paradox. A decision can never be "presently and fully just"[109] because there is no actual moment when the paradox of foundation and conservation is solved. Either the decision "has not yet been made according to a rule, and nothing allows us to call it just"[110] simply because it has not yet occurred, or "it has already followed a rule . . . which in its turn is not absolutely guaranteed by anything; and, moreover, if it were guaranteed, the decision would be reduced to calculation and we couldn't call it just."[111] The specific rule to which a decision adheres may or may not accurately reflect the minimization of violence and the maximization of justice—it is not guaranteed—but if the decision was guaranteed, if due to perfect information or whatever the correspondence of the rule to justice was known, the decision itself would not undergo the ordeal of the undecidable. Therefore the decision would be the mere mechanistic application of a rule, rather than an act of justice. It is this undecidability that opens the horizon of existence to personhood, which is predicated upon creating meaning and value out of the ordeal of the undecidable. If knowable Truth existed, personhood would devolve from creativity into the mere legalistic application of specific rules.

Accessing the same issue from the angle of the perspectival finitude of the face, Derrida argues that because the fundamental structure of our discursive experience is egoistic (to wit, perspectival and therefore finite), we are incapable of fully accepting others as sources of meaning. "Presence as violence is the meaning of finitude,"[112] because as finite we only experience through a positionality that denies the positions of others. In this formulation the positionality of discursive acts is the result of the violent finitude that results from egoity being the fundamental form of experience. Acts of justice, as acts of egoity and position in the face-to-face relationship, are no less discursive than any other acts, and as such they are subject to this same violent finitude. Justice as the full recognition of others as sources of meaning can never be fully achieved because acts of justice are fundamentally inscribed with the violence of discursive positionality—an economy of justice and violence.

IV. Getting Political

The overlapping intersubjective face-to-face relationships of daily life lead to a situation in which some persons are more recognized as sources of meaning, such that their positions are iterated more often than are the positions of others.[113] This inevitable situation constitutes a violence against the effaced position that is not iterated by others and leads proponents of the effaced position to call for justice. Those who are silenced always call for the justice that would mean the recognition of their voices, the recognition that they are "capable of a language in general"[114] and are therefore beings capable of producing meaning. Full justice therefore necessarily always has what Derrida calls an *avenir* [to come; has to come]—"it will always have it, this *a-venir*, and always has"[115] because the voices of some are always effaced in order for others to be heard. Justice is always "on the way," it is that which *must* always be on the way, in at least two ways. First, no one group in a society can experience perfect justice. Not only is the concept of full justice aporetic, but the existence of more than one group causes a struggle for power that is never settled. Second, there are always disadvantaged groups that lack an acceptable minimum level of the political voice that would constitute some measure of justice for them.

Law claims to create a situation of justice, but law itself manifests a paradox just as significant as that of positioning and iteration in discourse. In fact, inasmuch as law is discourse raised to the level of the political (or, that all discourse is itself political), the paradox within law is the same as that within all other forms of discourse. Law-creating, or revolutionary, violence is the political form of discursive positioning. In it, "a *coup de force*, of a . . . violence that in itself is neither just nor unjust and that no justice and no previous law with its founding anterior moment could guarantee or contradict or invalidate"[116] is perpetrated upon others.

Because this moment of revolutionary or institutional violence denies all previous laws, all prior discursively dominant positions, it exceeds the distinction between just and unjust. As institutional or foundational, law-creating violence can not appeal to the previous law that constitutes the legal, calculable side of the calculable/undecidable paradox of justice. Instead, as foundational, "revolutionary movements project ideals from within their present discourse,"[117] which is itself not founded upon anything prior.

Law-conserving violence, on the other hand, is the violence of the state—the political manifestation of arguing in favor of an accepted premise, ossified category, or conventional wisdom. It preserves the existing legal order and rejects the claims of the effaced others who seek to alter the basic discursive structures of their society. Because "position is already iterability, a call for self-conserving repetition," law-creating violence must itself become law-conserving in order to maintain what it has created, "turn[ing] against its original positing character"[118] as revolutionary, recalling the paradox within all discourse and thereby pointing to "a *differantielle* contamination"[119] between the two types of violence.

"Conservation in its turn refounds" by iterating from scratch through the ordeal of the undecidable, "so that it can conserve what it claims to found."[120] The decisions of a judge (as above), or other law-conservationists "must conserve the law and also destroy it or suspend it enough to have to reinvent it in each case, rejustify it, at least reinvent it in the reaffirmation and the new and free confirmation of its principle"[121] of justice.

Even if, hypothetically, the law does not aspire to justice, its conservation manifests this paradox of foundation and conservation because an interpretive moment is required for the application of the law. The person as face, as intersubjective, discursive creator of meaning, must decide whether and how to apply a given rule to a particular situation. This moment of decision, in which the ordeal of the undecidable resides, can not be limited "to putting into operation a determinable or determining knowledge"[122] because the application of the case to the rule must be made by the judge in a moment of the free iteration of the law.

This contamination or paradox between two types of violence in law breaks down law's claim to achieve justice. I shall focus here on four ways in which law's inadequacy can be analyzed. First, law is always an economy of violence in which some voices are heard and iterated, accepted as "a rule, a norm or a universal imperative,"[123] and others are effaced. According to Derrida, the law depends "on who produces it, founds it, authorizes it,"[124] in a discursive, and therefore inescapably egoistic, performative act. This act can never approach full justice due to the violent paradox inherent within the discursive face-to-face relationship, "for all law," like any discursive positioning, "is dependent on a positing, and no such positing manages without violence."[125]

Even though all law is based on the discursive positioning of particular persons in specific times and places, in order to be legitimate the law must deny its own history. This denial of history, the second reason why law can never achieve full justice, is necessary because "to be invested with its categorical authority, the law must be without history, genesis, or any possible derivation."[126] Derrida puts it best when he writes that "the story of prohibition is a prohibited story."[127] A law that admits to a historical genesis and change admits that it is not categorically valid, that it has been and can again be changed, an idea which reduces the law from transcendent truth to ubiquitously iterated performative act. By claiming to be without history the law hides its origins in the arché-violence of discourse, a violence which, according to the paradox of discourse, continues the moment of the founding violence of the law in each moment of its continued iteration.

Pursuant to its denial of its history and its inherent claim to universality, the law demands that it be iterated without aporia, without being questioned through an ordeal of the undecidable. By admitting the possibility of its own subjects suspending and re-founding it, the law would tacitly admit that it does not hold inevitable universal, categorical validity. An interesting example of this is the military: specifically tasked with defending a state from forceful overthrow, the military is one of the primary conservative forces of a state. Upon enlisting, members of the United States Army take an oath in which they swear to "support and defend the Constitution of the United States against all enemies, foreign and domestic; that I will bear true faith and allegiance to the same; and that I will obey the orders of the President of the United States and the orders of the officers appointed over me."[128] This is an oath of the purest possible conservative violence, in which one promises to forcefully assist the continued iteration of the law over all opponents. In training, members of the military are taught to follow orders without question or regard for personal safety. The perfect soldier is not a person, but an entity of an entirely legalistic, rule-governed, calculable, conservative, non-*épokhal* nature. Inasmuch as all persons retain some capacity to initiate an ordeal of the undecidable, this perfect military entity is not fully achievable with humans, although it certainly is with machines.

The Allied military commanders' collective discomfort at article 8 of the post-World War II Nuremberg International Military Tribunal Charter is an excellent example. Article 8 of the Tribunal's charter indicates that "the fact that the Defendant acted pursuant to order of his Government or of a superior shall not free him from responsibility, but may be considered in mitigation of punishment if the Tribunal determines that justice so requires."[129] This article frustrated many Allied military commanders, who worried that opening up military orders to individual soldiers' ethical calculations would destroy the chain of command by inviting the ordeal of the undecidable into the rigorously conservative and legalistic environment of the military chain of command.

Due in large part to the International Military Tribunal, members of many states' militaries are now officially allowed to disobey orders that are illegal. The United States' military provides a simple but instructive example. Although it is often stated that members of the US military are allowed to disobey orders that they consider immoral, this is not the case—such would open an unacceptable moment of *épokhè* within the conservation of the law. Article 90 of the Uniform Code of Military Justice makes it illegal for any member of the armed forces to willfully disobey "a lawful command of his superior commissioned officer;" article 91 covers obeying the orders of warrant, noncommissioned, and petty officers; and article 92 provides perhaps the most general statement, declaring that "any person subject to this chapter who . . . violates or fails to obey any lawful general order or regulation . . . shall be punished as a court-martial may direct."[130] Thus, members of the US armed forces are only allowed to disobey an order when that order itself violates the law of the United States. Conservation of the law remains paramount in both theory and practice, and any soldier who disobeys an order because she thinks it may be illegal acts at her own peril—article 90 provides for the death penalty if a legal order is disobeyed during time of war.

But the Uniform Code of Military Justice goes even further than this. Again showing that the law and the law's conservation do not structurally allow for any possibility of its suspension, article 134 makes it illegal for a soldier to make any statement "disloyal to the United States. Examples include praising the enemy, attacking the war aims of the United States, or denouncing our form of government . . . [Even] a declaration of personal belief can amount to a disloyal statement if it disavows allegiance owed to the United States by the declarant."[131] In its very structure, in the law itself, the law denies the agents of its enforcement and conservation the moment of aporia that full justice requires. The iteration of the law is not a just practice—it is a solely legal endeavor.[132]

Third, law contains "*in itself, a priori, in the analytic structure of its concept*, the possibility of being 'enforced,' applied by force."[133] The law contains within itself the notion of its being enforced by physical violence that "manifests itself in the purest fashion when violence is absolute, that is to say when it touches on the right to life and to death."[134] The executive and judicial powers of law enforcement, both integral to the very concept of law, are fundamentally based on violence perpetrated against those who commit infractions. The law can never achieve full justice as the recognition of all as sources of meaning because a law breaker, who essentially positions himself discursively as a potential revolutionary in opposition to the current law, is the subject of conservative violence by the law as it iterates itself upon its opponent.

Fourth, in its analytical enforcement of itself the law constitutes a "programmable application or unfolding of a calculable process"[135] which Derrida argues renders a decision legal but not just. A just decision is paradoxically both free and rule-governed, such that the position being iterated is re-decided from scratch as a free decision even while being the calculable application of a rule. Law is only the calculable half of this process, that unfree half that effaces the freedom of the judge in the making of his decision. Law demands a pure conservative violence and insists that its enforcement should not be a *decision*, a free moment that could be decided against law, thus constituting a new foundational moment; rather, law would have its enforcement be the mere inevitable unfolding of a mechanistic process which in its lack of the undecidable would render judicial action legal but not just.

Those who are silenced under a system of law call for the justice that would recognize their voices by breaking into the monologue of the dominant position. Just as in conversation a listener breaks into an ongoing monologue in order to contribute to the dominant story, so in politics does a disadvantaged group enact a revolution against the law. This revolutionary moment of the creation of a new law that favors the voices of those who were previously effaced is, as above, a moment of violence outside of the concept of justice, for "the operation that consists of founding, inaugurating, justifying law (*droit*), making law, would consist of a *coup de force*, of a performative and therefore interpretive violence that in itself is neither just nor unjust and that no justice and no previous law with its founding anterior moment could guarantee or contradict or invalidate."[136] This interpretive moment of revolution transcends the concept of justice because it is a radical break with the previous calculable content of law and a leap through the undecidable in a performative moment of new foundation. The dictates of previous law would be completely effaced as their iterative conservation/re-foundation was halted and a new foundation was made. The previous law, which embodied the particular structural, calculable aspect of justice would not merely be suspended, which would be unjust—the very concept of the calculable is rejected in a moment of total freedom that results in the foundation of a new calculable structure, a new law, at which point the concept of justice is re-instituted.

This moment beyond justice of the creation of a new law or story can also be explained as a time of undecidability between the constative and the performative. Derrida contends that in any successful revolution it is the confusion between these two structures that produces the necessarily paradoxical effect of foundation. In this discussion Derrida builds on Austin's distinction between constative and performative utterances. The former are descriptive claims that can be true or false, such as "the sky is blue." The latter are statements that do something in the stating: when one says "I promise," the very act of promising is constituted by the utterance of the promise.[137]

Derrida explains this undecidability between constative and performative in the foundation of a new state by examining the Declaration of Independence. The final paragraph of the Declaration states that "We, therefore, the Representatives of the United States of America, in General Congress, Assembled . . . do, in the Name, and by the Authority of the good People of these Colonies, solemnly publish and declare, That these United Colonies are, and of Right ought to be Free and Independent States." Although the political independence of the United States is declared by its representatives in the name of its people, the United States does not come into existence until after independence is declared. The People of the United States "do *not* exist as such as an entity, it does *not* exist, *before* this declaration,"[138] so they are therefore unable to authorize representatives to speak in their name and declare their independence. Before the Declaration there is no "they" to become independent: "The signature invents the signer," but because "henceforth, [they] have the right to sign, in truth [they] will already have had it" since they were able to give it to themselves.[139] The signer, in this case, is not the group of representatives, but the People who authorize them to sign in their name.

Herein lies the paradox. The Declaration can be considered constative, as the statement of a claim that can be either true or false—either the People of the United States are politically independent of Britain, or they are not. The fact that they were capable of stating and acting upon their independence would certainly support the notion that the Declaration is constative. In terms of the foundational/conservative aporia, the constative character of the Declaration is conservative. It continues to iterate the previously given fact that the People of the United States exist independently of Britain. But the Declaration can also be considered performative, since the act of stating independence and the formation of a new state creates what it claims to merely describe. The Declaration performed the foundation of the United States of America by rejecting the colonies' subjection to Britain and declaring independence. It is therefore impossible to decide "whether independence is stated or produced by this utterance,"[140] whether a declaration of independence is conservative or foundational. The speech act of declaring oneself is an act of creating oneself—in this case, the creation of the People of the United States who are capable of authorizing representatives. But it is also an act that would be unthinkable unless the declaring entity already existed, already had the power to declare or announce itself.

Because of this undecidability the declaration is simultaneously the comparatively innocuous description of an extant situation, as well as a "coup of force, which is also a coup of writing, as the right to writing" (or in this case, signing) in which "the *self* surges up here in all cases (nominative, dative, accusative)."[141] In fact, this undecidability is played out within the dual nature of the nominative itself, in which the self ("the People of the United States") is the subject of a verb ("to declare"), and is also named or nominated by itself in that act of declaration. The People of the United States are both creator and created, namer and named, nominator and nominee. This coup of writing is therefore a political coup in both the common strict sense, as a declaration of political independence, and in the broader sense of a coup of force that rejects the dominance of an other through a creation/assertion of selfhood.

In this decidedly political, but also ethical, moment of declaration, one person both takes possession of her personhood and creates that personhood where previously it did not exist. The new person begins in/as an act of meaning creation that is both law-creating and law-conserving violence against an oppressing person. Through an upsurge of creative personhood, the Americans, who had been considered inferior subjects by the British in the arché-violent usage of this work, and hence in the common political denotation of the term, founded a new corporate personhood in both the metaphysical and political senses that I have been using here. As a performative act of foundational violence, a declaration of independence rejects the continued iteration of the meanings of another person or the laws of another state and begins a new system of meanings and values in its own name.

But this moment of creation does not escape the aporia of law-creating and law-conserving violence. Even as they reject and exceed the law of the past and institute their own system of meanings, "the people" of the Declaration of Independence appeal to accepted principles of ethics to justify their break with the past. Not only are those "good people" free, but "of Right [they] ought to be" free and independent. They continue to conserve and iterate the law, but not as mere mechanistic restatement. Rather, in this "moment in which the foundation of law remains suspended in the void or over the abyss, suspended by a pure performative act that would not have to answer to or before anyone,"[142] they can undergo the ordeal of the undecidable and *choose* part of the law while rejecting another part. As they create themselves as an independent political entity, they re-accept the moral law in a free act of re-foundation. They simultaneously reject the iterations of past oppressions upon their independent personhood in an extra-legal way that can not be considered a mere domestic crime because it exceeds the system of meanings and values under which that crime exists. The founders of a new state (or law, or method of literary interpretation, etc.) thus play out the paradox of iterability that infests every new institution or claim.

Moving beyond Derrida's well-trodden idea that a moment of pure foundation is not possible due to the "*differantielle* contamination" between foundation and conservation,[143] the new system of law that a revolution erects is itself a new violence to replace the old. Revolution "inaugurates a new law . . . in violence" that "will in return legitimate, retrospectively" its new claims that arose through the ordeal of the undecidable.[144] For Derrida "a 'successful' revolution . . . will produce . . . proper interpretative models to read in return, to give sense, necessity and above all legitimacy to the violence that has produced, among others, the interpretive model in question, that is, the discourse of its self-legitimation."[145]

The new law that is instituted after a successful revolution serves to enforce the continued conservation (iteration) of the ideas it represents, and it does so by providing an interpretive framework that retrospectively legitimates the performative act of its own institution. This performative act of lawmaking is a violence perpetrated from the inescapable egoism of the face, it is a foundation/conservation that simultaneously creates a new structure and enforces its own universal iteration by effacing the positions of others. This new dominant position is no less violent than that which it overthrew: although the face has changed, the inevitability of the structure has remained the same.

Given this inescapable economy of violence, the best we can do within discourse is to approach justice as closely as possible. Recognizing that we are stuck within discourse and using the heliocentric metaphor of Western metaphysics, Derrida writes that

> one must combat light with a certain other light, in order to avoid the worst violence, the violence of the night which precedes or represses discourse. The *vigilance* is a violence chosen as the last violence by a philosophy which takes history, that is, finitude, seriously; a philosophy aware of itself as *historical*. . . . The philosopher (man) *must* speak and write within this war of light, a war in which he always already knows himself to be engaged; a war which he knows is inescapable, except by denying discourse, that is, by risking the worst violence.[146]

Because pure non-violence is impossible, the least violent option is one of great vigilance that continuously reminds all positions that they are finite, historical, and contestable. By undermining the fundamental bases of dominant positions in the name of repressed others and questioning the formers' claims to universality and inevitability, one can mitigate the violence—metaphysical as well as physical—that the dominant position would otherwise perpetrate upon those others in the name of its own iteration. Grammatically, this amounts to minimizing the forceful accusative and the objectifying attributive in favor of the peaceful recognition of the face-to-face relationship signified by the vocative and the dative.

By questioning the dominant position—the law—in the name of justice, deconstruction approaches justice by constantly revolutionizing discourse. Deconstruction does not try to simply destroy dominant positions, but instead "it positively renders justice possible by adopting an excessive and incalculable *responsibility* to the question" of justice.[147] This responsibility towards justice is at the heart of deconstruction, motivating the deployment of violence against violence and light against light to ward off the worst violence that would permanently efface all positions except one.

Deconstruction's vigilance, a counter-violence against greater violence, motivated by the responsibility to the *avenir* of justice, is operationalized by a methodological suspension of a dominant position and a radical questioning of its bases that opens room for the deployment of other positions. Derrida writes that

> The moment that an axiom's credibility is suspended by deconstruction, in this structurally necessary moment . . . this period of *épokhè* . . . this anxiety-ridden moment of suspense—which is also the interval or space in which transformations, indeed juridico-political revolutions take place—cannot be motivated, cannot find its movement and its impulse . . . except in the demand for an increase in or supplement to justice.[148]

Motivated by a demand for justice, a demand to have their positions recognized, the effaced do violence to the dominant position by suspending it, by refusing to iterate it themselves and by questioning any further conservation of it. The resulting period of *épokhè*, in which the automatic conservation of a position is suspended, is the space in which revolution occurs and justice can be done because the positions at stake undergo the ordeal of the undecidable. At this *épokhal* moment of suspension there is "a break in the programmatic such that law cannot easily calculate decisions," resulting in "the possibility of a relation 'to the other.'"[149]

Rather than being mindlessly iterated, the dominant position is questioned and given the opportunity to be justified, to be re-founded in a moment that approaches justice. By being evaluated from the positions of others and hence freed from its automatic iteration, the law is given the chance to move toward the justice that requires that each moment of iteration be re-decided from scratch as a free and incalculable decision. This suspenseful *épokhè* that breaks through law into justice, the result of a cry for increased justice, actually does justice to the given situation because it re-founds as it questions rather than just moving with discursive or legal inertia. In this revolutionary space both the law and its interlocutor are given the chance to give accounts of themselves and be evaluated through the ordeal of the undecidable that is demanded by justice.

Those deconstructors who do justice to the law and its interlocutors are consequently the most just of people. They do not move with inertia for or against a position—they are neither state security nor rabid rebellion. Instead they attempt to constantly question each iteration, actually choosing a position through a moment of discreet revolution that may in fact re-found the given law. Deconstruction does not try to overthrow positionality, it seeks to do justice to all positions (even dominant ones) by giving them the chance to be justified, to speak originarily for themselves and be chosen rather than enforced. This is why "deconstruction is justice."[150] Certainly deconstruction "assumes the right to contest . . . constitutional protocols, the very charter that governs reading,"[151] but it does not assume a position of overthrow—such would not do justice to the given, would not let the given speak on its own behalf. Deconstruction is justice (or at least, it approaches justice) because it suspends and questions *all* positions—and of course the dominant position must be suspended more thoroughly in proportion to its supposed self-evidence—and creates the space for every position to have a face (and every face to have a position), which is the ultimate demand of the justice that is each position's recognition that all others are their own independent sources of meaning.

V. Nietzsche

The foregoing all points to the notion that for Derrida human life—at least any human life we could comprehend, any life within discourse—is fundamentally about being a source of meaning. Violence, the "reduction of the other to a *real* moment of *my* life" and hence the denial that the other has its own independent existence, is antithetical to gaining "access to the egoity of the alter ego as if to its alterity itself . . . the most peaceful gesture possible."[152] This peaceful gesture would be an acceptance that the other is an independent entity capable of creating its own meanings and interpretations, rather than a mere extension of oneself that is bound to one's own ideas and categories.

Derrida writes that reduction of the other to "intraworldliness is the origin and very meaning of what is called violence"[153] because this reduction denies that the other is capable of any leaps through the ordeal of the undecidable. A thing that can not work through the ordeal of the undecidable can not move outside the merely calculable—it may be a legal entity, but it can never be a just entity. Justice involves not only a calculable application of law—it also requires a positive decision, a moment of the creation of meaning or value out of the ordeal of the undecidable. "As speech and glance the face is not in the world"[154] because the world is mere calculation. Glance and speech, the autonomous address and foundation/iteration of a perspective, are beyond the world of mere calculation, so reducing this face to intraworldliness is the direct denial that it is the seat of the presence of an autonomous other within the world of discourse.

Although Derrida's conclusions are decidedly un-Nietzschean, there are important but unexpected agreements and similarities between the two writers. For Derrida the being-in-the-world of the Person begins with the Face, in which a person "is given 'in person' and without allegory."[155] The Face institutes the person in the world as egoity, perspective, intersubjectivity, sensor, and speaker; thus the ethical nature of life begins with the physical construction of the person.

Nietzsche also claims that the physical nature of personhood explains both the general structure of intersubjectivity and ethics, but he goes further than Derrida by arguing that an individual's specific physiology conditions his or her specific moral nature. He claims that "morality is mere sign language, mere symptomatology,"[156] that "every 'though shalt' known to history or ethnology, requires first a *physiological* investigation and interpretation, rather than a psychological one."[157] Both the ideals of individual persons and the moralities of cultures "are resultant states," "translations of pleasurable or unpleasurable feelings"[158] into ideas that influence the actions of these physical bodies.

Physical life is the only type of life according to Nietzsche, who is well-known for his position that "the 'apparent' world is the only one: the 'true' world is merely added by a lie."[159] He reconfirms this idea in, for example, *Thus*

Spoke Zarathustra, in which Zarathustra himself proclaims that "the awakened and knowing say: body am I entirely, and nothing else; and soul is only a word for something about the body."[160] This worldly, physical life "operates *essentially*, that is in its basic function, through injury, assault, exploitation, destruction."[161] As part of nature, those persons who exhibit "a powerful physicality, a flourishing, abundant, even overflowing health"[162] are richest in life itself, "which aims at the expansion of power."[163] Thus Nietzsche arrives at one of his most famous concepts: "the will to power—the unexhausted procreative will of life."[164]

The will to power defines life itself. Because life itself is "the instinct for growth, for durability, for an accumulation of forces, for *power*,"[165] that which manifests will to power is living healthily, and that which does not manifest it is sick and decaying. This power is not constituted by a mere stagnant self-preservation; it is a constant striving "of the spontaneous, aggressive, expansive, form-giving forces that give new interpretations and directions"[166] to the world. Human life, defined by this constant struggle for increasing interpretive dominance among other wills to power, is for Nietzsche (as for Derrida) characterized by the will to be a creator of meaning, to dominate one's surroundings discursively. Will to power is therefore fundamental to all truly human life, as exemplified by the "the noble type" who Nietzsche says "experiences *itself* as determining values," as "*value-creating*."[167] But even the slavish and weak (which I shall define more thoroughly later) contain "the will to be master,"[168] though they may not realize it.

Bluntly stating one of the most constant themes throughout his work, Nietzsche proclaims that "*there are altogether no moral facts*."[169] Therefore "men gave themselves all their good and evil. Verily, they did not take it, they did not find it, nor did it come to them as a voice from heaven;"[170] humans are the creators of value and meaning in the world. They are not "contemplative," they are not mere "spectators" or "listeners"—humans are "poet[s] who [keep] creating this life"[171] in accordance with the basic nature of life as will to power. The scientist who claims to discover objective external facts is therefore a life-denying ascetic who does not understand that he is a creator and artist. Although an excellent scientist "is certainly one of the most precious instruments there are," thanks to his self-denied abilities to craft meaning into existence, "he belongs in the hand of one more powerful."[172] Because the scientist makes every effort to remove his subjectivity from his work—as immediately evidenced by the rejection of the use of the first person in scientific writing—he is, Nietzsche claims, using Kantian terminology, "no 'end in himself.'"[173] He is, rather, "an instrument,"[174] an advanced form of tool to be used by a joyful creator who, embracing life as the will to power, struggles for discursive dominance with other persons.

Each individual's ongoing creation of meaning is purely perspectival. "In the end, one experiences only oneself"[175] because "there is *only* a perspective seeing, *only* a perspective 'knowing,'"[176] which is not actually a 'knowing' at all. 'Knowing' would obviously imply the discovery of pure objective fact, as the scientist claims to accomplish, but "fact has to be interpreted: *in itself* it just stands there, stupid to all eternity, like every 'thing-in-itself.'"[177] Humans do not discover facts, they create meaning and value based on their individual perspectives, which are themselves conditioned by the physiological makeup of each person. As above, judgments "have value only as symptoms"[178] of one's physiology; discursive positions that embrace life as will to power are likely taken by strong, vibrant physical bodies, whereas positions against life result from having a weak or tired physicality.

Of course, this creates a potentially serious methodological dilemma for Nietzsche. By one account, he himself can not possibly be providing an objective account of the True nature of life and the universe, since such an account is impossible. On the other hand, he may contend that life as will to power and the subjectivity of all human "knowledge" may be the only objectively knowable facts in existence. The latter position is held by John Richardson, who claims that "Nietzsche's vision of a world of perspectives presumes that each of these has the essential structure of will to power [that is] 'objectively' true of them."[179] The content of each of these wills to power is determined perspectivally, but their essential structure as will to power is objectively true. Part of this essential structure of will to power is that it "views the world from its interests,"[180] creating its own meanings and values based on the "psychological fact [that] a condition of authority over other persons is our 'highest end,'" and that all our actions are "chosen and pursued only as means to this" end.[181]

Linda Williams argues an opposing position when she stresses that for Nietzsche "all human life is engaged in interpretation. Even the act of perception is an act of interpretation."[182] She believes that "what drives readers of Nietzsche's works crazy . . . is that Nietzsche does not feel the need to tell his readers that this is all from his perspective over and over again"—but that what Nietzsche writes are *his* Truths and his alone, and that although he may argue that they hold for all times and places that they are still only individualized interpretations.[183] According to Williams' perspective, what Nietzsche is trying to do is get his readers to ask why he interprets things in the ways he does, thus prompting them to examine their own creations and learn more about themselves in the process.

Although it is a very important exegetical issue, whether Nietzsche holds certain things as universal facts or if from his perspective the only universal is interpretation, both readings support my use of him. If will to power is objectively true, then Nietzsche explicitly holds that all life *is* a violent struggle for dominance. Therefore human life would objectively be about the creation of meanings and values in the pursuit of this overarching universal goal. But if Nietzsche does not believe in any nonperspectival truth, then his own claims to Truth—including his arguments about will to power, the master morality, et cetera—are all his own individualized creations of meaning and value. Others may disagree with his position, and claim that objective knowledge is possible, but those who make that claim would themselves also take their position based on their own individualized interpretations. For Nietzsche, either 1) objectivity is only possible enough to claim that all knowledge is interpretation, or 2) even that minimal level of objectivity is impossible, so everything, including the claim that all life is a drive to overcome and that all knowledge is perspectivally created, is interpretation. Either way, life is about the individualized, perspectival imputation of meaning and value into ideas and events that have no objective status outside of our interpretations of them.

Because the meanings and values persons create are conditioned by their physiologies, Nietzsche does not try to convince people to change how they value. Persuasion is pointless when free will is merely "the foulest of all theologians' artifices,"[184] when "one must first persuade the *body*"[185] in order to change the positions taken by the mind. The freedom of the will is a myth perpetrated by the weak and slavish as an excuse for punishing the strong and vibrant. If persons are considered free to choose how they esteem, if "the origin of every act [is] considered as lying within the consciousness,"[186] then they can be blamed and punished for their actions. In practical application, this amounts to the weak punishing the strong for the latter's actions that adversely affect the former.

These weak, slavish persons of whom I keep writing, whom Nietzsche is not trying to convince to embrace their nature as meaning-creators, are simply "human being[s] who [have] turned out badly."[187] These "despisers of the body," want to "die and turn away from life,"[188] because, due to their comparative weakness, life for them is pain and suffering. This slavish type is a creature of *ressentiment*, an impotent resentfulness that is "denied the true reaction, that of deeds,"[189] because of its weakness. The morality of *ressentiment*, called Slave Morality by Nietzsche, began when the weak and downtrodden rejected the suffering that was naturally inflicted upon them by those who were stronger. Their "*ressentiment* itself [became] creative and [gave] birth to values"[190] that in their first instance rejected the actions of the stronger as evil. This rejection, this focus on denial of an other instead of an affirmation of self, "is of the essence of *ressentiment*: in order to exist, slave morality always first needs a hostile external world . . . its action is fundamentally reaction."[191] Masterful persons, on the other hand, are like children: "The child is innocence and forgetting, a new beginning, a game, a self-propelled wheel, a first movement."[192] The child here represents action that is not reaction, a new beginning that propels itself based upon its own desires and interpretations. Slavish ideas begin not as a first movement or a new beginning, but a reaction to something else. Slaves are in this way only an advanced form of machine that responds to external stimuli, not true persons.

These slaves, faced with their own weakness and inability to revenge themselves upon their tormentors, turned this weakness into a virtue. Their *ressentiment* festered and caused the weak to dream of revenge against their oppressors. This stunted desire for revenge was forced into "hiding places, secret paths and back doors"[193] until, in an act of supreme cognitive dissonance, the "inability for revenge [was] called unwillingness to revenge, perhaps even forgiveness."[194] The main motivation behind all their actions was that "nobody should hurt them," so "they tr[-ied] to please and gratify everybody"[195]—thinking that they were good and virtuous while they were actually frightened and obsequious.

Caught in a desire for revenge but unable to fulfill this wish, downtrodden by the strong, and dreaming of a place where their suffering will abate, the weak were also the first to posit an afterlife. They "downgrade[d] physicality to an illusion"[196] and proclaimed "a god who would be truly a god for the sick, a healer and savior"[197] who would love and protect them for eternity. Although Nietzsche at first appears to completely despise these life-denying ascetics who "slander the world,"[198] he recognizes the necessity of these pleasant fictions for most people. The sickly, slavish priest who leads the weak in their adoration of religious fictions is not only an "enemy of life," he is also among "the greatest *conserving* and yes-creating forces of life"[199] because the weak can cling to his stories and find life slightly more livable than they would otherwise.

The passage in *The Gay* Science in which Nietzsche explains this question of the "value of values" most clearly is worth reproducing in full:

> Now something that you formerly loved as a truth or probability strikes you as an error; you shed [246] it and fancy that this represents a victory for your reason. But perhaps this error was a necessary for you then, when you were still a different person—you are always a different person—as are all your present "truths," being a skin, as it were, that concealed and covered a great deal that you were not yet permitted to see. What killed that opinion for you was your new life and not your reason: *you no longer need it*. . . . When we criticize something, this is no arbitrary and impersonal event; it is, at least very often, evidence of vital energies in us that are growing and shedding a skin.[200]

In this passage Nietzsche provides one of his clearest accounts of the value that values have for those who hold them. Different people require different types of meanings and values in order to survive, so truth is less important than believing what one has to believe in order to go on another day. Slavish persons require a belief in gods and afterlives if they are to sustain themselves through all their trials and tribulations, and priests help serve this important function. But Nietzsche does not teach atheism as any more eternally true than theism. Rather, he "would have men proceed 'as if' there were no God."[201] Masters require different beliefs to help them conduct the sort of lives that they must, given their physiologies and dispositions. The value of one's beliefs for oneself is more important than any question of the objective truth of those beliefs—even when the question is one of the objective truth of Nietzsche's position against the importance of objective truth.

Naturally, this raises the question of Nietzsche's value for any philosophical investigation. Similarly to the methodological dilemma I discussed above, Nietzsche may believe that all the ethical ideas he proposes are objectively true, or he may only consider them necessary for him to believe, irrespective of their likely unknowable ontological status. But as above, either position is acceptable for the use to which I put him. If his ethical ideas are objectively true, then there is no problem at all: it is objectively true that persons are meaning creators. If our ideas are only our own, which we consider universally true because they are necessary for the continuation of our lives, then they are still our individualized creations. Therefore persons are still the creators of meaning and value in the world.

Obviously, the slavish morality of the weak is not a morality of death. It falls within the definition of life as will to power because its creators posited new meanings and values, and tried to iterate those values as widely as possible. Although the weak find "blessedness (pleasure) only in no longer offering any resistance to anybody"[202] here in the temporary physical world, they stake this discursive position as a positive claim. Through history they "have turned the wolf into a dog and man himself into man's best domestic animal"[203]—they have won the struggle with the morality of the strong and propagated their assertion of passivity over the human race. The weak also seek to become "master[s] over *beasts of prey*"[204] in their posited afterlife. In their "kingdom of God" the weak "intend to be the strong,"[205] and plan to live forever in glorious peace with their god while they look down upon the hellish suffering of their former tormentors. Those who reject this slavish morality are subject to the revenge as punishment that the weak are now free to inflict upon those few noble-minded persons who remain. Punishment is exacted by the weak upon the noble because, thanks to the slavish doctrine of the freedom of the will, the former can blame the latter for acting against the dominant morality. "Punishment *tames* [these noble] men"[206] and attempts to force them to act as slaves, rejecting their noble morality of proud creation in favor of subjection to the iteration of the slave morality.

Those "noble, powerful, high-stationed and highminded"[207] masters whom the slaves overcame slowly through history by sheer force of numbers did not constantly compare themselves with others, as the slaves did. These masters "did not have to establish their happiness artificially by examining their enemies, or to persuade themselves, *deceive* themselves, that they were happy (as all men of *ressentiment* are in the habit of doing)."[208] They simply lived as their vibrant physiologies conditioned them to live, embracing life as will to power and understanding that "happiness should not be sundered from action."[209] Most importantly, these noble, value-creating persons silenced the "mole and dwarf" who proclaimed universal goods and evils by proclaiming to themselves "this is *my* good and evil."[210] Instead of adhering to the so-called universal laws announced by the slavish moralists, the noble masters struggled joyfully against each other as they asserted their individual positions and embraced the "fundamental instinct of life which aims at the expansion of power."[211]

Nietzsche argues that the slaves long ago defeated the masters. Today almost everyone adheres to the "'altruistic' morality" of the weak, "a morality in which self-interest wilts away"[212] and every one has an "'evil eye' for his natural inclinations."[213] One of Nietzsche's main goals is to reinvigorate those strong, noble persons who have been poisoned by the dominance of the slave morality. He speaks "of a 'return to nature,' although it is really not a going back but an *ascent*—up into the high, free, even terrible nature and naturalness,"[214] through which persons will once again embrace their nature as creators of meaning. "Another century of readers," another century of those who merely absorb and iterate the ancient universal laws of the slave morality, of the belief in objectivity and the discovery rather than the creation of meaning, "and the spirit itself will stink."[215] Nietzsche wants at least the strong to remember that the world revolves "around the inventors of new values."[216] These fully-human free creators become their own poles around whom orbit all those slavish folk who are incapable of transcending mere iteration and becoming truly human.

Those who do not create meaning for themselves are not fully human for Nietzsche. In complete persons "*creature* and *creator* are united: in man there is material, fragment, excess, clay, dirt, nonsense, chaos; but in man there is also creator, form-giver, hammer hardness, spectator divinity, and seventh day."[217] The human is both conservative and foundational, it is (in more Derridean terms) the constant overcoming of the ordeal of the undecidable that exists in the arché-violent tension within justice, which demands both the application of law and the freedom to create outside of any prescription. Those who slavishly accept the values they are taught deny that they themselves are sources of meaning—they are legal half-persons, beholden to the idols of the mind[218] and incapable of making the leap through the undecidable. True persons, those who contain both foundational and conservative drives, those in whom "creature and creator are united," give themselves their "own evil and [their] own good and hang [their] own will over [themselves] as a law."[219] They do justice to themselves and their situations by choosing freely, rather than adhering slavishly to the dominant position's self-lessness and ego-lessness. The meaning-creating person who rejects the calculable iteration of ancient value claims decides for himself what positions he will (re-)produce. For Nietzsche, this creator is free from the mindless mere legality of iterating the dominant position, for "to will is to create," therefore "to will liberates."[220]

Liberating oneself from the present and future meaning creations of others is certainly a sign of a true person, but freeing oneself from the past takes the exceedingly powerful sort of meaning creator that Nietzsche calls the "overman." Thus he writes that

> The stronger the roots of the inmost nature of a man are, the more of the past will he appropriate or master; and were one to conceive the most powerful and colossal nature, it would be known by this, that for it there would be no limit at which the historical sense could overgrow and harm him; such a nature would draw its own as well as every alien past wholly into itself and transform it into blood, as it were.[221]

The highest type of meaning creator is capable of appropriating even the past into himself and reading his own will, his own meaning creations, into the events of the past, as well as those of the present and the future. "All 'it was' is a fragment, a riddle, a dreadful accident,"—a collection of events that appear unchangeable, already written and passed, but which is reconceptualized by the greatest of persons who says "But thus I willed it."[222] The overman subsumes the past to his own creative discursive force by willing his own identity into it, such that the fragments of the past become a narrative with the great person as their culmination. The great person creates the present by struggling with and overcoming all other sources of meaning and value, the future by enforcing the iteration of his own meanings and values over time, and the past by reinterpreting it in retrospect such that it becomes the story of his own inevitable triumph.

VI. Derrida and Nietzsche at Play

Although for both Derrida and Nietzsche human life is about being a source of meaning, this premise leads each thinker in a completely different direction. The idea that humans are fundamentally sources of meaning leads Derrida to the conclusion that we should try to be as non-violent as possible by practicing deconstruction. By stripping away "law's pretension to be other than politics"[223] deconstruction shows that dominant positions are discursively bound to the particular positionality of their purveyors rather than being universal and incontestable ideals. Seen from the literary side, deconstruction can "counteract the aggression of speech as presence"[224] by reminding us that individual claims are not universal and all-encompassing, being bound by the necessary perspectivalism of egoity. "Since *finite* silence is . . . the medium of violence" as an enforced silencing of dissident voices in conversation or politics, "language can only indefinitely tend toward justice by acknowledging and practicing the violence within it."[225] Deconstruction does this by constantly overcoming dominant discourses in the name of the justice that is called for by those who are silenced.

If human life is fundamentally about being a source of meaning, deconstruction is as peaceful a gesture as one can make toward the humanity of each other because it promotes the reception of all voices in their individuality. Justice as the "rectitude of address"[226]—the addressing of an other as a being capable of approaching justice itself—"is always singular"[227] in that it addresses the legitimate uniqueness and fullness of the positionality of each particular other, thus preserving the primary nature of the other as an independent source of meaning. Mere law, on the other hand, "seems always to suppose the generality of a rule, a norm or a universal imperative,"[228] and therefore imposes perspectives upon others who are in the structure of this law denied status as meaning-creators independent of the presumed universality of the law.

Similarly, Nietzsche argues that each individual should embrace his meaning-creating nature and actively create his own law for himself, rejecting "the mole and dwarf who say, 'Good for all, evil for all.'"[229] Those sickly half-persons who can not reject this mole, and who live under the yoke of eternal laws, do no justice (in the Derridean sense) to themselves or their situations because they never exceed the calculable. Only those who are value-creating, who undertake "a strategy of rupture"[230] with the dominant discourses of the day, celebrate human life over the ascetic, legalistic ideals of those who treat "life as a wrong road"[231] and measure their lives not by the independent creation of value, but by selfless legal adherence to universals.

This celebration of individual lives as sources of meaning (wills to power) manifests itself for Nietzsche as a war of all against all in which only those who most manifest the fundamental principle of all life, to wit, the will to power, are capable and worthy of flourishing. The direction of his argument is perhaps seen most clearly in his statement that "a legal order thought of as sovereign and universal . . . as a means of *preventing* all struggle in general . . . would be a principle *hostile to life*,"[232] that is, hostile to the principle of will to power. In contradiction to Derrida's argument that because life is about being a source of meaning we must always choose the lesser of the necessary violences and allow everyone an independent voice, Nietzsche argues here that we should each embrace violence as the denial of the other as a source of meaning and attempt to overcome all other discursive positions with our own. Only in this way, Nietzsche argues, can we truly do justice to ourselves and the principle of life within ourselves and others. If each person takes his own life seriously he will reject the lives of all others as he lives out his own imperative of will to power. A universal legal order that prevents struggle is hostile to life because "to demand of strength that it should not express itself as strength, that it should *not* be a desire to overcome, a desire to throw down, a desire to become master . . . is just as absurd as to demand of weakness that it should express itself as strength."[233]

Any morality or legalism that demands that individuals not pursue their natural wills to power is not only absurd, it is unhealthy because it denies the natural function of the human organism by subsuming this "unexhausted procreative will of life"[234] beneath the slavish fiction of a universal law that enforces limits upon that will. Such a slavish system in effect sickens the human animal, reducing "the beast of prey 'man' to a tame and civilized . . . hopelessly mediocre and insipid man."[235] This mediocre creature willingly limits his own will to power, his own positionality and hence his own *life*, so that others in discourse may also live their stunted lives in relative peace.

This "democratic idiosyncrasy which opposes everything that dominates and wants to dominate," instead demanding compromise and cooperation with the mass of mediocre souls, "has permeated the realm of the spirit"[236] and tamed otherwise creative, dominating personalities. The triumph of this democratic idiosyncrasy in people's minds and the victory of democracy as a form of governance are still, however, the result of a violent positioning and the iteration of that position over others. As above, the slave morality is still itself a manifestation of that nature of persons as meaning creators, even if the slavish persons themselves reject that notion in favor of the ascetic ideas of objectivity and universality. Although they may believe that democratic societies were formed peacefully, resulting from the recognition of the independent voices of all persons, democracy is itself a repressive paradigm that rejects and oppresses those who seek to embrace life as will to power.

"Human society is a trial . . . and what it tries to find is the commander"[237]—but in democratic societies the slavish impulse for equality and herd animality has conquered those few noble souls who recognize and actively pursue life as will to power. According to Nietzsche, the "welding of a hitherto unchecked and shapeless populace into a firm form was not only instituted by an act of violence but also carried to its conclusion by nothing but acts of violence,"[238] all slavish rejections of the will to power notwithstanding. Society is therefore a "trial . . . and *not* a 'contract':"[239] it is the result of the struggle, victory, and iteration of some particular person's or persons' creations of meaning about how people should interact. Even so, the slavish safety and luxuries of the modern state allow for an increase in population that "reinforces the state because the state is needed to minister to the needs of those who can no longer be self-sufficient."[240] As the population of mediocre persons grows, the state becomes more and more entrenched as a new idol of the mind, reified for its preservative capacity that is really a coddling of the slavish herd that rejects the human creative nature and for its forceful and ubiquitous iteration of slavish ideals over potential creators of new values.

VII. The Economy of Violence

So beginning from the same premise that life is about being a source of meaning, Derrida and Nietzsche arrive at two different conclusions. Derrida argues that we should come as close as possible to respecting the face of each other as a sovereign face, and Nietzsche claims that because life is about being a source of meaning we should each embrace our own will to power and reject that of each other. These appear to be two perfectly different positions, Derrida stressing the importance of giving all others their due and Nietzsche focusing on giving oneself one's own due, but there may be a "*differantielle* contamination between the two"[241] such that each position is inscribed within the other.

The key to Nietzsche's position of overcoming is that it requires something to overcome. The struggle that slavish legal orders reject must be a struggle against something, of persons against one another. The will to power must be a power over something, and that something is precisely what has been overcome. The will to power is a "subduing, a becoming master"[242] that in its very structure as an overcoming requires "war and victory . . . conquest, adventure, danger,"[243] which necessitates a belligerent-*cum*-interlocutor. In fact, according to Nietzsche the struggle that is necessitated by the will to power should be embraced as a "joy in persecuting, in attacking"[244] rather than as a regrettable necessity.

The necessity of an interlocutor to be overcome means that Nietzsche's theory can not transcend the economy of violence of which Derrida speaks. Although Nietzsche would have us each try to completely efface the other or be effaced in the attempt, such struggle tacitly recognizes the humanity of the enemy as a source of meaning that must be overcome. As I shall revisit in my discussion of Hobbes' state of nature in the following chapter, this other is not struggled with and overcome if it is a mere mindless object, and indeed Nietzsche claims that the noble person "desires his enemy for himself,"[245] an enemy worthy of being attacked. These sought after enemies in which there is "*very much* to honor"[246] are recognized as strong independent sources of meaning, as people worthy of a fight and capable of making victory difficult and therefore precious. In fact, Nietzsche argues that "one's best enemy"[247] is one's best friend. Creators seek companionship in fellow creators, "not corpses, not herds and believers,"[248] because creators want to "strive against one another like gods"[249] and live out the principle of life as will to power. The very dominance that Nietzsche argues for requires the recognition (and indeed the companionship) of strong others. If only one ego existed, Nietzschean discursive dominance would not be possible.

This necessity for strong others is the point at which Nietzsche's thought is inscribed with the Derridean position of recognizing the face of the other as sovereign, because Nietzschean dominance is not possible unless it is dominance over such independent creators of meaning. If complete Nietzschean dominance were achieved and all others were effaced, this victory would cease to exist because the complete subjection of all others would destroy the very otherness that made them overcome-able. For the victory to continue to exist, for the victor to continue to be dominant *over* something, the vanquished must not be completely effaced. If the defeated were completely effaced, the victor could not be dominant over them because they could not be subjugated—objects that are not themselves independent sources of meaning can not be subjugated because they simply fall into line behind discursive inertia. In the very act of completely subjugating an opponent, of completely effacing that opponent in an act of pure violence, the victor would render his opponent incapable of being subjugated, and that opponent would slip through his grasp. Because this Nietzschean dominance is a discursive dominance over others, those others must continue to be capable of discourse, so they must not be completely effaced.

Given that the other can not be completely effaced within Nietzsche's idea of dominance through the will to power, the economy of violence remains inescapable for his thought, and his position is logically inscribed with Derrida's notion of respecting the face of the other. If the others' faces were completely subjugated—if Derrida's claim that the faces of others should be respected as sovereign was rejected and one succeeded in transcending discourse and annihilating the otherness of the others—the victor would be a god in an empty universe, as powerful as a person can be over merely phenomenal objects, but discursively dominant over nothing. For Nietzsche's victory and supremacy to remain as such, for the most masterful person to be the dominant source of meaning, that master must be the master over other persons who, although capable of becoming independent sources of meaning, have been subjugated by the victor. Thus they must be done justice (in Derrida's sense) to the extent that they are recognized as sovereign others rather than being reduced by the victor "to the state of empirical alter-ego."[250]

Recognizing the inescapable economy of violence within discourse, Derrida argues that we should pursue the least violence possible. Pure non-violence, "the nonrelation of the same to the other,"[251] is an impossibility, so what Derrida proposes is somewhat violent. Because of the paradox of pure violence and pure non-violence, the best Derrida can propose within discourse is a "violence against violence, light against light"[252] in which the dominant position (the law) is constantly revolutionized in the name of justice by those who are currently effaced. Because the origin of this new law is itself a "violent positioning"[253] it effaces the position of the previous law which it overcomes in the name of justice, thus doing violence to another in the name of justice for itself.

This new founding moment can not be criticized on the basis of any preceding legality because it "does not recognize existing law in the moment that it founds another."[254] The new law is a clean break with the past that neither seeks nor requires justification on the grounds of the previous law that it destroys. By effacing the previously dominant position, the new founding law does justice only to itself through its "performative force, which is always an interpretative force"[255] and is therefore reminiscent of Nietzsche's will to power which does violence to all others in the struggle for individual dominance. Through a continual "interrogation of the origin, grounds and limits of our conceptual, theoretical or normative apparatus"[256] Derrida is promoting a system whereby one will to power rises up and deconstructs the "constructed or interpretable and transformable textual data"[257] of the law through a new violent act of interpretation and effacement, only itself to be overcome eventually by its own adversaries. This inescapable economy of violence forces Derrida to accept Nietzsche's claims that life requires the violent overcoming that does no justice to others, only to itself.

VIII. Conclusion

Beginning from the premise that humans are sources of meaning, Derrida promotes an ethic of respect for the independent face of the other, which is peaceful relative to Nietzsche's ethic of face-to-face struggle and overcoming. Each position requires at least minimum respect for the other in order to maintain the otherness of the other and hence the ethical face-to-face relationship; they also need some level of violence for the promotion of the self or the repressed. Derrida argues for a relatively peaceful system in which individuals do justice to others by limiting the discursively violent promulgation of their own creations of meaning. Even so, he also recognizes that the revolutions that overthrow the meanings and values embedded within dominant monologues in the name of justice are violent acts that occur outside of the legal aspect of justice, and therefore can not appeal to justice for their legitimacy. Nietzsche's healthy persons who glory in the god-like struggle against each other for discursive dominance require worthy enemies/friends against whom to fight for mastery. These noble persons who revel in life as will to power do justice to themselves by striving to iterate their own meanings and values as vigorously as possible, just as they do justice to others by providing a worthy opponent with whom they can do battle. This economy of violence is inescapable—for both the peaceful ethics of Derrida and the violent ethics of Nietzsche, justice logically requires the presence of some level of discursive violence.

The economy of violence, discursive or otherwise, and its role in the formation of human communities, is the subject of the next chapter. In it, I intend to show that Thomas Hobbes' story of the social compact demonstrates how this paradox of interwoven violence and peacefulness plays out as persons force each other to recognize that they are meaning creators who demand a voice in the foundation and conduct of political living. The social compact itself is an agreement that results when meaning creators, recognizing that the basic problem with the state of nature is that there is no agreement on signification, establish a sovereign to act as the ultimate definer and arbiter of disputed meanings.

According to Hobbes, this play of violence and respect that results in the formation of the commonwealth is driven by those individuals whose better grasp of language gives them superior reasoning abilities. Hobbes' theory of the social compact thus sheds light on the decisions that different sorts of meaning creators make as they attempt to live out their creative nature, and the processes of the interplay of violence and respect at the founding of a society.

Notes

1 Jacques Derrida, *Writing and Difference*, trans. Alan Bass (Chicago: University of Chicago, 1978), 27.

2 Ibid., 115.

3 Ibid., 98.

4 Ibid., 143.

5 Jacques Derrida, *The Ear of the Other: Otobiography, Transference, Translation.* Otobiographies trans. Avital Ronell (London: University of Nebraska Press, 1985), 51.

6 Ibid.

7 Derrida, *Writing and Difference*, 113.

8 Ibid., 103.

9 Ibid., 98.

10 Ibid., 101.

11 Ibid., 115.

12 Ibid., 103.

13 Ibid., 95.

14 Ibid.

15 Ibid.

16 Ibid., 104.

17 Jacques Derrida, *Aporias*, Trans. Thomas Dutoit (Stanford, CA: Stanford University Press, 1993), 55.

18 Ibid., 52.

19 Good examples of such definitions can be found in: Ted Honderich, *Political Violence* (Ithaca, NY: Cornell University Press, 1976), and Robert Audi, "On the Meaning and Justification of Violence," in *Violence*, Ed. Jerome Shaffer (New York: David McKay Company, Inc., 1971). I will refer to both authors periodically during my discussion of Derrida and the concept of violence.

20 Giuliano Pontara, "The Concept of Violence," *Journal of Peace Research* 15, no.1 (1978), 24.

21 Derrida, *Writing and Difference*, 125.

22 Jean-Jacques LeCercle, *The Violence of Language* (London: Routledge, 1990), 234.

23 Ibid.

24 Ibid., 236.

25 Jacques Derrida, "The Force of Law: The 'Mystical Foundation of Authority,'" *Cardozo Law Review* 11 (November 1990), 983.

26 Ibid.

27 Aristotle, *Nichomachean Ethics*, Trans. Terence Irwin (Cambridge: Hackett Publishing Company, 1985), 1109b30.

28 Ibid., 1111b5-10.

29 Ibid., 1135a20.

30 Immanuel Kant, *Groundwork of the Metaphysics of Morals*, Trans. by H.J. Paton (New York: Harper and Row, [1785] 1964), 116.

31 Ibid., 114.

32 Ibid., 116.

33 Immanuel Kant, *The Metaphysics of Morals*, in *Kant: Political Writings*, Ed. Hans Reiss (Cambridge: Cambridge University Press, [1797] 1970), 145.

34 Ibid., 155.

35 Audi, 50.

36 John Harris, *Violence and Responsibility* (London: Routledge and Kegan Paul, Ltd., 1980), 19. Citing Harris, this language is also used by Vittorio Bufacchi, "Why is Violence Bad?" *American Philosophical Quarterly* 41, no. 2 (April 2004), 171.

37 Derrida, *Writing and Difference*, 125.

38 Ibid.

39 E.V. Walter, "Power and Violence," *American Political Science Review* (June 1964), 350.

40 Ibid., 148. At no point in this book have I altered any original italics.

41 Jacques Derrida, *Of Grammatology* trans. Gayatri Spivak, corrected edition (Baltimore: Johns Hopkins University Press, 1997), 110.

42 Derrida, *Writing and Difference*, 147.

43 Ibid., 103.

44 Derrida, *The Ear of the Other*, 50.

45 Derrida, *Writing and Difference*, 129.

46 Ibid., 133.

47 Ibid., 128.

48 Ibid., 103.

49 Ibid., 144.

50 Ibid.

51 Ibid., 91.

52 Ibid., 57.

53 Ibid., 95.

54 Ibid., 125.

55 I shall explore this idea much more thoroughly in my discussion of Nietzsche later in this chapter, as well as in the following chapter's examination of Hobbes' state of nature. In this latter discussion I shall show that the recognition of the personhood of an other may directly lead to physical violences toward that other, such as in Hobbes' state of nature.

56 Derrida, "The Force of Law," 997.

57 Derrida, *Aporias*, 19.

58 Ibid.

59 Jacques Derrida, "A Discussion with Jacques Derrida," *Theory and Event* 5, no.1 (2001), 36.

60 Derrida, *Writing and Difference*, 103.

61 Derrida, "The Force of Law," 963.

62 Richard Beardsworth, *Derrida and the Political* (London: Routledge, 1996), 12.

63 Ibid.

64 Friedrich Nietzsche, *On the Genealogy of Morals*, in *Basic Writings of Nietzsche*, trans. Walter Kaufmann, 4th edition (New York: The Modern Library, [1887] 1992), 515.

65 Derrida, *Writing and Difference*, 117.

66 Ibid., 146.

67 Ibid., 146-147.

68 Ibid., 95.
69 Derrida, *Aporias*, 72.
70 Ibid., 73.
71 Derrida, *Writing and Difference*, 124.
72 Ibid., 146.
73 Ibid., 128.
74 Ibid., 106.
75 Ibid., 138.
76 Derrida, "The Force of Law," 949.
77 Derrida, *Writing and Difference*, 125.
78 Harris, 49.
79 Ibid., 48-49.

80 This medical example evokes an interesting aside. One commentator on this work has suggested that although pure discursive non-violence may not be possible, pure physical non-violence is. He goes on to claim that the exercise of pure physical non-violence does not necessitate the exercise of pure physical violence, as it paradoxically would with discursive non-violence. I disagree with this assessment. Pure physical non-violence would require absolutely no physical intercession with the other under any circumstances—it would mean compete respect for the independent physical existence of the other, and an unwillingness to, as Locke might put it, mix one's own labor with the body of that other. Expressing oneself physically upon the other in any way would, like the machine in Kafka's "In the Penal Colony," iterate one's own physicality upon the body of an other in a direct physical analogue to a discursive imposition upon the independent meanings and values created by an other. Yet one who is unwilling to intervene physically under any circumstances would have to allow an other to be physically harmed, rather than come to that other's physical aid. This is one of the classic dilemmas of pacifism—a true pacifist might be implicated in the injury or death of an other upon whose behalf he is unwilling to intervene physically. Thus, pure physical non-violence contains an element of physical violence because it demands non-intervention under any circumstances, including those in which the health or life of the other may be at risk.

Physical intervention with non-violent intentions is therefore an imposition in itself, but it may also require more overt or banal forms of physical violence. Consider, for instance, health care professionals who regularly intervene physically to save the lives of others. Their intervention may be physically peaceful in that it saves patients' lives, but in order to save those lives health care workers must routinely perpetrate gruesome physical violences. The process of repairing a patient's body is may involve piercing, cutting, removing, implanting, and otherwise physically invading and manipulating that patient's body. Although the goal of physical repair is arguably peaceful (with Foucault's discussion of the social construction of 'health' as a pointed exception), the process by which this repair occurs is physically violent. Even pulling someone from the path of an oncoming vehicle may require a shove or yank. So pure physical non-violence is impossible—one must either refrain from physical intervention under any circumstances, even those in which one could protect the life of an other, or one must intervene with good intentions but physically infringe upon the other in order to do so.

81 Ronald B. Miller, "Violence, Force, and Coercion," in *Violence*, Ed. Jerome Shaffer (New York: David McKay Company, Inc., 1971), 20. Miller defines violence as "any act taken by A that 1) involves great force; 2) is in itself capable of injuring, damaging, or destroying, and; 3) is done with the intent of injuring, damaging, or destroying B (a being), or O (an inanimate object), where the damage or destruction of an object by A

is only an act of violence when it was not done with the intention of doing something of value for the object's owner (25-26)."

82 Audi, 56. On this very page, Audi admits that "the notion of vigorous or incendiary destruction or damaging is of course vague." Aqua Regia is a mixture of hydrochloric and nitric acids that is capable of dissolving even gold.

83 Piotr Hoffman, *The Quest for Power: Hobbes, Descartes, and the Emergence of Modernity* (New Jersey: Humanities Press, 1996), 8.

84 Thomas L. Dumm, "The Politics of Post-Modern Aesthetics: Habermas Contra Foucault," *Political Theory* (May 1988), 220. Notice, incidentally, the arché-violence of appellations that I have already done to Magritte. He is a Belgian, a Surrealist, a painter; his art is placed into the narrative (as though there is only one!) of 'postmodernity' in a certain way. These appellations do not call to the pureness of his being, they do not appreciate the fullness of his existence, but they are useful for promulgating my position on violence. To iterate my idea of violence I must perform violence itself. This points to the performativity of violence itself—"This is what violence is" is an at least economically performative utterance because as it purports to describe violence it carries it out through the more or less forceful iteration of its own definition. The only way to describe it is in fact to do it. A proposed definition of violence that was itself without violence could not be a definition of violence.

85 Theodore A. Gracyk, "Pornography as Representation: Aesthetic Considerations," in *Pornography: Private Right or Public Menace?*, ed. Robert M. Baird and Stuart E. Rosenblum (Buffalo, NY: Prometheus Books, 1991), 125.

86 I say that it "may," rather than it "does," encourage the physical violence of rape towards women, because to my knowledge there are conflicting research results on this point.

87 Susan Gubar, "Representing Pornography," In *For Adult Use Only: The Dilemmas of Violent Pornography*, Ed. Susan Gubar and Joan Huff (Bloomington: Indiana University Press, 1989), 52.

88 Jack J. Spector, *The Aesthetics of Freud* (New York: McGraw-Hill, 1972), 173.

89 Brian May, "J. M. Coetzee and the Question of the Body," *Modern Fiction Studies* 47.2 (2001), 409.

90 Alan Soble, *Sexual Investigations* (New York: New York University Press, 1996), 217.

91 Ibid., 218, 219.

92 May, 409.

93 Derrida, "The Force of Law," 961.

94 Ibid.

95 Derrida, *Writing and Difference*, 96.

96 Derrida, "The Force of Law," 947.

97 The reader will easily see that this brief discussion warrants an article in itself. I intend to write a full treatment of these issues in the near future, in which I shall address various Kantian objections to my characterization of his ethics as merely legalistic, such as his claim that the will can only be free when it follows the demands of the ethical law. Put all too briefly, Kant's conception of a free will under the categorical imperative is dependent upon his strict separation of the noumenal and empirical and his claim that causality only applies to the empirical. I believe I can show that his account of the affect of the categorical imperative upon the will begins a deconstruction of the distinction between the noumenal and empirical. In this more extensive treatment I shall also deal with Derrida's claim that "an immediate respect for the other himself . . . does not pass through the neutral element of the universal, and through respect—in the Kantian sense—

for the law (*Writing and Difference,* 96)." Simply, Derrida is here contradicting Kant's claim that "all reverence for a person is properly only reverence for the law (of honesty) and so on of which that person gives us an example (*Groundwork*, 69, footnote 2)." By Derrida's argument, treating the other as a node or example of the law is not calling to him in the vocative or accessing the uniqueness of his being.

98 Kant, *Groundwork*, 68.

99 Ibid., 66.

100 Ibid., 69n**.

101 Ibid., 29.

102 Immanuel Kant, *Critique of Practical Reason*, Trans. Lewis White Beck (Upper Saddle River, NJ: Prentice-Hall, Inc., [1788] 1993), 28-9.

103 Hoffman, 50.

104 Derrida, "A Discussion with Jacques Derrida," 36.

105 Hoffman, *Violence in Modern Philosophy*, 50-51.

106 Ibid., 51.

107 Derrida, "The Force of Law," 961.

108 Ibid, 1007-1008.

109 Ibid., 963.

110 Ibid.

111 Ibid.

112 Derrida, *Writing and Difference*, 133.

113 I shall discuss this much more rigorously in chapter five.

114 Derrida, "The Force of Law," 951.

115 Ibid., 969.

116 Ibid., 941/943.

117 Drucilla Cornell, "The Violence of the Masquerade: Law Dressed Up as Justice," in *Working Through Derrida*, ed. Gary B. Madison (Evanston, Ill.: Northwestern University Press, 1993), 92.

118 Werner Hamacher, "Afformative, Strike," *Cardozo Law Review* 13 (December 1991), 1134.

119 Derrida, "The Force of Law," 997. The term *differantielle* may translate literally as "differential," but here it is used as the grammatically proper form of *difference*, Derrida's term that invokes the mutual differing and deferring of different but related terms. This is Derrida's shorthand way of saying that each type of violence contains a constant deference and transition to/from the other.

120 Ibid.

121 Ibid., 961.

122 Derrida, *Aporias*, 17.

123 Derrida, "The Force of Law," 949.

124 Ibid., 993.

125 Hamacher, 1134.

126 Derrida, "Before the Law," in *Acts of Literature*, Ed. Derek Attridge (Routledge, NY, 1992), 191.

127 Ibid., 200.

128 United States Army, "Oaths of Enlistment and Oaths of Office," Last Updated 27 July 2004, http://www.army.mil/cmh-pg/faq/oaths.htm.

129 *Charter of the International Military Tribunal*, Article 8, http://www.yale.edu /lawweb/avalon/imt/proc/imtconst.htm.

130 *Manual for Courts-Martial United States*, 2000 Edition, IV-18—IV-23, http://usmilitary.about.com/library/pdf/mcm2000.pdf.

---

131 Ibid., IV-102—IV-103.

132 The law's demand to be iterated without *épokhè* is at the base of all insistence for unreflective subservience to authority. Consider the far-flung example of the beginnings of the Reformation in Europe. The fundamental affinity among the Allies' concern at the Nuremberg Tribunal's rejection of the excuse that someone was just following orders and the Catholic Church's anger that reformers were encouraging literate laypersons to read the Bible resides in this idea that the law, be it courtroom procedure, presumably Divinely-sanctioned canonical practice, or any other manifestation of legalism, be iterated without the épokhal suspension that opens even the mere possibility of its rejection.

133 Derrida, "The Force of Law," 925/927.

134 Ibid., 1005.

135 Ibid., 963.

136 Ibid., 941/3.

137 For a more complete description of this distinction, see J.L. Austin, *How To Do Things With Words*, (Cambridge, MA: Harvard University Press, 1975). Derrida's first deconstructive treatment of this distinction appears in the essay entitled "Signature/Event/Context," and began a fascinating, sometimes heated and personal, exchange between Derrida and Searle on the nature of context and other related linguistic matters.

138 Jacques Derrida, "Declarations of Independence," *New Political Science* 15 (Summer 1986), 10.

139 Ibid.

140 Ibid., 9.

141 Ibid., 10.

142 Derrida, "The Force of Law," 993.

143 Ibid., 997.

144 Ibid., 991.

145 Ibid., 993.

146 Derrida, *Writing and Difference*, 117.

147 Roberto Buonamano, *The Economy of Violence: Derrida on Law and Justice* (Oxford: Blackwell Publishers, 1998, 171.

148 Derrida, "The Force of Law," 955/7.

149 Derrida, *The Ear of the Other*, 173.

150 Derrida, "The Force of Law," 945.

151 Ibid., 997.

152 Derrida, *Writing and Difference*, 128.

153 Ibid., 57.

154 Ibid., 104.

155 Ibid., 100-101.

156 Friedrich Nietzsche, *Twilight of the Idols*, in *The Portable Nietzsche*, Trans. Walter Kaufmann (New York: Penguin Books, [1888] 1982), 501.

157 Nietzsche, *On the Genealogy of Morals*, 491.

158 Friedrich Nietzsche, *Thus Spoke Zarathustra*, in *The Portable Nietzsche*, trans. Walter Kaufmann (New York: Penguin Books, [1892] 1982), 499.

159 Ibid., 481.

160 Nietzsche, *Thus Spoke Zarathustra*, 146.

161 Nietzsche, *On the Genealogy of Morals*, 512.

162 Ibid., 469.

163 Friedrich Nietzsche, *The Gay Science*, trans. Walter Kaufmann (New York: Vintage Books, [1887] 1974), 291.

164 Nietzsche, *Thus Spoke Zarathustra*, 226.

165 Friedrich Nietzsche, *The Antichrist*, in *The Portable Nietzsche*, trans. Walter Kaufmann (New York: Penguin Books, [1888] 1982), 572.

166 Nietzsche, *On the Genealogy of Morals*, 515.

167 Friedrich Nietzsche, *Beyond Good and Evil*, in *Basic Writings of Nietzsche*, trans. Walter Kaufmann, (New York: The Modern Library, [1886] 1992), 395.

168 Nietzsche, *Thus Spoke Zarathustra*, 226.

169 Nietzsche, *Twilight of the Idols*, 501.

170 Nietzsche, *Thus Spoke Zarathustra*, 171.

171 Nietzsche, *The Gay Science*, 241.

172 Nietzsche, *Beyond Good and Evil*, 316.

173 Ibid.

174 Ibid., 318.

175 Nietzsche, *Thus Spoke Zarathustra*, 265.

176 Nietzsche, *On the Genealogy of Morals*. 555.

177 Ibid., 543.

178 Nietzsche, *Twilight of the Idols*, 474.

179 John Richardson, "Nietzsche's Power Ontology," in *Nietzsche*, ed. John Richardson and Brian Leiter (Oxford: Oxford University Press, 2001), 171.

180 Ibid., 169.

181 Ibid., 151.

182 Linda Williams, *Nietzsche's Mirror: The World as Will to Power* (Lanham, Maryland: Rowman and Littlefield, 2001), 89.

183 Ibid., 93.

184 Nietzsche, *Twilight of the Idols.*, 499.

185 Ibid., 552.

186 Ibid., 500.

187 Nietzsche, *The Gay Science*, 314.

188 Nietzsche, *Thus Spoke Zarathustra*, 147.

189 Nietzsche, *On the Genealogy of Morals*, 472.

190 Ibid.

191 Ibid., 473.

192 Nietzsche, *Thus Spoke Zarathustra*, 139.

193 Nietzsche, *On the Genealogy of Morals*, 474.

194 Ibid., 483.

195 Nietzsche, *Thus Spoke Zarathustra*, 282.

196 Nietzsche, *On the Genealogy of Morals*, 554.

197Nietzsche, *The Gay Science*, 328.

198 Nietzsche, *Thus Spoke Zarathustra*, 317.

199 Nietzsche, *On the Genealogy of Morals*, 557.

200 Nietzsche, *The Gay Science*, 246. This paragraph is worth reproducing in full because, as with some other major authors (including Derrida and Hobbes), many of his most cogent descriptions of otherwise difficult concepts are given in his less-read works. While its title is not as provocative as *Beyond Good and Evil* and much of its content is only interesting to serious students of Nietzsche, many a misunderstanding about Nietzsche could be cleared up if more people read *The Gay Science*.

201 Gregory Bruce Smith, *Nietzsche, Heidegger, and the Transition to Postmodernity* (Chicago: University of Chicago Press, 1996), 109.

202 Nietzsche, *The Antichrist*, 602.

203 Nietzsche, *Thus Spoke Zarathustra*, 282.

204 Nietzsche, *The Antichrist*, 590.

205 Nietzsche, *On the Genealogy of Morals*, 484.

206 Ibid., 519.

207 Ibid., 462.

208 Ibid., 474.

209 Ibid.

210 Nietzsche, *Thus Spoke Zarathustra*, 306.

211 Nietzsche, *The Gay Science*, 349. This silencing of the mole and dwarf is an example of doing violence to them, of rejecting their personhood. The noble-minded person who understands that all value is self-created and individualized creates values for herself, founding her own new line of iteration over that of the mole and dwarf. They are silenced by her, shouted down so that their position is no longer iterated by the noble-minded person who has overcome them.

212 Nietzsche, *Twilight of the Idols*. 535.

213 Nietzsche, *On the Genealogy of Morals*, 531.

214 Nietzsche, *Twilight of the Idols*, 552.

215 Nietzsche, *Thus Spoke Zarathustra*, 152.

216 Ibid., 243.

217 Nietzsche, *Beyond Good and Evil*, 344. Just what Nietzsche means by "seventh day" is, like so much in his works, open to interpretation. Although at first I was tempted to think of the seventh day in terms of culmination alone, it is now clear to me that Nietzsche most likely intends this as a reference to the repose of a creator after a great triumph or culmination. In this list of human attributes, the seventh day would then refer to the creative human act of giving rise to something great, looking upon it in triumphant rest, evaluating it, and then moving on to the next creative task.

218 "Idols of the Mind" is of course Francis Bacon's famous phrase from *Novum Organum*, which Nietzsche himself invoked for the title of his 1895 book *Twilight of the Idols*. This reference is particularly interesting, given Nietzsche's denigration of scientists as mere tools in the hands of real creators. It is also interesting to consider what Nietzsche would have thought of Bacon himself. Would Nietzsche simply cast him aside as another numb ascetic, or would he, as with Jesus, respect Bacon as a founder, even while criticizing the substance of his creation?

219 Nietzsche, *Thus Spoke Zarathustra*, 175.

220 Ibid., 318.

221 Friedrich Nietzsche, *On the Advantage and Disadvantage of History for Life*, trans. Peter Preuss (NY: Hackett Publishing Company, 1980), 10.

222 Nietzsche, *Thus Spoke Zarathustra*, 253.

223 Cornell, 77.

224 Buonamano, 175.

225 Derrida, *Writing and Difference*, 117.

226 Derrida "The Force of Law," 949.

227 Ibid.

228 Ibid.

229 Nietzsche, *Thus Spoke Zarathustra*, 306.

230 Derrida, "The Force of Law," 997.

231 Nietzsche, *The Genealogy of Morals*, 553.

232 Ibid., 512.

233 Ibid., 481.

234 Nietzsche, *Thus Spoke Zarathustra*, 226.

235 Nietzsche, *On the Genealogy of Morals*, 478-9.

236 Ibid., 514.
237 Nietzsche, *Thus Spoke Zarathustra*, 324.
238 Nietzsche, *On the Genealogy of Morals*, 522.
239 Nietzsche, *Thus Spoke Zarathustra*, 324.
240 Smith, 104.
241 Derrida, "The Force of Law," 997.
242 Nietzsche, *On the Genealogy of Morals*, 513.
243 Ibid., 532.
244 Ibid., 521.
245 Ibid., 475.
246 Ibid.
247 Nietzsche, *Thus Spoke Zarathustra*, 168.
248 Ibid., 136.
249 Ibid., 214.
250 Derrida, *Writing and Difference*, 128.
251 Ibid., 146-7.
252 Ibid. 117.
253 Derrida, "The Force of Law," 1005.
254 Ibid., 1001.
255 Ibid., 941.
256 Ibid., 955.
257 Ibid., 943.

Chapter Two
The Economy of Violence in Hobbes' Social Contract

I. Violence and the State of Nature

Hobbes and Derrida are both concerned with the inevitable difficulties of creation. Hobbes' story of the creation of a commonwealth and Derrida's investigation of the beginnings of discourse share the premise that persons are creators, rather than discoverers, of meaning and value in the world, and that therefore justice consists of respecting the independent status of others as meaning creators. For Hobbes, this natural human creativity leads to the brutalities of the state of nature and the necessity of a commonwealth grounded in enforced discursive unity. But even though the natural condition and the social compact are violent, Hobbes agrees with Derrida that pure violence, like pure justice, is a logical impossibility. Although Derrida discusses this "economy of violence" at length, this recognition is not immediately apparent in Hobbes. An examination of Hobbes' state of nature and the formation of the commonwealth in the light of this Derridean play of violence and justice reveals some surprising implications for Hobbes' system, which in turn provides an excellent story of the practicalities of the economy of violence and justice in action.

As I discussed in the previous chapter, for Derrida "all value is first constituted by a theoretical subject."[1] This arché-violence, which "is tied to phenomenality itself, and to the possibility of language,"[2] equals rejecting the other as an independent creator of meaning and value in the world. As the most primordial violence, arché-violence "appears with *articulation*,"[3] which itself is opened by the inescapable articulation required by discourse, which originally constitutes the relationship among persons. This originary violence is also constituted in "the necessity of speaking of the other as other, or to the other as other, on the basis of its appearing-for-me-as-what-it-is: the other,"[4] the additional. Because "the absolute form of experience"[5] is egoity, one can only conceive of the other from a position of one's one's finite perspective. Because personal existence is irreducibly perspectival, one's conception of the other is as an-other-to-oneself, an entity that exists only vis-à-vis oneself, such that oneself is the ontologically primary term of the binary. This "reduction of the other to a *real* moment of *my* life, its reduction to the state of empirical alter-ego, is an empirical possibility, or rather eventuality, which is called violence."[6]

By this inevitable violent move, the person, grounded in its own perspective, necessarily perceives the empirical existence of the other in reference to itself, thus reducing the other to mere phenomenality. A person is therefore "incapable of respecting" an other's "Being"[7] as an independent creator of meaning, instead reducing it "to intrawordliness," which "is the origin and very meaning of what is called violence, making possible all straitjackets."[8]

The necessity of position for articulation that is the root of arché-violence directly implies the iterability of that position, which, as I also examined in chapter one, is the key to why discourse is itself violent for Derrida. "Position is already iterability, a call for self-conserving repetition"[9] because any discursive position is a universal claim that in order to be universal must continually refound itself. This universal iterability denies in its structure the legitimacy of counter-claims made by others, thus denying that others are really persons, independent sources of meaning who are capable of their own independent creation of meaning.

At each moment of iteration, every discursive position must go through an Ordeal of the Undecidable—otherwise the statement would be mere inhuman, mechanistic calculation. "A decision that didn't go through the ordeal of the undecidable would not be a free decision,"[10] it would instead be the merely mechanistic application of a general rule. If a person is responsible for his or her decisions, if a person is capable of doing violence, then that person's decisions must not be "protect[ed] . . . by some theoretical assurance, or by the certainty of being right, of being on the side of science, of consciousness or of reason."[11] If they were protected or ensured, these decisions would not be free human actions. They would be the mere "deployment of a program . . . technical application of a rule or a norm, or . . . subsumption of a determined 'case.'"[12] But persons exceed mere phenomenality—they are the meaning-creating, value-instituting "origin of the world"[13] that intersubjectively create discursive positionality. Discourse is characterized by the creation of meaning and value, rather than by mere mechanistic calculation.

Because of this ordeal of the undecidable, each new iteration or moment of conservation within discourse is also an independent refounding. Even as one iterates and conserves a previously-given position, one re-decides anew as though it had not previously existed. Therefore each outcome of the ordeal of the undecidable is both conservative and foundational. The ordeal of the undecidable is hence the paradox inherent in any claim or counter-claim: an iteration of any previous position is both foundational in itself, re-decided anew from scratch in an act of meaning-creation, and therefore includes its own new claim to universal iteration, and is also conservative in that it is an iteration of a previous claim. This paradox also applies to a new discursive position, which as a foundation constitutes a new claim against the universal iteration of some opposing claim. Even so, a new position also contains within itself its own claim to universal iteration, a concept which it simultaneously stands against as it challenges the iteration of opposing claims.

So for Derrida, any discursive positioning is the outcome of an ordeal of the undecidable. Persons are the choosers, the creators, of discursive positionality. Violence is thus the unavoidable denial of the other as a source of meaning independent of oneself. Before returning to the specifics of the economy of violence later in this chapter, I shall lay out why Hobbes agrees that humans are the creators of meaning and value, and proceed from there.

Agreeing with both Derrida and Nietzsche, Hobbes states his position that persons are the creators of meaning and value most directly in *The Philosophical Rudiments Concerning Government and Society* (usually known by its Latin name, *De Cive*), in which he states that "to *know truth*, is the same thing as to *remember* that it was made by ourselves by the very usurpation of the words."[14] In fact, Hobbes here sounds rather like Nietzsche's Zarathustra, who proclaims: "Verily, men gave themselves all their good and evil. Verily, they did not take it, they did not find it, nor did it come to them as a voice form heaven. Only man placed values in things to preserve himself—he alone created a meaning for things, a human meaning."[15] "For Hobbes truth is a function of logic and language, not of the relation between language and some extralinguistic reality,"[16] so the "connections between names and objects are not natural."[17] They are artificially constructed by persons, based on individual psychologies and desires. These individual desires are for Hobbes the only measure of good and bad, because value terms "are ever used with relation to the person that useth them, there being nothing simply and absolutely so, nor any common rule of good and evil to be taken from the nature of the objects themselves."[18] Since "there are no authentical doctrines concerning right and wrong, good and evil,"[19] these labels are placed upon things by humans in acts of creation rather than discovered as extrinsic facts.

Elaborating on this, Hobbes writes that "the nature, disposition, and interest of the speaker, such as are the names of virtues and vices; for one man calleth *wisdom*, what another calleth *fear*; and one *cruelty* what another *justice*."[20] A more simplistic understanding of the brutality of the state of nature, which David Gauthier calls the "simple rationality account,"[21] has it that mere materialistic competition for goods is the cause of the war of all against all, but such rivalry is a secondary manifestation of the more fundamental competition among all persons to be the dominant creator of meaning. Certainly, Hobbes writes that persons most frequently "desire to hurt each other" because "many men at the same time have an appetite to the same thing; which yet very often they can neither enjoy in common, nor yet divide it; whence it follows that the strongest must have it, and who is strongest must be decided by the sword."[22] But this competition for goods only arises as the result of the more primary struggle that is inherent in the nature of persons of meaning creators. In the state of nature, "where every man is his own *judge*,"[23] persons will "mete good and evil by diverse measures,"[24] creating labels for things as they see fit, based on individual appetites.

One of the most significant objects that receives diverse labels in the state of nature is "threat." Even if most people happen to construe threat similarly, there will be serious disagreement regarding whether or not a specific situation fits a commonly-held definition. This is of course the key to the famous Security Dilemma that international relations theorists spend so much time trying to overcome[25]—certain perfectly innocent actions by one person (or state) can easily be construed, and rationally *must* be construed, as a threat. Furthermore, any attempt by one person to allay another's fears about the threatening nature of actions must be taken as strategic disinformation, rather than as genuine explanation. Even if "I agree with you in principle about your right to preserve yourself," this agreement is useless "if I disagree about whether this is the moment for you to *implement* that right."[26] Given that persons "are individual in experience, they are individual in their conceptions and in their speech. Their power of reasoning with words . . . dissociates them and provokes violent competition"[27] specifically because concepts that seem simple invoke very different interpretations. If there were some universally objective and knowable set of circumstances that constituted Threat as such, the rationally self-interested persons of the state of nature would not have to seek control over all things for their own protection. All persons could both avoid actions that would meet the universally objective and knowable definition of threat and shed the overbearing suspicion that, taken together, make the Hobbesian state of nature so unbearably brutish.

But even more significantly for his relationship with Derrida and Nietzsche, Hobbes argues that in the state of nature persons must not only try to control as many objects as possible—they must also try to control as many persons as possible. "There is no way for any man to secure himself so reasonable as anticipation, that is, by force or wiles to master the persons of all men he can, so long till he see no other power great enough to endanger him. And this is no more than his own conservation requireth, and is generally allowed."[28] While it is often assumed that by this Hobbes means a person will try to control others with physical force alone, when one approaches Hobbesian persons as meaning creators this control takes on a more discursive, arché-violent character.

"First," says Hobbes, "among [persons in the state of nature] there is a contestation of honour and preferment,"[29] a discursive struggle not over what physical objects each person will possess, but over who or what will be considered valuable. Persons, as rationally self-interested beings who "measure, not only other men, but all other things, by themselves,"[30] and value themselves above all others, attempt to force that valuation on others. "The human desire for 'glory', which," Gabriella Slomp reminds us, "in today's language translates not simply as the desire for prestige, but also the desire to acquire power over others,"[31] is therefore primarily about subsuming others beneath one's own personhood, as direct objects or merely phenomenal substances. As above, the inevitability of this situation is given by the fact that the primarily egoistic nature of all experience renders the other in a "state of empirical alter-ego"[32] to oneself.

Those who prefer a more directly materialistic reading of Hobbes may attempt to bolster their position by pointing to his comment from *The Rudiments* that "the most frequent reason why men desire to hurt each other, ariseth hence, that many men at the same time have an appetite to the same thing; which yet very often they can neither enjoy in common, nor yet divide it; whence it follows that the strongest must have it, and who is strongest must be decided by the sword."[33] This quote also supports my reading of Hobbes, because quite simply the primary thing all persons want but can never have in common is the status of the ultimate creator of meaning, the primary personhood, from which all other goods flow. Everyone, by their natures as creators of meaning whose "desire of power after power . . . ceaseth only in death,"[34] tries to subsume others beneath their own personhood in order to control these others and glorify themselves. As Piotr Hoffman puts it, "every individual acting under the right of nature views himself as the center of the universe; his aim is, quite simply and quite closely, to become a small "god among men," to use Plato's phrase."[35]

Incidentally, this natural human desire to subsume others beneath one's own personhood, to dominate their systems of signification (which I shall revisit in chapter four, suggesting that it may be developed into a theory of power) is one of the most obvious, but rarely explicated, affinities between Hobbes and Nietzsche. Not only do both authors famously consider life as the ongoing struggle for power—both also argue that the most fundamental method of control consists in controlling signification. Hobbes' notion that persons in the state of nature are engaged in a constant contest for power as the domination of the personhood of others is matched by Nietzsche's claim that all life is "a subduing, a *becoming master*, and all subduing and becoming master involves a fresh interpretation, an adaptation through which any previous "meaning" and "purpose" are necessarily obscured or even obliterated."[36]

Hobbes argues that this discursive struggle rapidly becomes physical when he writes that "every man thinking well of himself, and hating to see the same in others, they must needs provoke one another by words, and other signs of contempt and hatred, which are incident to all comparison, till at last they must determine the pre-eminence by strength and force of body."[37] The ultimate violence, the surest and most complete way of removing a person's ability to create meaning, is to kill that person, and the escalating contentiousness of the state of nature makes life short in the war of all against all. But this does not render the fundamental reason for this violence any less discursive, any less based on "one's sense of self-importance in comparison with others"[38] or human nature as a creator of meaning.

If humans did not create meaning and value, but rather were all somehow privy to nonperspectival, universally valid meanings, the state of nature would not be a state of unmitigated war. Except during direct competition for some specific scarce good, such as water or shelter, the laws of nature would usually be enough to maintain peace because every person would know exactly what single Meaning each situation contained. For Hobbes, this is impossible because "evil, and contemptible are ever used with relation to the person that useth them, there being nothing simply and absolutely so, nor any common rule of good and evil to be taken from the nature of the objects themselves."[39] Because each person imputes perspectival meaning and value to given situations,[40] in which "there are no objective facts to which to appeal in order to resolve,"[41] a state of war arises based on each person's inability to know the meanings and intentions of others. As Hobbes argues, this makes preemptive attacks rational in the state of nature, in which whether the means a person chooses to use, "and the action he is performing, be necessary to the preservation of his life and members or not, he himself, by the right of nature, must be judge."[42]

By way of example, consider again the concept of "threat." Every individual in the state of nature may independently arrive at the same concept, but this will still not lead to peace. Even though everyone may agree on the concept of threat, the application of this term will remain intractably perspectival, so that individual persons may disagree as to when a specific situation should be labeled a threat. In fact, simply agreeing on the parameters of the situation to be defined may prove impossible because, of course, the borders of a subject or situation are no more objective than its other characteristics. If, on the other hand, a nonperspectival usage of "threat" were possible, all persons in the state of nature would know what actions constituted a threat, and they could refrain from taking certain actions that participated in this Form. The security dilemma that makes preemptive strikes rational would not come about, and the state of nature would be a much more peaceful place because actions that constituted objective threat would only be taken during actual competition for scarce goods. Matthew Kramer has even proposed that the laws of nature actually worsen the strife of the state of nature by "lending themselves to hosts of clashing interpretations and by therefore incensing the proponents of each interpretation—who presume that supporters of the countless other interpretations are not merely self-interested and hostile, but likewise grossly devoid of prudence and moral insight."[43] Whether or not they actually increase the danger inherent in the linguistic/conceptual freedom of the state of nature, the inevitably perspectival application of the laws of nature must be overcome if peace is to be achieved.

Hobbes' Laws of Nature may be attempts to provide the nonperspectival, universally valid definitions that are necessary, but not sufficient, for peace. He speaks of them as "all the right reason we have," "the infallible rule[s]"[44] that "declare unto us the ways of peace, where the same may be obtained, and of defence where it may not."[45] But he also seemingly recognizes that these laws would be subject to the same difficulties that I elaborated above, for he writes that "though all men do agree in the commendation of the foresaid virtues, yet they disagree still concerning their nature, to wit, in what each of them doth consist."[46] For example, in his first law of nature Hobbes says that "*every man ought to endeavour peace, as far as he has hope of obtaining it,*"[47] which both lays down the universal principle that persons should seek peace and recognizes that the pursuit of peace is based on individualized hope, which is itself based upon the individual perspectival imputation of meaning to certain events in the state of nature. Similarly, Hobbes suggests that "*a man be willing, when others are so too, as far-forth as for peace and defence of himself he shall think it necessary, to lay down this right to all things.*"[48] Here, as above, the law of nature sets out a supposedly universal demand, but also recognizes that this demand will be carried out by individual, self-interested, creators of meaning. Each individual must decide for himself if others appear for him as willing to give up the state of nature.

All of the foregoing points to the conclusion that in the commonwealth the sovereign's first and most fundamental job is to be the ultimate definer. Several other commentators have also reached this conclusion. By way of elaborating upon the importance of the moderation of individuality in Hobbes' theory of government, Richard Flathman claims that peace "is possible only if the ambiguity and disagreement that pervade general thinking and acting are eliminated by the stipulations of a sovereign."[49] Pursuant to debunking the perennial misinterpretation of Hobbes' mention of people as wolves, Paul Johnson argues that "one of the primary functions of the sovereign is to provide the necessary unity of meaning and reference for the primary terms in which men try to conduct their social lives."[50] "The whole *raison d'être* of sovereign helmsmanship lies squarely in the chronic defusing of interpretive clashes,"[51] without which humans would "fly off in all directions"[52] and fall inevitably into the violence of the natural condition.

It is not surprising that so many noted students of Hobbes have reached this conclusion, given how prominently he himself makes this claim. According to Hobbes, "in the state of nature, where every man is his own judge, and differeth from others concerning the names and appellations of things, and from those differences arise quarrels and breach of peace, it was necessary there should be a common measure of all things, that might fall in controversy."[53] The main categories of the sovereign's tasks are "to make and abrogate laws, to determine war and peace, [and] to know and judge of all controversies,"[54] but each of these duties is a subspecies of its ultimate duty to be the sole and ultimate definer in matters of public importance. It is only through the sovereign's effective continued accomplishment of this duty that the people of a commonwealth avoid the definitional problems that typify the state of nature.

Judging controversies, which Hobbes lists as the third main task of the sovereign, is the duty most obviously about being the ultimate definer. In fact, Hobbes declares it a law of nature that "*in every controversy, the parties thereto ought mutually to agree upon an arbitrator, whom they both trust; and mutually to covenant to stand to the sentence he shall give therein.*"[55] As I repeatedly alluded to above, this agreement to abide by the decision of a third party arbitrator, a sovereign in the commonwealth, is necessary because of the fundamentally perspectival and relative nature of persons' imputations of meaning and value into the situations they construct. Hobbes understands this problem, as evidenced by his claim that "seeing *right reason* is not existent, the reason of some man or men must supply the place thereof; and that man or men, is he or they, that have the sovereign power"[56] to dictate meanings that will be followed by all. The sovereign is even protected from potential democratic impulses, by which a 'true' meaning would be that agreed upon by the greatest number of people. Because "no one man's reason, nor the reason of any one number of men, makes the certainty," they will still "come to blows . . . for want of a right reason constituted by nature"[57] unless both the majority and the minority agree to abide by the meanings promulgated by the sovereign.

This is also the main reason why Hobbes prefers a monarchical sovereign. In *Leviathan*, he is clear that whether the sovereign is organized as a monarchy, an aristocracy, or a democracy, the powers of that sovereign remain the same. "The difference between these three kinds of commonwealth" consists rather in "the difference of convenience, or aptitude to produce the peace, and security of the people; for which end they were instituted."[58] Of the six advantages to a monarchy, the fourth is "that a monarch cannot disagree with himself . . . but an assembly may; and that to such a height, as may produce a civil war."[59] Although an assembly may itself constitute a sovereign, it is a sovereign whose internal parts may disagree, resulting in renewed violence and the collapse of the commonwealth. Hobbes ensures peace by protecting the sovereign against itself, as well as against its subjects' impulses for a democratic construction of truth.

These meanings are usually created and promulgated by the sovereign in the form of laws, another of the tasks with which Hobbes charges it. In one of his clearest explanations of the law, Hobbes writes that "it belongs to the same chief power to make some common rules for all men, and to declare them publicly, by which every man may know what may be called his, what another's, what just, what unjust, what honest, what dishonest, what good, what evil; that is summarily, what is to be done, what to be avoided in our common course of life."[60] The civil law is the set of the sovereign's definitions for ownership, justice, good, evil, and all other concepts that are important for the maintenance of peace in the commonwealth. When everyone follows the law (that is, when everyone follows the sovereign's definitions) there are far fewer conflicts among persons because everyone appeals to the same meanings. This means that people know what meanings others will use to evaluate the actions of themselves and others, so the state of nature's security dilemmas and attempts to force one's own meanings upon others are overcome.

There is to be no question of the truth or falsity of the sovereign's definitions because "there are no authentical doctrines concerning right and wrong, good and evil, besides the constituted laws in each realm and government."[61] In fact, Hobbes specifically says that one of the "*diseases* of a commonwealth" is that "*every private man is judge of good and evil actions*."[62] Only when individual persons agree to follow the meanings promulgated by the sovereign, which of course includes refraining from trying to impose their own meanings on others, can persons live together in peace—when they take it upon themselves to impose meaning on situations of public import, they descend into violence again.

Hobbes also says that sovereignty includes the ability to "give titles of honour, and to appoint what order of place and dignity each man shall hold, and what signs of respect, in public or private meetings, they shall give to one another."[63] This is necessary so that private individuals all follow the same system of meanings where respect and honor are concerned. If they maintained their own individual meanings, a hand raised in greeting could easily be taken for an insult, and medals of honor would be indistinguishable from scarlet letters. Again, the state of nature would be the result.

After exploring the difficulties raised by the nature of persons as creators of meaning, Hobbes grants the sovereign "the right to decide among irresolvably contested truths: to provide the authoritative criteria for what is and thus to remove people from the state of epistemic and ethical anarchy that form the basis of the state of nature."[64] Only by appointing a sovereign to dictate meanings and values to them can persons live together in relative peace—a fundamentally political solution to a metaphysical crisis that Richard Tuck claims is Hobbes' "most distinctive contribution to political theory."[65]

The foregoing all points to the conclusion that a Hobbesian commonwealth is best described as a group of persons who all live by a single system of meanings and values, created and promulgated by a sovereign that they have agreed upon. In this way Hobbes' definition is pseudo-Augustinian: In *City of God* XIX, Augustine describes a "people" as an association united by agreement on the "objects of their love," but in Hobbes' association people are united by agreement on the (enforced) *meaning* of objects and other signs. Hobbes defines the commonwealth explicitly as "one person, of whose acts a great multitude . . . have made themselves every one the author, to the end [the sovereign] may use the strength and means of them all, as he shall think expedient, for their peace and common defence."[66] This one corporate person, symbolized most clearly by the image of a king whose body is composed of innumerable smaller bodies, which appears on *Leviathan*'s frontispiece, coalesces out of the sovereign's single, dominant, enforced, system of meanings. Exactly how a person, and one person rather than another, achieves the position of sovereignty, is the subject of the next section.

II. The Economy of Violence at the Formation of the Commonwealth

In the final words of my above reiteration of Derrida's argument, I discussed how every act of arché-violence, every ascription of meaning, is paradoxically both institutive and conservative of a rule or claim. This paradoxical stance of any positioning points to Derrida's claim that discourse "is *economy*: violence against violence, light against light."[67] According to Derrida, discourse is always violent to some extent because in making a universally iterable claim one always does violence to another by denying that other as a source of meaning. Yet because "like pure violence, pure nonviolence is a contradictory concept"[68] discourse can never be completely violent or nonviolent. Discourse always consists of an economy of violence. As I elaborated in chapter one, Derrida makes this claim because "pure violence, a relationship between beings without face, is not yet violence, is pure nonviolence. And inversely: pure nonviolence, the nonrelation of the same to the other . . . is pure violence."[69] Thus, both pure violence and pure nonviolence are paradoxical.

Violence, which I earlier defined as the denial of the other as a source of meaning, can therefore never be a pure violence. That would require the complete denial of the other's similarity to oneself as a being capable of creating meaning. It would constitute the complete denial that the other is an alter-*ego*, leaving one with no relation to the faceless other, who would not even be recognized as a person against whom violence could be perpetrated. No discursive relationship between the two would be possible. On the other hand, complete nonviolence (complete justice to the other) would necessitate the complete recognition of the similarity between oneself and the other as fundamentally sources of meaning. One would identify with "the other immediately and originally, silently, in communion with the other's own experience" to the extent that the other "would cease to be the other."[70] This self-identical dyad could not maintain a discursive relationship because pure identity would deny the independent positionality of the two.

Therefore all persons necessarily practice arché-violence through the pre-ethical structure of their discursive relationship, but they practice it economically. One "*let[s]* be [the] other in their truth," in their independence as sovereign sources of meaning, to the extent that one comes "as close as possible to nonviolence."[71] The full achievement of this impossible nonviolence would "gain access to the egoity of the alter ego as if to its alterity itself,"[72] respecting its nature as a face and calling to it as an independent ego rather than objectifying it as a mere phenomenal object.

Discourse is increasingly violent to the extent that it "*reduces* the other" to a mere object or attribute of one's own life, "when it *leads* the other, whether through psychology, demagogy, or even pedagogy which is not instruction."[73] Conversely, the violence in intersubjective language is minimized to the extent that it is characterized by a "'letting-be' of an existent (an other) as something existing outside"[74] of oneself as an independent, meaning-creating person. Justice, as the respect for the other as a creator of meaning, is manifested in a "*rectitude* of address"[75] towards the other "as other, irreducible to *my* ego, precisely because it is an ego,"[76] a sovereign person rather than a mere phenomenal object, such as a simple rock or vegetable.

In one of his more famous passages, Hobbes ostensibly claims that all persons are basically mentally equal. He writes: "as to the faculties of the mind—setting aside the arts grounded upon words, and especially that skill of proceeding upon general and infallible rules called science . . . as being not a native faculty (born with us), nor attained (as prudence) while we look after somewhat else—I find yet a greater equality amongst men than that of strength."[77] Strangely, as Gary Herbert has pointed out, Hobbes' argument here actually tends to affirm a conclusion opposite to that which Hobbes claims it affirms. According to Herbert, "Hobbes begins, incredibly, by abstracting from the inequalities of mind, that is, from the inequality of imagination and reason that he elsewhere says is as natural to man as are the passions."[78] That is, Hobbes sets aside precisely those faculties of the mind that are of primary importance for all other mental faculties, then claims that if we do not consider those that persons are about equal.

Elsewhere in the corpus of his work, Hobbes makes a more nuanced (and interesting) claim about mental equality. In *The Rudiments* he argues that if "men be equal by nature, the equality is to be acknowledged," but that if persons are "unequal, because they are like to contest for dominion, it is necessary for the obtaining of peace, *that they be esteemed as equal*."[79] It is therefore "a precept of the law of nature, *that every man be accounted by nature equal to another*."[80] This claim is repeated in *The Elements of Law*, where he writes that "as long as men arrogate to themselves more honour than they give to others, it cannot be imagined, how they can possibly live in peace: and consequently we are to suppose, that for peace sake, nature hath ordained this law, *That every man acknowledge others for his equal*."[81] It appears that Hobbes' actual claim is that whether or not persons are mentally equal, they must assume that they are, for otherwise the state of nature will be inescapable.

It is interesting to note that although Nietzsche agrees with Hobbes that violence is inescapable as long as persons reject equality, he considers it slavish to *want* to escape this violence. For Nietzsche, those who would refuse to embrace their (real or self-perceived) superiority are deniers of life as will to power. In Nietzsche's unparalleled prose: "'He is so polite.'—Yes, he always carries a biscuit for Cerberus and is so timid that he thinks everyone is Cerberus, even you and I. That is his 'politeness.'"[82]

Actually, Hobbes tacitly accepts that persons are mentally unequal, for he states that the "difference of wits are in the passions," and that those passions most responsible for this admitted difference of wits are "the more or less desire of power, of riches, of knowledge, and of honour. All which may be reduced to the first, that is, desire of power. For riches, knowledge, and honour are but several sorts of power."[83] The specific disposition of each person's passions "proceedeth, partly from the different constitution of the body, and partly from different education."[84]

These wits, these "arts grounded upon words, and especially that skill of proceeding upon general and infallible rules" that persons have in unequal amounts, are of course none other than "reason, which is grounded on the right use of speech, and produceth the sciences."[85] Words are the building blocks of reason, which Hobbes identifies as "nothing but *reckoning* (that is, adding and subtracting) of the consequences of general names"[86] that we, as persons, create. Since "our reliance upon the prelinguistic modes of cognition does not allow us to order experience in a rational manner,"[87] reason for Hobbes emerges only with the use of language. Therefore greater reason must be "attained by industry," by educational labor, instead of "by experience only,"[88] as is mere animalistic prudence.

It is, in fact, reason that separates persons from animals. Although Hobbes states this quite clearly in several places, none are clearer than a passage from *Leviathan*, in which he writes that "for besides sense, and thoughts, and the train of thoughts, the mind of man has no other motion, though by the help of speech and method the same faculties may be improved to such a height as to distinguish men from all other living creatures."[89] Similarly, in *Liberty, Necessity, and Chance*, Hobbes claims that

> The truth is, that man is a creature of greater power than other living creatures are, but his advantages do consist especially in two things: whereof one is the

> use of speech, by which men communicate one with another, and join their forces together, and by which also they register their thoughts that they perish not, but be reserved, afterwards joined with other thoughts, to produce general rules for the direction of their actions.[90]

Just as the power of language and the Reason that it engenders separate persons from animals, it seems certain that high levels of language (and therefore reasoning) ability distinguish exceptional persons from lesser persons. As I discussed above, Hobbes does accept that some persons have better language and reasoning abilities than others, but he argues that in the state of nature persons should all assume, for the sake of peace, that they are equal. Even so, "beasts, for want of" the "advantage of *names*" are not "capable of *science*."[91] By analogy, those persons who are more capable in language and reason—those areas that distinguish persons from animals—are higher or better persons than those who have lesser abilities in language and reason. Although Hobbes never actually lays this out explicitly, he does come close to stating it overtly near the beginning of *Leviathan*, where he compares those with lesser amounts of reason to children, who themselves "are not endued with reason at all, till they have attained the use of speech, but are called reasonable creatures for the possibility apparent of having the use of reason in time to come."[92] Most persons, being like children, "have the use of reasoning a little way," which "serves them to little use in common life" because "as for science"—which is based on the use of language—"or certain rules of their actions, they are so far from it that they know not what it is."[93] These childlike persons are inferior to other persons in exactly those characteristics that distinguish persons from other animals, so the former are lesser persons than the latter.

The difference between Hobbes and Nietzsche on this point is instructive. Although both contend that there are greater and lesser types of persons, they have nearly opposite conceptions of each. First, whereas Hobbes claims that superior persons are those with greater language and reasoning abilities, Nietzsche maintains that those are characteristics of the slavish. For Nietzsche, the intricacies and subtleties of reason are not natural for persons—they arise as necessities for those lesser persons who are "denied the true reaction, that of deeds."[94] These weaker beings, lacking the ability and the will to strike back at their tormentors, are "cleverer than any noble race . . . honor[ing] cleverness . . . as a condition of existence of the first importance."[95] As I will discuss below, the distinction between Hobbes and Nietzsche on this point may indicate that, from a Nietzschean perspective, Hobbes' philosophy does not penetrate the core of human nature. Rather, it may only encompass the slavish bulk of humanity.

Gabriella Slomp has very convincingly explained how, even though there are superior and inferior persons in Hobbes' system, the state of nature makes it nearly impossible for those with greater cognitive abilities to use those abilities to their great advantage. She argues that because the state of nature is so chaotic and brutal, "the distinctive ability of the mind to detach itself from the present and to plan the future is wasted . . . their mind[s] being completely absorbed in the present."[96] Although Hobbes does not overtly discuss this direct result of the conditions found in the state of nature, he implies it very strongly when he writes that in the natural condition "there is no place for industry . . . no knowledge of the face of the earth, no account of time, no arts, no letters."[97] Those few superior persons who are capable of seeking the "continual and indefatigable generation of knowledge,"[98] which Hobbes elsewhere calls the "great and master-delight,"[99] do not have the opportunity to pursue these higher intellectual abilities because the exigencies of constant fear and chaos keep them too grounded in the practicalities of the present. As Hobbes writes, "leisure is the mother of philosophy,"[100] and the state of nature does not allow for any rest in which superior persons would be able to engage in such high-minded endeavors. Being forced by their situation to live for the moment, they are left unable to realize their greater abilities.

Even though the superior persons can not engage in philosophy or other intellectual pursuits in the state of nature, they are likely to be the first to realize that it is possible to leave the natural condition and live more commodiously. Although "all men easily acknowledge this state [of nature], as long as they are in it, to be evil, and by consequence that peace is good,"[101] those persons with the greatest reasoning abilities are likely to be the first to figure out exactly how this peace can be accomplished. They will quickly come to understand that disagreement about definitions is the root difficulty in the state of nature, leading to the war of all against all, and that the only way to achieve peace is by instituting a supreme definer, the Leviathan. Those who realize this will then have to convince others to leave the state of nature and create a commonwealth, "the mother of peace and leisure,"[102] and hence the grandmother of philosophy and other high intellectual pursuits.

This is a part of the story that Hobbes himself seems to leave out. He discusses both the state of nature and the commonwealth at length, but he does not dwell on the process by which a group of people all arrive at the same place at the same time and all agree to "give up [their] right of governing [themselves] to this man, or to this assembly of men."[103] Hobbes distinguishes between commonwealths by institution and by acquisition.[104] The former are covered more extensively by Hobbes, and constitute what we generally think of as a state created by a social compact. In commonwealths by institution, "men agree amongst themselves to submit"[105] to a sovereign that they themselves create. Commonwealths by acquisition, on the other hand, are formed when the sovereign power is "acquired by force . . . when men . . . for fear of death or bonds do authorize all the actions of that man or men"[106] who is already in a position of relative advantage.

But there are far fewer differences between the two than the casual reader might think, for Hobbes continues by claiming that the only difference between the two forms of commonwealth is that "men who choose their sovereign do it for fear of one another, and not of him whom they institute," but in a commonwealth by acquisition "they subject themselves to him they are afraid of."[107] Even in the case of commonwealth by acquisition, when a person is given the choice between death and subjecthood, the situation remains one of choice. "The rights and consequences of sovereignty are [therefore] the same in both"[108] types of commonwealth. Thus, after this comparison the commonwealth by institution comes to look more like a special case of the commonwealth by acquisition than like a distinct species of society. All commonwealths are founded on fear and force—commonwealths by institution are based on the mutual fear and force of each against all, and commonwealths by acquisition are founded upon the fear a group has of the force of one.

In fact, as Richard Flathman notes, given everything Hobbes says about the state of nature and the human condition, it appears that "commonwealth[s] can get started only through the highly uncertain process of 'acquisition' by one or more powerful individuals."[109] Gary Herbert agrees, claiming that "it is unlikely that any civil society has ever come about by an original, contractual act of institution. Most likely, the emphasis on sovereignty by institution in *Leviathan* is Hobbes's way of legitimizing sovereignty by acquisition."[110]

There are two reasons for one to claim that Hobbesian persons in the state of nature can never come together to form a commonwealth by institution. Most obviously, in the natural condition it is rational for each person to distrust every other person, given that no social compact has been concluded and everyone retains a right to all things, including the bodies of others. As Gauthier explains, according to the "simple rationality account" this distrust would be the result of the scarcity of the material means of preservation, while the "subversive passions account" holds that "subversion by the passions" destroys "what would otherwise be rational agreement on peace."[111] It is highly unlikely that a group of persons in the state of nature could ever carry out the discussions and negotiations necessary to the formation of a commonwealth by institution.

But behind both of these accounts lies a discursive difficulty that threatens to unravel any possibility for commonwealth by either acquisition or institution: How would persons in the state of nature actually communicate with one another? Even if a group of persons managed to all arrive at the same place at the same time and not immediately kill each other, how would they actually discuss the formation of a commonwealth, given the differences of signification among them? Identifying and expounding upon this difficulty is the focus of Matthew Kramer's work, in which he concludes that "a sharing of key assumptions for interpretation and reasoning must guide the establishment of the social contract but must fail to materialize until that contract has already achieved its force."[112] In his and others' views, the social compact is dependent upon the very structures of mutual intelligibility that it must create, but I intend to show how this problem can be overcome by meaning creators acting within the economy of violence. When we examine the matter in light of the discursive violence inherent in all personal relations, the incremental creation of the commonwealth by acquisition appears as the most likely possibility.

Hobbes himself alludes to this linguistic difficulty when he writes in *De Homine* that "it is incredible that men once came together to take counsel to constitute by decree what all words and all connexions of words would signify."[113] This issue also arises in *Leviathan*, in which Hobbes writes that without mutually intelligible speech humans could create "neither commonwealth, nor society, nor contract, nor peace."[114] That is, it is unlikely that a social compact to institute a meaning-enforcing sovereign could have ever occurred. The sovereign would have to have already existed! Words for things common in the state of nature (such as rock, tree, fear, or threat), are invented independently by many persons of all linguistic/mental capacities, but those words that are iterated most widely are forced on others by those persons who have the greatest capacity for language and reason. These latter persons are most capable of muddling through the problems of diverse signification in the state of nature and slowly forging agreement on language through "psychology, demagogy, or even pedagogy which is not instruction."[115] As superior persons force their own significations upon others, spreading agreement on language, their victims (rather than "students") are convinced of the truth or accuracy of positions that they would not otherwise hold.

But before there is any violently instituted agreement on any name, there are simply two persons confronting each other in the state of nature and the economy of violence. Neither Hobbes nor his most eminent commentators speak directly of this important theoretical moment, when two fearful persons confront each other in the natural condition, each knowing that the other is a person but naturally conceiving of that other as the inferior term of the dyad dominated by oneself. Most likely, this confrontation will end in violence, with one party dying, the other victorious but still terrified, and both of their muddy intellects trying to figure out exactly how this happened.

On the other hand, if one of these persons has, thanks to her grasp of language, a sufficiently high reasoning ability, she may be able to deceive and capture the other person and begin the process of training him in the use of her own system of signification. At this point the inferior person is like a child who, having not yet "attained the use of speech," is "not endued with reason at all . . . but [is] called [a] reasonable [creature] for the possibility apparent of having the use of reason in time to come."[116] The superior person may act as a parent to this child, using "psychology, demagogy, or even pedagogy which is not instruction"[117] to begin laboring upon this proto-person, indoctrinating/instructing him in the use of language as the superior person sees fit. Of course, Kramer may object that it is impossible for this indoctrination to proceed before both parties agree on the meanings of words, but he would be missing the point. It is not as though two persons with an advanced use of language fight each other until one agrees to the other's definition of "happiness" or "success." Rather, the superior person, playing the role of parent to the inferior person who has only a very basic use of language "for *marks*, or *notes* of remembrance,"[118] slowly indoctrinates him into the use of her own system of linguistic signification. This happens countless times around the world every day, as children learn to use language and reason in the way their parents or caretakers (and other socializing influences) do. While this process remains somewhat of a mystery, it is a mystery for developmental neurophysiology and early childhood studies, not ethics or political philosophy.

"Because all men be not alike affected with the same thing," and "seeing all names are imposed to signify our conceptions . . . when we conceive the same things differently, we can hardly avoid different naming of them."[119] Therefore the inferior person can not truly have "those thoughts which the words of [the superior person's] speech, and their connexion, were ordained and constituted to signify,"[120] until the inferior person's personhood is subsumed beneath the superior's, such that he will be "alike affected with the same thing[s]"[121] and hence agree with the superior person's system of significations.

Again using the concept of "threat" as an example, the inferior person will agree with the superior's exact use of the word only when the former's personhood is subsumed beneath the latter's. At that point the inferior person will in effect see "threat" through the eyes of the superior, using and understanding this and other terms in the same way. This amounts to a "reduction of [the inferior person] to a real moment of [the superior person's] life"[122] which is, of course, the very definition of violence. By rejecting another person's creations of meaning and forcing him to submit to her own creations, the superior person causes him to become less an independent person and more a phenomenal iteration of herself. As agreement on language is spread by the violences of superior persons, the basis for commonwealth is itself extended. The superior person who forcefully subsumes others' creations of meaning beneath her own ensures that all those influenced by her maintain "opinions and beliefs"[123] based on her own conceptions that keep the peace among them all, literally on the dominant creator's "own terms."

To explain how superior persons would convince their inferiors to join a commonwealth based on this spread of one superior person's discursive dominance, Hobbes writes that "we get a right over . . . the persons of men . . . by force and natural strength."[124] This implies what I alluded to above—that intellectuals could force others to join by deploying both discursive and physical violence. "The common people's minds . . . are like clean paper, fit to receive whatsoever . . . shall be imprinted in them"[125] by the discursive (or perhaps physical) violence perpetrated upon them by those more potent meaning creators who are trying to construct commonwealths.[126] "Seeing all *delight* is *appetite*, and presupposeth a *further* end, there can be no contentment but in *proceeding*,"[127] so certainly superior persons would not simply wait (perhaps in vain) for the others to realize that a social contract is necessary. Because they comprehend that they would be able to use the greater part of their reason in the commonwealth, thus both putting them at an advantage to the inferior persons and opening up new avenues for their own continued creations of meaning and other forms of struggle, the superior persons would certainly try to bring about the creation of commonwealths as quickly as possible. Their desire to create commonwealths thus "proceedeth from the imagination or conception of [their] *own power* above the power of [they] that contendeth with [them]."[128]

At this point it is easy to distinguish a major similarity between Hobbes and Nietzsche, one that sets them in economical opposition to Derrida. Although I will save a detailed examination of the topic for another project, it is interesting to note that for both Hobbes and Nietzsche it is both natural and appropriate for superior persons to force their personhoods upon lesser entities. As above, these authors have nearly opposite views of what constitutes a superior person, but within their respective systems, they each consider it expedient for the superior to impose themselves upon the inferior. This similarity between Hobbes and

Nietzsche is perhaps most clearly demonstrated by Nietzsche's pronouncement that "the lordly right of giving names extends so far that one should allow oneself to conceive the origin of language itself as an expression of power on the part of the rulers: they say 'this is this and this,' they seal every thing and event with a sound and, as it were, take possession of it."[129] Broadly agreeing with Hobbes, Nietzsche here makes a succinct statement of his idea that agreement on meaning, rather than being natural or objective, is a creation that is imposed upon the inferior by the superior.

Even so, the motivations for this imposition by Hobbesian and Nietzschean superior persons are quite different. For Hobbes, superior persons pursue the possibility of peaceful coordination created by forced agreement on meaning because of fear of death and desire to develop their intellectual abilities even further. According to Nietzsche, who is "delighted with all who love . . . danger, war, and adventures, who refuse to compromise, to be captured, reconciled, and castrated; we count ourselves among the conquerors,"[130] these are slavish reasons to seek power over others. Those who seek peace to allay their fears are "simpletons [who] want a single thing most of all: that nobody should hurt them,"[131] and those who desire peace to pursue intellectual endeavours are "fragments and limbs and dreadful accidents"[132] who wish only to lock themselves away with their studies, rather than vibrant human conquerors and embracers of life.

Again, it may appear that Hobbes' philosophy only addresses Nietzsche's slavish type. Although some may find this unlikely, given that although Hobbesian sovereigns dominate others for ignoble reasons rather than revelry in life as the will to power, these sovereigns do dominate nonetheless. But recall that Nietzsche affirms that the slavish are also creators, even though they do not recognize this inescapable fact. *All* life is will to power, and the slave morality is no less creative than the master morality. The slave morality "begins when ressentiment itself becomes creative and gives birth to values,"[133] and these values are imposed upon others no less than are those of the master morality.

In Derrida's terms, the process by which a Hobbesian superior person imposes her sovereignty is inscribed throughout with the economy of violence. Although the superior persons do (at the very least) discursive violence to others as the former attempt to force the latter to participate in a commonwealth, this can never be a pure violence. The superior persons must recognize that certain creatures are capable of the creation of meaning and value, that they are in fact persons, before they will attempt to do violence to them in the creation of a commonwealth, as Hobbes himself recognizes. He declares that "no man can compact with him who doth not declare his acceptance; and therefore we cannot compact with beasts, neither can we give, or take from them any manner of right, by reason of their want of speech and understanding."[134] "The self-centered attitude of an agent bent at absorbing everything within his power is due not," as Piotr Hoffman puts it, "to a lack of clear awareness of other people's independent standing in the world; rather, it is a way in which the agent responds to the very real and very acute knowledge of the others as power centers representing a constant threat to him."[135] Only upon appreciating that he is surrounded by others who are also capable of violence (discursive or otherwise) does a person perpetrate violence against them in an attempt to force them to adhere to his own system of meanings. Interestingly, this means that the fact that the lesser persons are actually persons of some sort is what causes them to be the subject of this violence. If they were more superior persons, they would have been among the first to understand the necessity of the commonwealth, so they would likely be perpetrating violence against others. If they were not persons at all, they would, "by reason of their want of speech and understanding,"[136] not be subject to any violence at all.

In their relatively limited capacity, the inferior persons may be convinced that a commonwealth is necessary, but they may also recognize that their superiors would use it to increase their own relative advantage. Put differently, the superior persons may be able to force their definitions upon their inferiors, thus violently infringing upon, changing, and supplementing the inferiors' reasoning processes. The inferiors would then, due to this (again, at least) discursive violence, be convinced that a commonwealth is to their advantage. But the inferior persons might also realize that the commonwealth will provide a framework under which their intellectual superiors could extend and enhance their relative advantage, since the commonwealth would free them from the necessity of living in the practicalities of the present moment.

Therefore, the inferior persons are faced with a choice: they can choose to remain in the free but frightening state of nature, or they can accept becoming second-class citizens in a commonwealth. When making this decision, they act out an economy of violence towards themselves. Full justice is an impossibility in this situation because some aspects of the fullness of each inferior person's existence as a meaning creator must be the subject of violence; no choice will result in one's full self-recognition. They can be somewhat just to themselves by not simply giving in to the system of meanings that the superior persons try to force upon them, but run the risk of being killed or enslaved; or they can be somewhat just to themselves by being safer, but subject themselves to a commonwealth that reduces their equality with their most potent others. Since for Hobbes "every man is presumed to seek what is good for himself naturally,"[137] each inferior person will make the choice that he considers best overall, but either way they do a violence to themselves.

If a person chooses to join a growing commonwealth, that person will be doing violence to his existence as a meaning creator, because he will be willfully subjecting himself to the meaning creations of a sovereign. The inferior person will be voluntarily reducing his personhood by giving up the right to decide his own meanings and values. If the person chooses to reject the commonwealth, that person retains his natural right to meaning creation, but runs the risk of being enslaved or killed, which would obviously completely destroy any further possibilities of creating meaning or value. If one follows Derrida's advice to always seek the lesser of the necessary violences in an economy of violence, one would likely choose to live as a strictly circumscribed person in a commonwealth, but if one was of a more Nietzschean bent one might choose the less circumscribed but more dangerous life of the state of nature.

Either way, violence is an unavoidable aspect of human existence for Hobbes. Although it is common for commentators to claim that Hobbes' sovereign puts an end to violence, when we recognize that violence is fundamentally a rejection of an other's nature as a creator of meaning and value it becomes clear that the commonwealth may be *more* violent than the state of nature. In the state of nature, one is free to be an independent creator, but this creativity may lead to conflict among persons. But in the commonwealth, where "it is annexed to the sovereignty to be judge of what opinions and doctrines are averse, and what conducing, to peace,"[138] one is constantly subject to the sovereign's rigorous mental and physical disciplining that itself constitutes a significant level of violence. Because "every man by right of nature, is judge himself of the necessity of the means, and of the greatness of the danger,"[139] one may or may not choose the perhaps more predictable and assured violences of the commonwealth over those of the state of nature. But either way, there is no escape from violence.

III. Hobbesian Justice

By minimizing the violence they do to themselves and others, Hobbesian persons approach justice. But Hobbes' conception of justice is one of his most misunderstood ideas. First, it is easy to show that Hobbes agrees with the classic definition of justice as giving each person her due. He states it plainly both when he writes that justice "signifies a steady will of giving every one his *own*,"[140] and when he states the reverse of this, that justice consists "in taking from no man what is his."[141] Of course, the problem with this definition throughout the history of ethics is that it requires one to determine what exactly is owned by and owed to each particular person.

In one of his most controversial ideas, Hobbes seems to determine that nothing is owed to a person before the conclusion of a contract that is, nothing is owed to any by nature, by the simple fact of his or her humanity. He puts this most bluntly in *Leviathan*, in which he writes that "injustice is no other than *the not performance of covenant*," and he expands this idea by explaining that "where no covenant hath preceded, there hath no right been transferred, and every man has right to everything; and consequently, no action can be unjust."[142] Elsewhere Hobbes writes that "the breach or violation of covenant, is that which men call *injury*, consisting in some action or omission, which is therefore called *unjust*,"[143] which again shows that no person owes or is owed anything at all by nature, that is, before expressly agreeing to it.

While this sort of position has caused discomfort among many ethicists, some of Hobbes' commentators see the advantages of his thinking. Flathman notes that in Hobbes' "radically voluntarist doctrine" all persons "make their own obligations for themselves."[144] Alan Ryan also praises this system, in which "nobody is obliged but by some act of his or her own."[145] Hobbes' notion of justice provides the fewest limitations on the personhood of the natural person—by living in this way a person comes perhaps as close as possible to doing perfect justice to herself by reveling in the virtually complete absence of obligation to the personhood of others. In the state of nature, before all contracts, a person "hath right to all things, that is to say, to do whatsoever he listeth to whom he listeth, to possess, use, and enjoy all things he will and can."[146] Upon entering into a contract, the parties to that contract agree to very specific and circumscribed relations that lay out exactly what is owed to each by each, a process that imbues the generic definition of justice with certain specific content that relates only to those parties to the contract. For whatever rationally self-interested reason they derive from their situations, each party to a contract chooses exactly how far to limit herself, exactly how much and in what ways to respect the existence of the other parties as meaning creating entities in their own right. Obviously, each contracting party therefore retains a maximum amount of independent selfhood while still making herself tolerable to the other persons with whom she interacts.

Perhaps the best example of Hobbes' selfhood-maximizing theory of justice is that even within a commonwealth, the product of the broadest and deepest contract, individuals retain the right to defend themselves against attack by the sovereign to which they have pledged their allegiance and subsumed the bulk of their potential personhood, even if the sovereign is simply trying to enforce a law that that person has broken (and which, incidentally, the person herself indirectly authored, according to Hobbes). No one ever agrees to give up his or her life, no person ever contracts to have her personhood completely violated through death, so even that "*Mortall god*,"[147] the Leviathan that is the supreme definer and enforcer in a commonwealth, is not owed it.

So in Hobbes' system, before entering into a contract a person does near-total justice to himself, while doing near-total violence to others by living out his natural "right to everything," including the bodies of others.[148] Even so, this situation remains an economy of justice and violence, and not a pure manifestation of either. Doing pure violence to an other is a paradoxical notion, for pure violence would constitute the complete rejection of the other as an alter-*ego*, as an independent creator of meaning. Such a rejection would render the other no longer an other to oneself, but simply a purely phenomenal object to which the concept of violence does not apply. In Hobbes' case, the inevitability of the recognition of others in the state of nature occurs in two separate but related aspects of the situation. First, as Hoffman puts it, "the self-centered attitude of an agent bent at absorbing everything within his power is due not to a lack of clear awareness of other people's independent standing in the world; rather, it is a way in which the agent responds to the very real and very acute knowledge of the others as power centers representing a constant threat to him."[149] A person is forced to struggle for discursive and physical dominance in the state of nature precisely because that person recognizes that other persons are contending for mastery as well. A person who did not recognize the independent egoity of others would not act as a Hobbesian individual does; such a person would not comprehend that "the very same powers that [he has] are turned against"[150] him in a struggle for control. As this recognition occurs it "translates itself immediately into an acknowledgment of [the other's] autonomy. As a force equal with [oneself] the other can not be absorbed within [one's] own ends-means sequence."[151]

The other provides a positive resistance to any attempts to force it into one's own system of signification as just another purely phenomenal object.

Second, Hobbesian persons specifically *do* recognize that they are locked in a struggle with alter-egos, based on their natures as meaning creators and the resulting dilemmas of signification and security. The ultimate evidence that they recognize the existence of others as meaning creators is that they attempt to contract with them to set up an ultimate definer and a formalized system of rules of justice. One would not attempt to conclude a contract with a rock or a dog, objects unable to create or share meanings, and hence incapable of the very essence of consent. To "*authorize and give up [one's] right of governing*" oneself, and to demand that others give up their "*right to him, and authorize all his actions in like manner,*"[152] requires both personhood and the recognition of the personhood of the others of which one is making the demand. One can not demand that a llama give up its right to independent meaning creation, just as one would not obligate oneself to a waterfall. In Hobbes' system, both the existence of struggle in the state of nature and the conclusion of contracts show that even persons in the state of nature, existing in an overwhelmingly selfhood-maximizing framework, are still within the economy of violence.

Notes

1 Derrida, *Writing and Difference*, 27.

2 Ibid.

3 Ibid., 148.

4 Ibid., 129.

5 Ibid., 133.

6 Ibid., 128.

7 Ibid., 91.

8 Ibid., 57.

9 Derrida, "The Force of Law," 997.

10 Ibid., 963.

11 Derrida, *Aporias*, 19.

12 Ibid.

13 Derrida, *Writing and Difference*, 103.

14 Thomas Hobbes, *Philosophical Rudiments Concerning Government and Society* (1650), XVIII.4.

15 Nietzsche, *Thus Spoke Zarathustra*, 171.

16 Michael Williams, "Hobbes and International Relations: A Reconsideration," *International Organization* (Spring 1996), 217.

17 Piotr Hoffman, *The Quest for Power: Hobbes, Descartes, and the Emergence of Modernity* (New Jersey: Humanities Press, 1996), 4.

18 Thomas Hobbes, *Leviathan*, Ed. Edwin Curley (Indianapolis, IN: Hackett Publishing Company, Inc., 1994), VI.7. The same point is made in XI.19.

19 Hobbes, *Rudiments*, xiii. Hobbes states this point again in *Human Nature*, VII.3.

20 Hobbes, *Leviathan*, IV.24.

21 David Gauthier, "Hobbes's Social Contract," in *Perspectives on Thomas Hobbes*, ed. Rogers and Ryan (Oxford: Oxford UP, 1988), 127. Gauthier also discusses the "subversive passions account (129)," by which war results from passions, such as vain-glory,

overcoming the rational movement toward peace. My account does not seem to fit within either of these two models.

22 Hobbes, *Rudiments*, I.6.

23 Thomas Hobbes, *The Elements of Law, Moral and Politic*, IV.6.

24 Hobbes, *Rudiments*, III.31.

25 It is not my intention to imply that we should (or should not) directly apply Hobbesian ideas about individual relations to state relations. I simply provide this analogy because readers unfamiliar with Hobbes may be familiar with the security dilemma, prominent as it is in some political science literatures.

26 Richard Tuck, *Hobbes* (New York: Oxford UP, 1989), 59.

27 Paul J. Johnson, "Hobbes and the Wolf-Man," in *Thomas Hobbes: His View of Man*, ed. J.G. van der Bend (Amsterdam: Rodopi, 1982), 41. The small volume in which this article appears does not seem to be very popular reading for students of Hobbes, but it contains some very interesting short articles on several aspects of his thought.

28 Hobbes, *Leviathan*, XIII.4

29 Hobbes, *Elements*, V.5.

30 Hobbes, *Leviathan*, II.1.

31 Gabriella Slomp, *Thomas Hobbes and the Political Philosophy of Glory* (New York: Macmillian Press, Ltd., 2000), 33.

32 Derrida, *Writing and Difference*, 128.

33 Hobbes, *Rudiments*, I.6.

34 Hobbes, *Leviathan*, XI.2.

35 Hoffman, 53.

36 Nietzsche, *On the Genealogy of Morals*, 513.

37 Hobbes, *Elements*, I.4.

38 Hoffman, 20.

39 Hobbes, *Leviathan*, VI.7.

40 This is an interesting turn of phrase, since by Derrida's, Nietzsche's, and Hobbes' accounts a situation is not "given," but rather constructed by each individual.

41 Williams, 230.

42 Hobbes, *Rudiments*, I.9.

43 Matthew H. Kramer, *Hobbes and the Paradoxes of Political Origins* (New York: St. Martin's Press, Inc., 1997), 83.

44 Thomas Hobbes, *The Questions Concerning Liberty, Necessity, and Chance* (1656), Animadversion XIV.

45 Hobbes, *Elements*, II.1.

46 Hobbes, *Rudiments*, III.32.

47 Hobbes, *Leviathan*, XIV.4.

48 Hobbes, *Leviathan*, XIV.5.

49 Richard E. Flathman, *Thomas Hobbes: Skepticism, Individuality, and Chastened Politics* (London: Sage Publications, 1993), 75.

50 Johnson, 43.

51 Kramer, 89.

52 Alan Ryan, "Hobbes and Individualism," in *Perspectives on Thomas Hobbes*, ed. Rogers and Ryan (Oxford: Oxford UP, 1988), 87.

53 Hobbes, *Elements*, Part 2, X.8.

54 Hobbes, *Rudiments*, VI.18.

55 Hobbes, *Elements*, IV.6.

56 Ibid., Part 2, X.8.

57 Hobbes, *Leviathan*, V.3.

58 Ibid., XIX.4.
59 Ibid., XIX.7.
60 Hobbes, *Rudiments*, VI.9.
61 Ibid., Preface xiii.
62 Hobbes, *Leviathan*, XXIX.6. He makes a similar claim in *Rudiments*, XII.1.
63 Ibid., XXXVIII.14.
64 Williams, 219.
65 Tuck, 57.
66 Hobbes, *Leviathan*, XVII.12.
67 Derrida, *Writing and Difference*, 117.
68 Ibid., 146.
69 Ibid., 146-147.
70 Derrida, *Writing and Difference*, 124.
71 Ibid., 146.
72 Ibid., 128.
73 Ibid., 106.
74 Ibid., 138.
75 Derrida, "The Force of Law," 949.
76 Derrida, *Writing and Difference*, 125.
77 Hobbes, *Leviathan*, XIII.2.
78 Gary B. Herbert, *The Unity of Scientific and Moral Wisdom* (Vancouver, Canada: UBCP, 1989), 137.
79 Hobbes, *Rudiments*, III.13.
80 Ibid.
81 Hobbes, *Elements*, IV.1.
82 Nietzsche, *The Gay Science*, 237.
83 Hobbes, *Leviathan*, VIII.14 and VIII.15, respectively.
84 Ibid., VIII.14.
85 Ibid., XIII.2 and VIII.13, respectively.
86 Ibid., V.2.
87 Hoffman, 3.
88 Hobbes, *Leviathan*, V.17.
89 Ibid., III.11.
90 Thomas Hobbes, *The Questions Concerning Liberty, Necessity, and Chance*, Animadversion XIV(h). For similar sentiments, see *Leviathan*, II.10., and *Human Nature*, V.4.
91 Thomas Hobbes, *Human Nature, or the Fundamental Elements of Policy* (1640), V.4.
92 Hobbes, *Leviathan*, V.18.
93 Ibid.
94 Nietzsche, *On the Genealogy of Morals*, I.10.
95 Ibid.
96 Slomp, 20.
97 Hobbes, *Leviathan*, XIII.9.
98 Ibid., VI.35.
99 Hobbes, *Elements*, X.6. I first encountered the juxtaposition of these two excellent quotes when reading *The Unity of Scientific and Moral Wisdom*, by Gary B. Herbert.
100 Hobbes, *Leviathan*, XLVI.6.
101 Hobbes, *Rudiments*, III.31.
102 Hobbes, *Leviathan*, XLVI.6.

103 Ibid., XVIII.13.

104 Ibid., XVIII.

105 Ibid., XVIII.15.

106 Ibid., XX.1.

107 Ibid., XX.2.

108 Ibid., XX.3.

109 Flathman, 132.

110 Herbert, 158.

111 Gauthier, 126-129.

112 Kramer, 68.

113 Hobbes, *De Homine*, X.2.

114 Hobbes, *Leviathan*, IV.I.

115 Derrida, *Writing and Difference*, 106. It is useful to note that "pedagogy which is not instruction" can range from "hard sell" sales tactics to physical torture that results in the victim's real assent to the truth of a given proposition. Of course, the forceful pedagogies with which we are familiar all occur within easily recognizable language. They are therefore impossible in the state of nature, which is characterized by a lack of agreement on the meanings of words. Although I hesitate to discuss such earthy things in an academic work, convincing others to agree with one's own system of significations is possible without the use of any language other than that which Hobbes says is naturally part of human nature. If, given the "similitude of the thoughts and passions (*Lev.*, Introduction)" of all persons, a superior person is able to "read in himself (Ibid.)" all of humanity, he might be able to manipulate the desires and aversions of an inferior person. Imagine, for example, that superior person A captures an inferior person B in a pit trap. Person A lets person B grow hungry and thirsty, then approaches the edge of the pit with some food and water. Person A points to himself and says "Bob," to which person B responds with a stream of yelling that person B assumes is probably vulgarities. Unhappy with this response, person A departs out of sight, taking the food and water with him. Some time later, Bob returns and tries again. Eventually person B will have to make a free choice—refer to his captor as Bob, or die of thirst and hunger. Most people will choose to call their captor Bob, and hope to receive sustenance in return. Thus begins an incremental agreement on signification that may end with person B subsuming a great deal of his personhood beneath Bob. If, whether out of intransigence or lack of linguistic capacity, the captured inferior person never figures out what Bob is trying to accomplish, he will likely die in the pit. Bob will find another inferior person, and try again.

116 Hobbes, *Leviathan*, V.18.

117 Derrida, *Writing and Difference*, 106.

118 Hobbes, *Leviathan*, IV.3.

119 Ibid., IV.24.

120 Ibid., IV.22.

121 Ibid., IV.24.

122 Derrida, *Writing and Difference*, 128.

123 Mary G. Dietz, "Hobbes's Subject as Citizen," in *Thomas Hobbes and Political Theory*, ed. Mary Dietz (Lawrence, KS: University of Kansas Press, 1990), 96.

124 Hobbes, *Rudiments*, VIII.10.

125 Hobbes, *Leviathan*, XXX.6.

126 Physical violence is a manifestation of the pre-ethical arché-violence played out by the creation of meaning and the nature of persons as value creators. Perhaps Derrida's best treatment of the derivative nature of physical violence is contained in his article, "The Force of Law," which I treat extensively in chapter one. Put less technically,

though, we can simply recognize that war is diplomacy by other means—that both convincing and what is more commonly termed forcing (convincing with a gun) share the same core idea, that you will do what I demand. Certainly, physical violence is generally more overtly gruesome than psychological, emotional, or other forms of discursive violence, and murder is the ultimate violence because it completely obliterates the personhood of the other, but they both derive from the pre-ethical inevitability of arché-violence.

127 Hobbes, *Human Nature*, VII.6.

128 Ibid., IX.1.

129 Nietzsche, *On the Genealogy of Morals*, I.2.

130 Nietzsche, *The Gay Science*, 377.

131 Nietzsche, *Thus Spoke Zarathustra*, 282.

132 Ibid., 250.

133 Nietzsche, *On the Genealogy of Morals*, I.10.

134 Hobbes, *Rudiments*, II.12. For a similar passage, see *Leviathan*, XIV.22.

135 Hoffman, 8.

136 Hobbes, *Rudiments*, II.12.

137 Ibid., III.21.

138 Hobbes, *Leviathan*, XVIII.9.

139 Hobbes, *Elements*, I.8.

140 Hobbes, *Rudiments*, Epistle Dedicatory.

141 Hobbes, *Leviathan*, XXX.12.

142 Ibid., XV.2.

143 Hobbes, *Elements*, III.2.

144 Flathman, 71.

145 Ryan, 91.

146 Hobbes, *Elements*, I.10.

147 Hobbes, *Leviathan*, XVII.13.

148 Ibid., XV.2.

149 Hoffman, 8.

150 Ibid., 27.

151 Ibid.

152 Hobbes, *Leviathan*, XVII.13.

Chapter Three
Isaiah Berlin and the Search for a Final Answer

I. Re-Iteration

In chapter one I explained how Derrida's and Nietzsche's different concepts of violence and respect for others as meaning creators are at odds with each other, even though the economy of violence that is inscribed within them keeps them from being completely opposed. For both, justice requires treating others as independent creators of meaning and value, but the form taken by this respect differs in each author. Derrida argues that a person respects others as creators when he voluntarily limits his own creations of meaning and allows the others to create independently. On the other hand, Nietzsche claims that we respect others as creators when we "strive against one another like gods"[1] and challenge their creations with our own.

Given the economy of violence, each theory contains elements of both respect and disrespect for the nature of an other as a meaning creator, but one theory's respect is the other's disrespect. In Derrida's self-limiting justice, we show respect for the other by voluntarily limiting our own propagations of meaning and value, by maintaining a "rectitude of address"[2] and calling to the other in the vocative rather than acting upon him in the accusative. Nietzsche scoffs that this attitude is appropriate only when dealing with the sickly or incompetent: such "cowardly compromise[s]"[3] obscure the fact that "the really fundamental instinct of life . . . aims at the expansion of power."[4] Truly respecting the creative nature of life implies that "in a friend one should have one's best enemy,"[5] a person who is willing to live as a creator among creators, struggling discursively with them rather than allowing them to remain unchallenged. For Nietzsche, Derrida's treatment of "the other as other, irreducible to *my* ego,"[6] and hence not to be put in danger of discursive defeat, is tantamount to treating him as a mere phenomenal object rather than as a person who naturally engages in discursive struggle. Nietzsche's attitude here reflects Hobbes' notion, which I discussed in chapter two, that the violence of the state of nature results not from the rejection of the personhood of others, but from the recognition that others are persons who are themselves capable of violence. Respect for the dangerous independence of the personhood of others necessitates a violent struggle for dominance.

Their conceptions of disrespect—the failure to recognize the other as a meaning creator—are also opposed. Whereas Derrida's idea of disrespect involves an attempted "reduction of the other to a real moment of my life,"[7] that same reduction constitutes Nietzsche's idea of respect. By attempting to iterate our own creations over those of an other, which necessitates denying that other's status as a legitimately independent source of meaning, we respect that other as one of the "spontaneous, aggressive, expansive, form-giving forces that give new interpretations and directions"[8] to existence. For Derrida, such aggression and struggle against the other constitutes a denial of his legitimacy, but Nietzsche argues that leaving the other to independent creation without struggle is to treat him as a child at whom we smile when he thinks he is asserting his intelligence, rather than struggling against him and helping him (and oneself) become better in the process.

I have also already explained how Derrida's and Nietzsche's conceptions of justice exist within an economy of violence that rejects the logical possibility of pure violence and pure nonviolence. Although Nietzsche argues in favor of joyful struggle among creators who are all trying to subsume their others beneath their own systems of signification, the key to this theory of overcoming is that it requires other persons to overcome. This struggle, rejected by that slavish legalism that prefers stagnant mediocrity, must be a struggle against something, of persons against one another. The will to power must be a power over something, and that something is precisely what has been overcome. The will to power is a "subduing, a becoming master"[9] that in its very structure as an overcoming requires "war and victory . . . conquest, adventure, danger,"[10] which itself necessitates a competitive interlocutor. Although Nietzsche would have us each try to completely efface the other or be effaced in the attempt, such struggle tacitly recognizes the humanity of the enemy as a source of meaning that must be overcome. If complete Nietzschean dominance were achieved and all others were effaced, this victory would cease to exist because the complete subjection of all others would destroy the very otherness that made them capable of being overcome. For the victory to continue to exist, for the victor to continue to be dominant *over* something, the vanquished must not be completely effaced. If the defeated were completely effaced, the victor could not be dominant over them because they could not be subjugated—they would be mere phenomenal objects, and hence outside of discursive intersubjectivity. Objects that are not themselves independent sources of meaning cannot be subjugated because they simply fall into line behind discursive inertia. In the very act of completely subjugating an opponent, of completely effacing that opponent in an act of pure violence, the victor would render his opponent incapable of being subjugated, and that opponent would slip through his grasp. Because this Nietzschean dominance is a discursive dominance over others, those others must continue to be capable of discourse, so they can not be completely effaced.

Similarly, although he proposes we be as peaceful as possible by letting the other be an independent source of meaning, Derrida recognizes that the complete recognition of the other as a source of meaning would necessitate the complete recognition of the similarity between oneself and the other as fundamentally sources of meaning. In this situation one would identify with "the other immediately and originally, silently, in communion with the other's own experience" to the extent that the other "would cease to be the other."[11] A complete unity would deny the possibility of calling to or addressing the other just as much as it would reject the possibility of doing violence in the accusative or attributive cases because there would be no other at all. Given that one thing can not simultaneously hold conflicting attributes, this denial of the difference between oneself and other would thereby do violence to one's own unique identity. This self-identical dyad could not maintain a discursive relationship because pure identity would deny the independent positionality of the two.

Given his understanding that pure non-violence is not possible, Derrida favors a deconstructive political system that uses "violence against violence, light against light,"[12] in which the dominant position is constantly revolutionized in the name of justice by those who are currently effaced. As I shall allude to repeatedly, this dominant position is the *law*. That body of statutes that we commonly refer to as law is not the law in its entirety—it is that subset of the dominant positionality that is codified in a governmental manner and enforced by the state. Statutes (or common law) do not encompass the entire realm of the dominant positionality. Statutory law, common law, ethical law, social mores, and other forms of dominant positionality all fall within the broader category of law as I use it here. Because the origin of any type of new law, whether it be the criminalization of human cloning or a newly dominant definition of "literature," is itself inevitably a "violent positioning,"[13] it effaces the position of the previous law which it overcomes in the name of justice, thus doing violence to another in the name of justice for itself.

Those who perform deconstructions do justice to the law and its interlocutors, and are therefore the most just of people. Not subject to the discursive inertia either for or against a position, they instead attempt to constantly question each iteration, actually choosing a position through a moment of discreet revolution that may in fact re-found the given law. Rather than trying to overthrow all positionality, deconstruction seeks to do justice to all positions (even dominant ones) by giving them the chance to be justified, to speak originarily for themselves and be chosen, rather than being mechanistically, legalistically enforced. Certainly deconstruction "assumes the right to contest . . . constitutional protocols, the very charter that governs reading,"[14] but it does not assume a position of overthrow—such would not do justice to the given, would not let the given speak on its own behalf. Deconstruction is justice because it suspends and questions *all* positions—its interrogations becoming increasingly vigorous in proportion to a position's dominance and supposed self-evidence—and creates the space for every position to have a face (and every face to have a position), which is the ultimate demand of the justice that is each position's recognition that all others are their own independent sources of meaning.

Nietzsche, on the other hand, would welcome "a more virile, warlike"[15] social environment, in which each person—to the extent that he is capable—embraces violence as the denial of the other as a source of meaning and attempts to overcome all other discursive positions with his own. Only in this way, Nietzsche argues, can we truly do justice to ourselves and the principle of life within ourselves and others. "A legal order . . . as a means of *preventing* all struggle in general . . . would be a principle *hostile to life*"[16] because "to demand of strength that it should not express itself as strength, that it should *not* be a desire to overcome, a desire to throw down, a desire to become master . . . is just as absurd as to demand of weakness that it should express itself as strength."[17]

For Nietzsche, Derrida's "democratic idiosyncrasy which opposes everything that dominates and wants to dominate,"[18] is not only absurd, it is unhealthy because it denies the natural function of the human organism by subsuming our "unexhausted procreative will of life"[19] beneath a slavish system that in effect sickens the human animal. This system of mediocrity and equality reduces "the beast of prey 'man' to a tame and civilized . . . hopelessly mediocre and insipid man"[20] who voluntarily limits his own will to power, his own positionality and hence his own *life*, so that others in discourse may also live their stunted lives in relative peace. This is why Nietzsche says that the state is "where all drink poison, the good and the wicked; state, where all lose themselves, the good and the wicked; state, where the slow suicide of all is called 'life.'"[21] In the state all people, both the weak and the potentially great, reject life as the will to power and instead elect to lead lives of mediocrity, devoid of the creative godly combat that characterizes healthy organisms.

But just as Derrida's deconstructive, self-limiting peacefulness remains within the economy of violence by inevitably containing an element of counterviolence against greater violence, motivated by the responsibility to the *avenir* of justice, so Nietzsche's bestial, self-asserting violence maintains within it the peacefulness of one struggling creator recognizing her greatest enemy as her greatest friend. Whereas Derrida demands we choose the lesser of the violences available to us within our discursive, creative existence, Nietzsche suggests we battle each other as *inaugural* beings[22] who each strive to become the universally dominant creator of meaning, while still recognizing that such a life requires the recognition that even the discursively defeated are still potential creators.

If we are stuck within the economy of violence and peacefulness, such that pure violence and pure peacefulness are impossible, what is the most just balance between peacefulness and violence? Should we tend towards Derrida's proposals and strive to choose the most peaceful of the available violences, or lean in Nietzsche's direction by becoming as violent as possible while still recognizing that we are struggling with and against other creators? Is justice the recognition of others as meaning and value creators that we manifest when we voluntarily limit our own propagations of meaning, thus allowing others to live as relatively unmolested independent creators, or is justice the recognition of others as creators whose nature it is to strive against other creators in a fight to become the dominant creator of meaning? To preview my response (which must be obvious by this point), there can be no final answer. Justice as the recognition of others as creators of meaning and value in the world has no exogenous, independent existence outside of the content given it by each person as an independent source of meaning. If humans are the creators of meaning, justice has no Platonic Form that we can intuit and try to match as closely as possible. We each create it for ourselves (or are educated, convinced, or forced to accept someone else's definition of it). And yet, paradoxically, justice does have a definite content—respecting others as creators of meaning and value. This dual nature and the violences within it are necessary to the existence of justice—we should embrace their inevitability as the necessity of an economy of violence and peacefulness.

But given that there is no final answer, do we endure this play in either Derridean or Nietzschean modes, or follow Hobbes by trying to use force to impose one strict set of definitions? This distinction between Derrida and Nietzsche on the one hand, and Hobbes on the other, may be one of the most practical ways to distinguish between the formers' postmodernism and the latter's modernity. By this point it is clear that Derrida, Nietzsche, and Hobbes all agree that an economy of violence and peacefulness through which we play out our creative natures (an ongoing process that I shall later call politics), is inevitable for intersubjective relations. Whereas Derrida and Nietzsche embrace this political play, Hobbes dreams of ending it. Derrida would have us deploy "violence against violence, light against light,"[23] and Nietzsche argues for a world in which we "strive against one another like gods,"[24] but they both embrace this economy of violence and respect as a joyful, quintessentially human, activity. Hobbes, while recognizing the inevitability of this economy, dreams of a world in which this politics, this ongoing play of violences, has been arrested by the creation of a supreme sovereign monarch who completely subjugates all others beneath her own system of signification. Only then would humanity, if in fact it could still be called humanity, step back from the brink of chaos.

But all this is still quite a leap. In order to get closer to the non-solution or closed road, the aporia, that I have proposed as the answer to the question of justice, I intend to examine the work of Isaiah Berlin, who spent much of his considerable body of literature arguing against those whose belief in a final answer led them down the path to totalitarianism. Although at first glance their political conclusions may appear somewhat Nietzschean, these ethical monists are excellent examples of those who Nietzsche derisively calls ascetics. Berlin's conclusions about justice as a combination of negative liberty and the positive liberty of cultural belonging remain within the economy of violence, and his intellectual honesty regarding the fundamental baselessness of his positions goes a long way toward demonstrating that there is no final solution to the question of justice.

II. Positive and Negative Liberty

As Berlin describes in his most famous work, *Two Concepts of Liberty*, the pursuit of positive liberty, favored by those Berlin calls rationalists and monists, is made up of three common philosophical premises:

> First, that all men have one true purpose, and one only, that of rational self-direction; second, that the ends of all rational beings must of necessity form into a single universal, harmonious pattern, which some men may be able to discern more clearly than others; third, that all conflict, and consequently all tragedy, is due solely to the clash of reason with the irrational or the insufficiently rational . . . when all men have been made rational, they will obey the rational laws of their natures, which are one and the same in them all.[25]

The first assumption, that rationality is the sole *telos* of humanity, is at least as old as Plato's argument in *The Republic* that it is in everyone's best interests for the appetitive and spirited masses to follow orders given by the rational, wise philosopher-kings who have perceived the Forms.[26] In this and all related conceptions of a single good or proper life, "freedom is not freedom to do what is irrational, or stupid, or wrong. To force empirical selves into the right pattern is no tyranny, but liberation"[27] from our base, appetitive, subhuman impulses. For the ethical monists who believe this, the only "true way of living a good life"[28] is to achieve "self-mastery . . . defined as the realization of one's intrinsic nature, the eternal dictates of reason."[29]

Indeed, the monists' belief in eternal, universal rational principles leads them to claim that a perfectly reasonable social or political system will be without conflict. Because "truths cannot logically be incompatible,"[30] when every person acts according to his or her true rational nature all our actions are perfectly coordinated, and there is conflict over neither means nor ends. But in order to attain this system of perfectly peaceful, universally valid rationality, those who have not achieved their own true natures must be coerced into, at best, realizing their latent rationality and choosing the universally objective principles of humanity, or, at worst, avoiding punishment by simply doing what the rational leaders order, without understanding why. In the terms of *The Republic*, the guardian class remains ready to use physical force when pedagogical violence fails, but the Noble Lie is usually sufficient to indoctrinate the unphilosophical masses into following the orders of the philosopher-kings. Berlin's point here is that the monists' belief in "the existence of *the right answer* to questions of how we are to live . . . inevitably leads" them "down the road to paternalism."[31] This paternalism has often been used to justify lies and deceit in both political theory and daily governmental practice, such as *The Republic*'s noble lies, the Soviet Union's practice of covering up its own commercial airline crashes, or US government's claim that it did not have nuclear weapons in Southeast Asia during the Vietnam War. In cases like these, governments use the paternalistic rationale of objectively knowing the "public good" to justify their own deceptions. By the rulers' accounts, their respective publics could not possibly understand the deep rationale for the way things are, so deception is warranted to keep the public on the path to Truth. As Plato explains in the Allegory of the Cave, if the wise tried to free the people from their government-sponsored ideological chains and show them the truth, the people would be unable to understand why things must be as they are. They would rebel, destroying Truth and plunging society into chaos in the name of "freedom."

In an essay that looks back on his own body of work, Berlin writes that positive liberty supports "the naïve notion that there is only one true answer to every question: if I know the true answer and you do not, and you disagree with me, it is because you are ignorant; if you knew the truth, you would necessarily believe what I believe; if you seek to disobey me, this can be so only because you are wrong, because the truth has not yet been revealed to you as it has been to me."[32] Plato's *Republic* is again archetypical of this attitude: If you disagree with the Philosopher-kings' ethical principles, you are simply incorrect, for they have conceived of the Forms and are therefore in possession of the Truth. If you insist on trying to live as you, in your ignorance, prefer to live, then the Guardians will deal with you as the animal that you are.

A different sort of example comes from the *Laozi* (also commonly called the *Dao De Jing*), a classical Chinese philosophical work, in which it is said that an effective ruler empties the people's "minds but fills their bellies, weakens their wills but strengthens their bones"[33] in an attempt to make them as simple and natural as possible. In this state, in which their human, personal facets of mind and will are suppressed but their animal, phenomenal aspect is satiated, the people are easy for the ruler to control because they are closer to nature. Thus "of old those who excelled in the pursuit of the way did not use it to enlighten the people but to hoodwink them. The reason why the people are difficult to govern is that they are too clever,"[34] but when the ruler limits them to simple phenomenality they will conform "to the way . . . [and be] gladly accepted by the way."[35] They will not seek to suspend and interrogate the *Dao* (the Way), but, bereft of will and mind, will flow with this universally objective natural principle, as do all other creatures. As in *The Republic*, those wise sage rulers who know the eternal Truths of human existence are justified in circumscribing and guiding lesser persons' sovereign creativity so that they will conform to the immutable Truth.

For the monists, institutions (such as the *Republic*'s Guardians and its system of enlightening education, or the *Laozi*'s sage rulers) that bring out the universalizable rationality in persons are both necessary and liberating. Because our true nature as persons is to be found in this monistic rationality, "to obey these institutions is but to obey ourselves, and therefore no slavery, for these institutions embody ourselves at our best and wisest."[36] Because they are enslaved by their appetites or incorrect conceptions of human ends and principles, the uneducated "cannot be expected to understand or co-operate with the purposes of their educators,"[37] and may struggle against the enlightenment of correct education. They must be, as Rousseau says, "forced to be free,"[38] which amounts to forcing them to live as the monists believe that all persons should, regardless of how they, in their ignorance, childishness, or animality, want to live.

Berlin points out that these are the arguments "used by every dictator, inquisitor and bully who seeks some moral, or even aesthetic, justification for his conduct. I must do for men (or with them) what they cannot do for themselves, and I cannot ask their permission or consent, because they are in no condition to know what is best for them."[39] In the name of freeing people, a person enslaves them to his own definition of a good or proper life. "This monstrous impersonation, which consists in equating what X would choose if he were something he is not, or at least not yet, with what X actually seeks and chooses,"[40] is a totalitarian system that denies that persons are the creators of meaning and value, rather than the subjects of some single universally valid concept of the Good. But for the monists, anyone who does not agree with their conception of the *telos* of humanity is obviously either still a child, as yet incapable of living without the benevolent oppression of the Wise, or a sub-human who must be tightly controlled or destroyed for both his and polite society's sake. Both those who are swayed and those who remain unconvinced are dehumanized by their monist masters who deny the creative nature of personhood, instead "manipulat[ing] men . . . [and] propel[ling] them towards goals which" only the dictators see, rejecting the creative "human essence, to treat them as objects without wills."[41]

Although at first glance this may appear a very Nietzschean ideal, given Nietzsche's celebration of discursive dominance, it is actually an excellent example of the intellectual asceticism that he so despises. The rationalists against which Berlin writes do not understand that "men gave themselves all their good and evil,"[42] rather than discovering exogenous, universal ideals. For Nietzsche, persons are not "contemplative," as the monists believe, they are not mere "spectators" or "listeners"—humans are "poet[s] who [keep] creating this life"[43] in accordance with the basic nature of life as will to power. These monist dictators who claim to discover objective external facts are therefore life-denying ascetics who do not understand that they and all people are creators and artists, rather than mere discoverers.

Nor are Berlin's monistic, ascetic totalitarian rulers examples of Hobbes' Leviathans. Although Hobbes' sovereigns may appear similar to monistic rulers because both groups force their subjects to live according to their single unified set of meanings and values, Hobbes' sovereigns are more Nietzschean because they do not seek to justify their laws through appeals to exogenous universal verities. Knowing that "*right reason* is not existent," Hobbes' sovereigns realize that "the reason of some man . . . must supply the place thereof; and that man or men, is he or they, that have the sovereign power."[44] As I described in chapter two, these sovereigns are those persons who have the greatest linguistic, and hence the greatest reasoning, abilities. They understand that "the [only] measure of good and evil actions is the civil law,"[45] and that they, as the persons most capable of creating sets of meaning and value within a world devoid of universal definitions, can impose these sets upon less capable persons. This imposition of these created laws produces the peace that the sovereigns desire for the pursuit of felicitous lives. Thus these sovereigns are more Nietzscheans than positive libertarians because they know that they are the creators, rather than the discoverers, of the systems of meaning and value that they impose upon their subjects.

The monists ruthlessly put down rebellions against their rule, which Nietzsche can respect as a natural part of will to power, but they rule in the name of fictitious universal ethical principles and functions of humanity, rather than embracing their own natures as creative wills to power. Their stagnant rationalist rule "brings all change, all re-learning, all self-transformation into *ill repute*,"[46] training persons to be "function[s] of the herd and to ascribe value to [themselves] only as a function"[47] of inescapable universal principles. The assumption of the rationalists that "the rational ends of our 'true' natures must coincide, or be made to coincide, however violently our poor, ignorant, desire-ridden, passionate, empirical selves may cry out against this process,"[48] is thus life-denying for Nietzsche, who writes that a legal system that functions "as a means of *preventing* all struggle in general . . . would be a principle *hostile to*"[49] our nature as creative wills to power. Even so, such a system may serve a function similar to that which Nietzsche attributes to priests, providing a concrete, reassuring system that keeps the slavish masses appeased for the present and hopeful for a better future. By creating conditions of surety and conformity, rationalists and priests conserve not only the monistic law—they are also "among the greatest conserving and yes-creating forces of life"[50] itself, ensuring a tolerable life for those who are incapable (or unwilling, which of course amounts to the same thing) of creation.

In Derridean terms, the monistic system of positive liberty is pure legalism, without the *épokhè* required for law to become justice. As I explained in chapter one, justice is aporetic because it requires both the legalism of following a rule and the re-creation of this rule's substance as though from scratch. A just decision is paradoxically both free and rule-governed, such that the position being iterated is re-decided anew as a free decision even while being the calculable application of a rule. Justice for meaning creators has a definite content—respecting others as meaning creators—but if that content is not suspended in the moment of decision and re-decided as though it had never existed, the act of carrying out justice loses its character as a free decision by creators. An act of justice, in which the content of justice is re-created by a person, would instead become the mere mechanistic application of a rule by an effaced unperson, a non-creative node or servant of that law.

As its mechanistic aspect, law is only the calculable half of justice, that unfree half that effaces the freedom of the judge and predetermines his decision because the absolute objective knowledge of the Truth or the universal law renders a judge's freedom a fall away from the definitely determined path of correctness. The mere legalistic application of a rule as the perfectly calculable unfolding of some mechanistic process can thus not be a just act in itself. A simple example might be elementary school zero-tolerance weapons and drug policies. Occasionally a top student is expelled from her elementary school because her mother includes a flimsy plastic knife (like the kind distributed with meals on commercial aircraft) in her lunch bag, or a young boy is expelled from his school for taking a single aspirin that his mother has given him for a headache. In cases like these, the principles involved argue that their hands are tied, that they are not free to dispense justice because they are bound to mechanistically enforce the law of zero-tolerance. The general public outcries over these sort of legalistic travesties demonstrate the difference between the mechanistic application of a law, in which the enforcer is reduced from a creative person to the active node of a perfectly calculable system, and the justice that would result from a momentary suspension of the rule—a "period of *épokhè* . . . [an] anxiety-ridden moment of suspense"[51]—in which a "human element" was brought to bear. Within this moment of undecidability justice is done to the law itself as it is questioned and either re-iterated or discarded.

Under a system of positive liberty, this human element is ignored and a door is "opened wide to the rule of experts"[52] who debate only means, not ends. This occurs because in a monistic system "where ends are agreed, the only questions left are those of means, and these are not political but technical . . . capable of being settled by experts or machines, like arguments between engineers or doctors."[53] There is no moment of *épokhè*, no ordeal of the undecidable in which pre-given conclusions are suspended, rather than being "protect[ed] . . . by the certainty of being right, of being on the side of science, of consciousness or of reason."[54] The creative nature of persons is rejected in favor of the unquestioned, unexamined, calculable application of a single system of rules organized by rationalist monists who resemble Nietzsche's scientific ascetics who, while still persons and thus at least potential active creators, deny their natures and instead claim to discover and enforce the universally identical dictates of human living. The result is a merely legal "authoritarian State obedient to the directives of an elite of Platonic" philosopher-kings.[55]

By this point it is obvious that for Isaiah Berlin, as for Derrida, Nietzsche, and Hobbes, humans are creators of meaning and value in the world. He makes both this and his reasoning for rejecting the legalistic conformity of positive liberty clear in his statement that

> if the essence of men is that they are autonomous beings—authors of values, of ends in themselves, the ultimate authority of which consists precisely in the fact that they are willed freely—then nothing is worse than to treat them as if they were not autonomous, but natural objects, played on by causal influences, creatures at the mercy of external stimuli, whose choices can be manipulated by their rulers, whether by threats of force or offers of rewards.[56]

The monists' positive freedom is grounded in the idea that there is a single human *telos*, one universal definition of the good life, to which we must all conform. Berlin, on the other hand, argues that persons are the creators of values and individual purposes, and that forcing them to adhere to one unified conception of existence, "shaping them against their will to your own pattern, all thought-control and conditioning, is, therefore, a denial of that in men which makes them men and their values ultimate."[57] The ascetic totalitarianism of positive liberty destroys individuals' capacities and desires to create their own lives and systems of signification for themselves, treating them as mere phenomenal objects, rather than the inventors that they truly are.

Because persons are creators, the monistic belief in a single correct way of living is simply one idea among the many that exist within a universe of value pluralism. Pluralism "recognise[s] the fact that human goals are many," and it does not "deprive men, in the name of some remote, or incoherent, ideal, of much that they have found to be indispensable to their life as unpredictably self-transforming human beings."[58] In a world without pre-given truths, an acceptance of the necessity of choice and self-creation seems to Berlin "a truer and more humane ideal than the goals of those who seek in the great disciplined, authoritarian structures"[59] a single unified truth and purpose to life. The only truth to human nature is that persons are creative entities, inventing individualized ways of living that do not necessarily combine into one coherent universal system. John Gray puts this idea into what he insists on calling the "*jargon* of post-modernism by saying that it is a consequence of the conception of human beings that [Berlin] invokes that they should tell a diversity of narratives about themselves, none of which has the authority of a meta-narrative."[60]

Many of the meanings, values, and narratives that persons create may conflict with one another. Whereas the monists "took it for granted all too easily that all good things were certainly compatible, and indeed interlocked, with each other,"[61] Berlin recognizes that a pluralistic universe of individual choice and creativity is characterized by a distinct lack of agreement. The essence of human existence is that persons and groups may base their lives on fundamentally incommensurable values and ideals. "To believe that there can ever be a condition of life in which the collisions of values are for ever forestalled and the painful choices permanently avoided"[62] may be a pleasant dream for some, but trying to create such a utopia requires doing violence to persons as creators. In fact, the complete realization of a world without violence would necessitate the paradoxical and unachievable complete effacement of the meaning creating natures of all persons except one—an idea tritely but effectively pronounced by the semi-popular bumper sticker "End Racism—Kill Everyone."

This value incommensurability is not only a part of social life; it occurs within individual persons, as well. Creative persons rapidly realize that some of their creations are incompatible with each other, and they are pulled in several mutually exclusive directions by the values they have made or reiterated. "The need to choose" from among incommensurable goals and values, "to sacrifice some ultimate values to others, turns out to be a permanent characteristic of the human predicament."[63] For example, a woman may want to be both an effective mother and a successful businesswoman, but the paths to these two ends do not generally coincide. This woman's inescapable pain at having to choose between the two is called "agonistic" by John Gray, who writes that Berlin's theory is one of "conflict and unavoidable loss among rivalrous goods and evils."[64]

If Berlin is correct, the necessity of choice is made even more agonistic by the fact that there is no "external standard, no 'super-value', according to which values can be rationally ranked."[65] The human creativity that gives rise to a universe of pluralistic, incommensurable values can never justify choices by reference to some overarching universal principle. If such a principle existed, the monists would be correct, and the only correct way of living would be in accordance with it. Without such a principle, the incommensurable meanings and values that persons construct are ultimately unjustifiable, so although there is no way to validate one's own choices, there is also no reason (other than one's own unjustifiable positions) to persecute someone else's choices.

Because he believes that humans are the creators of meaning and value, because "we are faced with choices between ends equally ultimate, and claims equally absolute,"[66] Berlin argues that persons should be left free to create and live as they see fit. He calls this principle negative liberty, and it asserts that "if I am prevented by others from doing what I could otherwise do, I am to that degree unfree."[67] Rather than denying that persons are value creators and forcing them to pursue one ideal in the name of freeing them from their incorrect appetites and desires, negative liberty frees individual persons to create and live out their own meanings and values. But "it is the actual doors that are open that determine the extent of someone's freedom, and not his own preferences,"[68] so even if an individual simply follows local tradition, never taking advantage of the opportunity to strike out on his own, he still experiences negative liberty to the extent that he is free from obstacles that would impede him from doing so. By maintaining these options and accepting the incommensurable nature of a value-pluralistic universe, negative freedom respects the creative nature of all persons, even those who hardly ever choose to do something revolutionary. As John Gray puts it, negative liberty "facilitates human self-creation by choice-making among goods and evils that are rationally incomparable."[69]

Some commentators have questioned Berlin's distinction between negative and positive liberty. In a classic article, Gerald McCallum denies that these two senses of liberty are separable by arguing that "freedom is always *both* freedom from something and freedom to do or become something."[70] Because a desire for freedom is always a desire to be free from obstacles specifically in order to be able to do something that one wishes, Berlin's separation of negative and positive liberty is artificial. Similarly, Gary Frank Reed claims that "to be uncontrolled by others and in control of oneself *are* just two ways of saying the same thing,"[71] so again Berlin's distinction between negative liberty's freedom from external control and positive liberty's freedom to become truly rational (however it is defined by the local philosopher-kings) is not useful in practice.

Berlin does concede the point that the question "Who is master?" which interrogates positive liberty, and "'Over what area am I master?'" which addresses negative liberty, "cannot be kept wholly distinct"[72] in practical considerations. Given that Berlin says that "the essence of the notion of liberty, in both the 'positive' and the 'negative' senses, is the holding off of something or someone,"[73] he seems to admit that keeping the two theoretical concepts completely separated is impossible in any but purely theoretical undertakings, since any instance of "holding off" in likely to be analyzable from the perspectives of both positive and negative liberty. For instance, Berlin himself argues that "the case for social legislation or planning, for the Welfare State and socialism, can be constructed with as much validity from consideration of the claims of negative liberty as from those of its positive brother."[74]

Even so, Berlin addresses McCallum directly when he writes that "a man struggling against his chains or a people against enslavement need not consciously aim at any definite further state. A man need not know how he will use his freedom; he just wants to remove the yoke."[75] Berlin rejects McCallum's argument on the grounds that one can indeed work for negative freedom without having any notion to what use he will put that freedom once he has it. The idea behind positive liberty, that one has the freedom to do or become some specific thing, is necessarily bound to negative freedom neither logically nor practically. Negative and positive liberty fulfill distinct tasks: the former "would preserve the ground of politics on which conflicting human ends grow, so that our ability to choose is preserved" and our nature as meaning creators is respected, and the latter "would harmonize human ends" by molding a group's ideals into the same general shape.[76] Although McCallum's argument is formally effective, it fails "because it does not get below the surface of the logical form of statements of freedom to the political question of who shall choose the ends of life for each person."[77]

Whereas positive liberty is a manifestation of the mechanistic legalism that effaces the creative nature of persons, negative liberty is an example of the pure *épokhè* that embraces persons as meaning and value creators. By arguing that the absence of any overarching arché-value by which to compare different value systems renders our creations and choices ultimately unjustifiable, Berlin holds that there is an ultimate undecidability to our decisions. The "assurance of presence, [of] any certitude or any supposed criteriology that would"[78] guarantee the correctness of our position is "only a craving for the certainties of childhood or the absolute values of our primitive past."[79] By liberating human creative freedom from the (false/inhuman) knowledge of positive liberty's always-already decided ethical truths and universally correct ways of living, negative liberty frees us to "really do what we are forced to do as human beings: make choices between valuable ends"[80] that we create for ourselves.

In Derrida's terms, Berlin's positive liberty represents "decidable knowledge and certainty in a realm that structurally remains that of the undecidable."[81] Under a system of positive liberty, rulers or other dominant creators form their own ideals out of the value-pluralistic uncertainty of a world without objective exogenous values, then impose those creations on their people as a definite structure of life. This is what Derrida calls Mythic Law (*droit*), a "juridical fiction" created by persons that "will have 'bastardized'"[82] the fundamental undecidability of creative existence by denying the ordeal of the undecidable to those who live under this fictitious certainty. The creative nature of the law's subjects is effaced by the artificial certainty imposed upon them by their discursive leaders. Thus, these subjects live with the decidable, known, legalism of the promulgated law that itself exists in a realm of irreducibly undecidable human creativity.

By contrast, negative liberty is the realm of "decision . . . beyond *droit* and the state . . . without decidable knowledge . . . without decidable certainty."[83] When persons are freed to live out their natures as meaning and value creators, rather than being forcefully subjected to determinate answers from their local philosopher-kings or sage-rulers, they are denied "the metaphysical comfort . . . whereby their particular forms of life are accorded a universal authority by being underwritten or guaranteed by a rational or natural or historical order."[84] Persons then exist in a state of complete creative freedom, in which all decisions may be suspended within a moment of *épokhè* and no decision is free from the recognition of the structural undecidability of personal existence. But *épokhè* can not be sustained—a decision, ultimately ungrounded in any universal principles, objective reason, or determinate knowability, is nevertheless necessary.

Contrary to what may appear obvious upon first reading Berlin, he does not promote a system of pure negative liberty. Instead, he argues for a combination of negative and positive liberty because "the satisfaction that each of them seeks is an ultimate value which, both historically and morally, has an equal right to be classed among the deepest interests of mankind."[85] Berlin recognizes that pure negative liberty would be unsatisfying to persons, who often want to pass on their own value systems and live among others who think as they do, just as much as they want to be free to create their own values and purposes in life. Furthermore, by his own account of persons as creators in a world without pre-given values, Berlin can not justify a universal dominance of negative over positive liberty. "The notion of freedom in its 'positive' sense that is at the heart of the demands for national or social self-direction"[86] is a desire to protect valuable but marginalized or oppressed forms of life from being diffused into an increasingly homogenized and imposed global culture. Just as persons have a right to exist without being coerced into living according to someone else's conception of the good life, so persons also have a right to maintain the discursive (and geographic) borders of their own traditional communities when they are being leeched away by an encroaching neighbor.

Persons who fight for negative liberty for a group with whom they identify do not simply fight for a pure vacuum of undecidability. They fight for "the right to be governed by themselves or their representatives"[87] and for "recognition—of their class or nation, or colour or race —" of those with whom they identify (for whatever reason) "as an independent source of human activity."[88] That is, they fight for justice, for the belief in the *avenir* of justice. Even if the members of a subgroup that does not agree with the system of law under which it is forced to live are generally left to their own devices, they are still left without the opportunity to fully live out their own meanings and values. Because our creative nature makes "participation in self-government . . . a basic human requirement, an end in itself,"[89] the full recognition of the personhood of these groups requires their freedom from even benevolent outside domination and the liberty to pursue their own self-prescribed purposes. Thus Berlin defends the existence of Israel on the grounds that those who identify themselves as Jews should have a place of freedom to "grow and flourish within the framework of a settled and familiar way of life,"[90] rather than simply being tolerated but still ultimately ruled by those they consider outsiders.

Some have challenged Berlin on this point, arguing that it is paradoxical for him to pursue both negative liberty as individual creative freedom and positive liberty as cultural belonging. Axel Honneth writes that Berlin is both a liberal and a communitarian, and that "you can't on one hand defend a radical, far-reaching notion of negative freedom and on the other hand emphasize the right of the individual to live in his or her own culture. The latter can only be guaranteed if some people's options are radically reduced in order to obtain the symbolic, immaterial and social resources for the reproduction of those cultures in danger of dissolution."[91] Similarly, Gary Frank Reed maintains that negative liberty constitutes an "absolute claim for individuality which is irreconcilable with the absolute claim for solidarity made by the ideal of belonging"[92] to a culture or community with which one identifies. This leads him to argue that, while the competing but psychologically required claims of negative and positive liberty are subject to some form of compromise within each individual person, one is ultimately either a member or an individual.

Berlin's own position that positive freedom as "self-government is a fundamental human need, something valuable in itself, whether or not it clashes with the claims of negative liberty or of any other goal,"[93] lends further credence to Reed's argument. Negative and positive liberty are values that may roughly coexist within a single human life, but they are ultimately incommensurable. A person may be torn between the desire to belong to a traditional social group and a wish to strike out on her own, but this in itself does no great damage to Berlin's system, in which the existence of incommensurable values and purposes is, as John Gray puts it, an "agonistic," but unavoidable part of personhood. By this account, we often harbor competing identities, values, and purposes that all carry equal weight, and are forced to make *épokhal*, ultimately unjustifiable, decisions from among them.

Berlin himself agrees that, given his positions on the incommensurability of some values and the lack of any ultimate guarantor of correctness in creativity and decision-making, he cannot provide any good reason for preferring negative to positive liberty. If "the very desire for guarantees that our values are eternal and secure in some objective heaven is perhaps only a craving for the certainties of childhood or the absolute values of our primitive past,"[94] Berlin can provide no real justification for his claim that negative liberty is more respectful than positive liberty to the creative nature of persons, or even that we should care at all about respecting other persons' creative natures. Perhaps the main reason why this relativistic conclusion does not bother Berlin is because he believes that there is a limited field of values that it is possible for persons to hold. Although he "feel[s] no certainty" about the universality and eternality of commonly accepted values, he does wonder "whether men and their outlooks have differed, over wide stretches of space and time, as greatly as has at times been represented"[95] by anthropologists, historians, and philosophers. "By virtue of [our] shared humanity," we have a shared "spectrum of values" in which "the possibility of understanding, if not necessarily agreement is always present."[96] Within this range, even if we do not agree with another's framing of the situation or his exact choices within it, we still recognize him as a value-creative person.

If the range of likely human creative life is limited, general agreement on values is likely to exist, and only relatively minor details would remain contentious. Occasional spectacular disagreements by a few persons do not disprove this theory; rather, everyone else's unified response against such widely divergent values can be seen as evidence of the truth of Berlin's claim. As an example, consider how virtually all persons' condemnation of murder is brought into high relief when a new serial killer becomes active. Similarly, the existence of widespread agreement on international values and norms is evidenced when many countries condemn the actions of a "rogue state."

But Berlin's final reply to Reed's assertion that persons must be fundamentally either individuals or members, negative or positive libertarians, lies deeper than this. The logic of Berlin's argument points to both negative and positive liberty, to both individuality and membership, as the incommensurable and aporetic but nevertheless mutually necessary requirements for the life of a person.

III. Berlin's Economies and Aporias

Berlin's defense of a combination of negative and positive liberty comes not only from an understanding that persons tend to desire both the freedom to create their own meanings and values, as well as the freedom to make their way in the world among others who think similarly. His defense of the combination of negative and positive liberty is a recognition of their inseparability in the natures and lives of persons as creators and an understanding of the economy of violence played out between and within them. Whereas positive liberty is representative of rules, legalism, definitiveness, iterability, and membership, negative liberty represents *épokhè*, revolution, undecidability, and individuality. *Both* sides are structurally required by the nature of discursive human existence.

The economy of peacefulness and violence is played out within both negative and positive liberty, as well as between them. Negative liberty, which maximizes the "area within which the subject . . . is or should be left to do or be what he is able to do or be, without interference by other persons,"[97] is obviously peaceful in that it allows persons to live out their natures as meaning and value creators. Recognizing that others are meaning creators, persons voluntarily limit their own creations of meaning and value and open a respectful sphere around each other person in which their human creative nature remains unmolested. This is also the realm of J.S. Mill's defense of free expression on the grounds that it is essential "to the mental well-being of mankind."[98] Although Mill does not agree that persons are meaning and value creators, he does argue that there are four grounds on which the negative liberty of free expression is essential to the development of both humanity in general and each individual person in particular:

> First, if any opinion is compelled to silence, that opinion may, for aught we can certainly know, be true. To deny this is to assume our own infallibility. Secondly . . . since the general or prevailing opinion on any object is rarely or never the whole truth, it is only by the collision of adverse opinions that the remainder of the truth has any chance of being supplied. Thirdly, even if the received opinion be . . . the whole truth; unless it is . . . vigorously and earnestly contested, it will, by most of those who receive it, be held in the manner of a prejudice, with little comprehension or feeling of its rational grounds. . . .

> fourthly, the meaning of the doctrine itself will be in danger of being lost, or enfeebled, and deprived of its vital effect on the character and conduct.[99]

For those who regard persons as creators, Mill's third and fourth reasons carry the most weight. When persons are allowed to propose and debate their own positions, the reasoning behind them remains robust and nuanced, and the meanings of these ideas retain vitality that would be lost without the contestation opened by negative liberty. Justice is done to these ideas because they are not allowed to fall into mindlessly iterated dogma—in order for ideas to survive, persons must do justice to them by proposing and defending arguments in their favor. The process of debate that occurs among negatively free persons is an ordeal of the undecidable in which every creation is tested via its suspension in a moment of *épokhè* and either re-iterated or discarded by each person independently of the others.

In this very same moment of free discussion, negative liberty also shows the violence of rejecting the necessary iteration that is implied by all positionality. Because every discursive positioning structurally implies its universal iteration over the counter-claims of others, there is a struggle inherent in inter-personal discourse. If one allows the other's assertions to go unchallenged out of a respect for the other's creative sovereignty, one in fact denies that creativity by denying the struggle among competing positions that is inherent in all discourse among persons. As I also discussed in chapter two, by rejecting the necessity of struggling against the implied iteration of the other's statement, one denies that the other's statement is the discursive positioning of a creative entity. This respect-induced violence reduces the other to a sub-person whose statements do not carry the implication of universal iterability, and thus do not warrant a counter-assertion. Of course, if one chooses to challenge another's position in a Millian moment of productive debate, one plays out the violent rejection of the positionality of that other in yet another manifestation of the inevitable (economic) violence of discourse.

Berlin himself explicitly recognizes that negative liberty can be oppressive in practice. As a system of laissez-faire in which governmental coercion is minimized in the name of allowing individual liberty, negative freedom has been "used to support politically and socially destructive policies which armed the strong, the brutal and the unscrupulous against the humane and the weak, the able and ruthless against the less gifted and the less fortunate."[100] When persons are free to create and choose as they see fit, they are free to do violence to one another, and a government (or other structure of intersubjective mediation) that allows this to continue in the name of negative liberty is guilty of abetting the destruction of most persons' creative freedoms. Similarly, Herbert Marcuse has recognized that if tolerance, as an operationalization of negative freedom, is to maintain itself, it must not be extended to those who would use it against itself. If the early Nazis had not been given the negative freedom to build their ideology of intolerance and positive liberty, "mankind would have had a chance of avoiding Auschwitz and a World War."[101] According to this argument, the survival of a system of negative freedom depends upon limiting its applicability to those persons who support it. Structurally, negative liberty is violent because it constitutes a denial of the other as an independent source of discursive positioning that demands a response; practically, negative freedom can open an arena of unbridled oppression such that "freedom for the wolves" means "death to the sheep."[102]

Another contemporary manifestation of violence practiced as an integral part of negative freedom is identified in Slavoj Žižek's claim that we often now say that "you're free to decide" on ethical and political matters, "on condition that you make the right choice."[103] Persons are given the negative freedom to form their own values and positions and to live their lives as they see fit, unless they create and live ideals that the majority of the dominant group considers improper, in which case they obviously do not deserve these freedoms of creation and choice because they will only use them improperly. Contemporarily, this violence within negative freedom can be seen "with the choice 'democracy or fundamentalism'. . . Is it not that, within the terms of the choice, it is simply not possible to choose 'fundamentalism'?"[104] There are two violences within Žižek's example. The first violence is that to which Marcuse pointed, in which tolerance must not be extended to the enemies of tolerance because they will destroy it if they can. Thus the enemies of liberal democracy (and the negative liberty it presumably practices) must not be allowed negative freedom—to paraphrase a popular bumper sticker, their intolerance will not be tolerated—because these 'fundamentalists' will use this tolerance as a foothold from which to try to destroy such freedom. The second violence in Žižek's example is the dehumanizing violence of totalitarian positive liberty, in which if you fail to live as the Wise have ordained as True, "you have not listened to your own inner reason . . . [and] like a child, a savage, an idiot, you are either not ripe for self-direction, or permanently incapable of it."[105] This sub-person did not decide to become, as Emile did, what they have made him—thus he is incapable of being a full person and therefore does not deserve to be treated as one.

Positive liberty also contains an economy of peacefulness and violence. The peace contained within positive freedom consists in the Derridean recognition that the creative discursive positionings of the other structurally imply their own universal iterability. These necessarily self-conservative positionings therefore require other creators to assert counter-positions as statements of their own status as independent meaning creators. Even if one agrees with an other's position, one must restate that position as the result of one's own moment of *épokhè*, as the outcome of one's own ordeal of the undecidable, rather than simply reiterating that position legalistically and hence doing violence to one's own nature as a meaning creator. The logic of the economy of violence shows that negative freedom does violence to the other's creative nature by not accepting that his positions are the universal claims of a discursive assertion. Positive freedom, on the other hand, calls for the Nietzschean discursive struggle that results when one creator recognizes that he faces another creator whose claims carry foundational discursive force (as, for example, in my discussion of violence in Hobbes' state of nature in chapter two). By this account, when one recognizes that the violence of this implied iterability seeks to overcome all others' contrary positionalities, one takes the others' claims seriously, thus respecting him as a creator. One would then strive to arrest and overcome the others' discursive positions by attempting to impose her own positions upon him. Under the violence within negative liberty this does not happen because the structurally implied universal iterability of the others' claims is rejected, which is tantamount to rejecting that the other is a discursively active creator of meanings and values. By calling for a recognition of the creative nature of the other and a struggle against him for the assertion of one's own creative nature, positive liberty respects the power of the other's nature as an independent creator of meaning and value and calls upon persons to "strive against one another like gods."[106]

This struggle, created by the peaceful recognition of the other as a source of meaning whose creations demand a response, is also an act of violence. The goal of the discursive struggle between meaning creators is the overcoming of one's other and the subsumption of his personhood beneath one's own. Although because the intersubjective nature of violence (because it is a concept that only applies among persons as creators, as in chapter one) renders complete violence against the other asymptotic, overcoming an other's creative nature and crushing his personhood beneath one's own system of signification and valuation tends to reduce him to the pure intraworldiness of a mere phenomenal object. A complete violence that utterly destroyed the personhood of the other would cease to be a violence because the other would no longer have the capacity to create meanings and values, but the various lesser violences of positive liberty perpetrated by philosopher-kings still do significant violence to persons' abilities to realize "themselves in as many directions as freely, variously and richly as they can."[107]

By forcing those under them to live according to their masters' ideas and values rather than letting these others live out their natures as independent creators, philosopher-kings and Leviathans do violence to the personhoods of their subjects. But the economy of violence and peacefulness within positive liberty remains, because they only seek to dominate the minds of those who they recognize as having the potential to create new discursive positions at odds with the law. A person does not argue with a cactus or a lamp, mere phenomenal objects incapable of a moment of *épokhè* and the resulting discursive positioning with its structurally necessary universal iteration, so in the act of struggling violently against the possibilities of new discursive creations by their subjects philosopher-kings and Leviathans make peaceful gestures of tacit acceptance of the creative personhoods of these subjects. Even so, as Žižek points out, a subject's independent use of his *épokhal* nature to institute a new claim is often met with increased violence because the subject is using his freedom "incorrectly" or "irresponsibly." In the minds of the monists, the only appropriate use of one's creative freedom is to reify the existing law.

One place this manifestation of the economy of violence appears is in Berlin's idea that we "must give up some of our [negative] liberty to preserve the rest."[108] "In so far as some minimum degree of prevalence of rules is a necessary condition for the existence of human societies,"[109] the violence of positive liberty's enforcement of community standards upon dissenters is grounded in the recognition of the dissenters' ability to create and promulgate new meanings and values that would be harmful to the unity and tranquility of the community. This violent enforcement, engendered by peaceful recognition, is necessary to fulfill the natural human desire for a life among like-minded persons that "both historically and morally, has an equal right to be classed among the deepest interests of mankind,"[110] as evidenced for Berlin by the creation of the sovereign Jewish community of Israel. Positive freedom is also necessary to maintain at least some element of order, to arrest the chaos and destruction of negative liberty that would paradoxically result from the existence of pure negative liberty, without the ordering and tempering effects of positive liberty. This situation would parallel Hobbes' state of nature because the brutality and lack of freedom of both conditions results from the unfettered freedom of all persons to do as they choose. The necessity of positive liberty's violent suppression of some level of difference for the preservation of the incommensurable but equally supreme values of negative freedom's individualism and positive freedom's community constitutes for Berlin an "overwhelmingly strong" argument for this "intervention, by the State or other effective agencies"[111] into persons' individual creative natures.

The economy of violence within both negative and positive freedom is also played out between the two. As a system in which one is "free to go down this or that path without being prevented from doing so by man-made institutions or disciplines, or by the activities of specific human beings,"[112] negative freedom tends toward the highest degree of peacefulness possible within discourse. Again, this is not a complete peacefulness, because the complete recognition of the other as a source of meaning would necessitate the complete recognition of the similarity between oneself and the other as fundamentally sources of meaning. In this situation one would identify with "the other immediately and originally, silently, in communion with the other's own experience" to the extent that the other "would cease to be the other"[113] and the concept of violence would cease to apply. On the other hand, positive freedom tends toward violence as the rejection of the other as an independent creator of meaning and value, but pure violence would require the complete denial of the other's similarity to oneself as a being capable of creating meaning. In this situation one would have no relation to the other, who would not even be recognized as a person against whom violence could be perpetrated.

Negative and positive freedom thus always contaminate each other. Necessary to positive freedom's struggle for discursive dominance (a struggle that has always already been won by those who rule) is negative freedom's recognition of others as sources of meaning and value, as persons capable of creating new discursive positions and thus worthy of having one's own system of signification and valuation imposed upon them. Negative freedom's recognition that "we do justice to actual men and women by respecting their particular creations"[114] still contains within it the kernel of positive freedom's violence because it still proclaims that negative liberty is the one true way to live. In the name of Truth and Justice, negative liberty demands a universal iteration of itself that would efface the positions of those whose ways of life contradict the dictates of negative liberty.

Although Berlin's "belief that one way of life (the liberal value-set) was of greater value than the others . . . remained elusive,"[115] at least one defense that he seems to momentarily propose further demonstrates the economy of violence between negative and positive liberty. If it is true that "unless there is some sufficient reason not to do so, it is 'natural' or 'rational' to treat every member of a given class (in this case, men) as you treat any one member of it,"[116] negative liberty could be defended on the grounds that its respect for others as meaning and value creators treats all persons equally. By assuming an equally realizable capacity for creation, one would follow this naturally default position of treating everyone equally. The first problem with this notion is that it is just as possible to treat everyone equally oppressively as it is to treat them equally respectfully. And because equality is one incommensurable value among many, it "cannot itself be defended or justified, for it is itself that which justifies other acts,"[117] such as respect or effacement.

Second and at least as significantly, the equal treatment of all persons is inhabited by both peacefulness and violence. In the more obviously respectful liberal (i.e., negative freedom-oriented) equalities, peacefulness is easily recognized in the equally high recognition of others as creators, but the violence of equality itself is hidden and, in Nietzsche's words, "secretly vengeful."[118] The first hidden violence is the limitations that equality presents to those who have the capacities to become more dominant creators. By treating all persons equally, one disrespects those with greater abilities and hence effaces them to the degree that equality stifles their potentialities. Nietzsche considered an enforced equality of creativity a most "poisonous poison" and argued (similarly to Aristotle, who said that justice consists not only in treating equals equally, but in treating unequals unequally) that doing justice to those with greater capacities demands that we "never make equal what is unequal."[119] By treating equally those who have the ability to live out the nature of persons as creators most fully, "the tyrannomania of impotence clamors out of" those slavish "preachers of equality"[120] who are themselves incapable of such heights.

Another violence hidden within equality is one's disregard for the egoistic structure of existence. As finite, perspectival egos, we experience existence through a positionality that structurally denies the positions of others and conceives of them as the inferior terms of dyads in which we are primary. Justice as the full peaceful recognition of others as sources of meaning can never be fully achieved because all our acts are fundamentally inscribed with the violence of discursive positionality and egoistic perspectivalism. Treating others with complete equality to oneself is therefore impossible because others always constitute the secondary, inferior position in the face-to-face relationship.

Positive and negative freedom do not only play out an economy of peacefulness and violence between and within themselves—as I explained above, they also trace the aporia of justice itself. As Derrida explains, justice is inscribed with a deep aporia because "to be just or unjust and to exercise justice, I must be free and responsible for my actions, my behavior, my thoughts, my decisions . . . but this freedom or this decision of the just, if it is one, must follow a law or a prescription, a rule."[121] In order for an act to be just it must be an act of independent meaning-creation on the part of the actor, for otherwise the act would not be the result of a free decision. As Derrida puts it, the act "might be legal" as the mindless, decisionless iteration of an enforced rule, but "it would not be just."[122] On the other hand, an action that does not adhere to a rule or law is not just, either. Because justice itself is the recognition of the other as a source of meaning, an individual act must conform to, must iterate, this rule in order to be called "just." A just act therefore requires a moment of *épokhè* that suspends all previously iterated rules of respect for the other and a new creation/decision to re-initiate the iteration of this rule. If one emerges from this *époklhal* moment and proposes a new rule that does not respect the creative nature of others, one has freedom without law; if one mindlessly iterates a rule of respect for others' creative natures, one has law without freedom. In neither case has one achieved justice.

Positive liberty as Berlin described it, in which the Wise who rule a society believe that persons are the discoverers rather than the creators of meaning and value in the world, represents the legalistic aspect of justice. Above I discussed how Berlin critiques the totalitarian rule of these philosopher-kings on the grounds that they tend to reduce their subjects to objects by rejecting and forcefully overcoming their natures as meaning creators, but the violence of positive freedom remains even in Berlin's rejection of it. By arguing that because persons are by nature creators we should act so as to respect their creative capacities, Berlin is proposing a monistic rule as strict as those iterated by repressive philosopher-kings. His assertion that persons are "autonomous beings. . . authors of values"[123] and that they must therefore be free to live "their life according to their lights, and in developing whatever faculties they possess"[124] either individually or in groups, effaces the claims of those who take contrary stances. Berlin's negative liberty is therefore a single case of positive liberty. This is not a failure—rather, it is inevitable given the structure of discursive existence, in which all claims imply their own universal iteration over the counter-claims of others.

Put another way, Berlin's positive claim about negative liberty is one side of the two competing violences at the heart of the aporia of justice. Positive liberty's demand for legalistic certitude is what Derrida calls "decidable knowledge and certainty in a realm that structurally remains that of the undecidable"[125] because all decidability is created by persons and hence devoid of exogenous guarantee. Whether one takes the Platonic stance that the only acceptable way for persons to exist is for each to live within the political class that best suits their philosophical abilities, or that the sole true and just political organization is one in which each person can create as she sees fit, the claim is a definitive statement. For Berlin, the decidable, iterable content of his claim that persons are creators exists in a world without exogenously pre-given truths. Even though Berlin avoids making specific policy proposals for universal levels of negative and positive liberty or forms of government that best respect persons as creators, "since in his view that would depend on the moral values of the community involved,"[126] his claims about human nature, the best general ways to do justice to it, and his positive stance that there are no universal standards for the application of these ideas all take the structure of universally iterable discursive positions.

The legalistic definitiveness of Berlin's claim about the human creative nature and the resulting necessity of negative liberty, both of which are inescapably authoritarian given the structure of discourse, is only the decidable aspect of justice. As representative of *épokhè*, the ordeal of the undecidable, and creative freedom in a world without pre-given meanings and values, negative liberty is, in Derrida's words, "the certainty of the undecidable but without decision."[127] It is the paradoxically definite knowledge that there is no definite knowledge, no decidability, and the resulting (non-)decision to stake no universal claims that would violate this knowledge of undecidability. By arguing that persons "are autonomous and self-determining beings who can choose, and wish to choose, their purposes and values"[128] rather than mechanistic (legalistic) objects or creatures that discover the one true way to live, Berlin makes a claim for the certainty of the undecidable in a universe without meaning or value. His conclusion that we must therefore respect others by allowing them to live as independent sources of meaning and value is a decision to make no decision, to place no restraints on the natural creative freedom of persons. Negative freedom is that *épokhal* aspect of justice that stands entirely outside the legalistic decidability of the state's law-conserving violence that stamps out new creations in the name of community unity and a single truly human way of life.

IV. War and Festivals

The necessity of both law and freedom for justice constituted by the aporia of justice requires Berlin to pursue, as I discussed above, a combination of both positive and negative freedom. One of the reasons John Gray and Robert Kocis have argued that Berlin's "pluralism and liberalism might be competitive,"[129] that his *épokhal* and decidable aspects might conflict, is because "either the rationalists are right that we can discover some order to our values which best guarantees our humanity, or he cannot insist that negative liberty is 'a truer and more humane ideal' than any other."[130] They are concerned that if Berlin claims that negative liberty is the only acceptable way to live, then he is no better than the oppressive philosopher-kings against whom he fights; but if Berlin makes no claim about any way to live, then he must accept the legitimacy of totalitarian regimes as well as negatively liberal democracies. But this aporia within Berlin's work is not a fault or a failure—it is what gives his work the force of justice.

It is only by embracing the aporia of justice as the necessity of both law and freedom, of both positive and negative liberty, that Berlin takes seriously the aporetic nature of justice as respecting others as independent creators of meaning and value in the world. If he removed from his thought the aspect of positive liberty as law or rule he would remove the possibility of all positionality, destroying his ability to claim that justice *is* any thing at all. As the law's conservation of itself through universal iteration, positive liberty makes positionality possible by tracing the "the violence of difference, of classification, and of the system of appellations"[131] within discursive positioning itself. Without a positive claim that implies its own conservation through universal iteration, Berlin's speech "would determine nothing . . . would say nothing"[132] because such speech would not take a position or make a determination, and would hence be outside of discourse. It would not be speech at all.

If Berlin removed the *épokhè* and undecidability of negative freedom, he would be left with the pure determinism that he contends "is not compatible with beliefs deeply embedded in the normal speech and thought of either ordinary men or historians."[133] Such legalistic determinism and complete rote decidability completely rejects the nature of persons as creators of meaning and value, or even as beings capable of autonomous choice outside the mechanistic inevitability of physics, reducing them to mere phenomenal objects. This "reduction to intrawordliness"[134] falls far short of justice because it does not recognize the creative nature that constitutes the essence of the other, or of oneself.

Because he incorporates both negative and positive freedom into his conception of a fully human life, Berlin avoids the traps of both excessive violence to the nature of persons as creators and excessive peacefulness as the complete lack of intersubjective discourse, both of which would render his ideas uncompelling. A just life, and a just political system, requires both negative and positive liberty as *épokhè* and decidability, as law and freedom.

It is easy to say that justice requires both legalism and undecidability, and that all violence and peacefulness are economical rather than pure, but this still leaves the problem of how much of each to allow. Towards the end of chapter one I described (and since then I have never stopped describing) how both Derrida and Nietzsche begin from the premise that humans are sources of meaning and value, but use it to move in economically opposite directions. Derrida promotes an ethic of respect for the independent face of the other, which one might consider peaceful relative to Nietzsche's ethic of face-to-face struggle and overcoming. Each position requires at least minimum respect for the other in order to maintain the otherness of the other and hence the ethical face-to-face relationship; they also need some level of violence against the personhood of the other for the promotion of the self or the repressed who would otherwise be completely effaced. Derrida argues for a relatively peaceful system in which individuals do justice to others by limiting the discursively violent promulgation of their own creations of meaning, but he also recognizes that violence as articulation and as law is an inevitable structural element of justice. Nietzsche's healthy persons who glory in the creative, god-like struggle against each other for discursive dominance nevertheless require other persons, capable of their own creations and positions, as worthy interlocutors against whom to fight for mastery. Both theories of justice require peacefulness and violence, negative and positive freedom, creativity and decidability. The economy of violence between those two theoretical poles is inescapable—for both the peaceful ethics of Derrida and the violent ethics of Nietzsche, justice logically requires the presence of some level of both violence and peacefulness.

This leads to the inescapable fact that there is no final answer to the question of justice for persons as independent sources of meaning. If Plato's philosopher-kings and Berlin's positive libertarians are correct, and "a single answer to questions of truth and meaning can be discovered,"[135] then humans are simply the discoverers of some higher or prior eternal moral verities, and there is only one correct answer, one universal law or rule. An *épokhal* suspension of this rule would perhaps be considered unnecessary, because any true person would inevitably choose to re-iterate this universal law after suspending and interrogating it. This is the violence of which Žižek accuses some of us: any true person who puts the currently dominant thinking through the ordeal of the undecidable will inevitably choose to re-iterate it. Therefore, it is pointless to waste time and effort questioning the law because, if we are real persons, we will simply re-justify it. Those who suspend and question the prevailing positionality and conclude that it should be changed are obviously sub-persons, incapable of recognizing the Truth of the law.

An *épokhal* suspension of this rule might also be considered potentially inhuman (i.e., irrational, etc.) because even the theoretical suspension of the eternally valid moral law would provide an opportunity for a fall into the evil of error. Thus a classic Daoist text states that "it was when judgments were made that the Tao [Dao] was damaged."[136] Simply thinking and judging, asserting one's own will rather than being "innocent of knowledge and free from desire,"[137] can damage one's naturalness and cause one to fall out of harmony with the universal law and into the degradation of artificiality. Once within this contrived human world outside the Dao, persons construct an increasingly intricate and unnatural web of virtues, mores, and rites, but for all their critical ingenuity they fail to "embrace the uncarved block"[138] of effortless unity with the Dao. The only way for such a fallen person to correct his errors is to cease questioning and judging the Dao and subsume himself beneath its eternal ebbs and flows.[139] Edmund Burke presents a more common example in his defense of prejudice. He argues that conservatives "are afraid to put men to live and trade each on his own private stock of reason; because [conservatives] suspect that this stock in each man is small, and that the individuals would do better to avail themselves of the general bank and capital of nations and of ages"[140] represented by traditional prejudices (broadly construed). Those who reject the combined wisdom of the ages, the dominant positionality, and instead proceed based upon their own individual reason are more likely to fall in to error, since their own wisdom can not possibly match the aggregate experience and consideration of generations.

Suspending and interrogating the law could also be dishonorable and blasphemous, since it is far above a mere human's station to question God, Nature, or the Forms. Obviously this is the attitude of, for instance, Christian fundamentalists who argue that because "the Bible is the inerrent word of God" . . . we "must trust Him to know what is best for [us], as He determines [our] role and purpose in life."[141] Any person who performs a procedural *épokhal* evaluation of the law of the Christian god as revealed objectively in the Bible "makes his decisions . . . independently of God,"[142] which is totally inappropriate for an entity that is comparatively so radically inferior, and in fact beholden to that god for his very existence. The influential ancient Chinese author Zhuangzi presents a similar attitude at the beginning of his classic book, where he describes a vast bird, thousands of miles across, an ancient creature for which half a millennium is but a single season. "The understanding of the small," Zhuangzi argues, "cannot be compared to the understanding of the great. A few years cannot be compared to many years." Persons are the small and young, like cicadas which do "not know of spring and autumn, for theirs are but short lives."[143] Thus Zhuangzi claims that mere persons should not mistake themselves for vast, aged, or wise creatures that are capable of significant understanding. Questioning the Dao (or Reason, or the Law, etc.) is far above our station—we should content ourselves with doing as it tells us, and not presume to suspend or question it. "When heaven and humanity are not in dispute, then we can say this is really the true man;"[144] when a small, insignificant person presumes to question the Dao, his arrogance will be his destruction.

But if individual persons are independent sources of meaning and value, rather than the subjects of some higher or prior authority, there can be no final answer because all creations are perspectival, transient, and naturally, necessarily, in the very structure of their intersubjective essence, contested. Politics is therefore, in the compelling words of Robert Kocis, "necessary not because we are weak and irrational" and need to be guided to the Truth by the Wise; "rather, politics is needed because human dignity entails that each person is capable of his or her own ends, which no authority can dictate."[145] Isaiah Berlin agrees, arguing that politics is not the result of some persons' intellectual inadequacies, blindness to "divine revelation," or any such "final solution . . . in the mind of an individual thinker, in the pronouncements of history or science, or in the simple heart of an uncorrupted good man."[146] For Hobbes, too, the politics of continually working out significations and values is an inevitable part of the human condition. The violence of the state of nature results from a lack of purely objective meanings, a situation that can only be overcome by a new violence of imposition by the sovereign, who enforces a certain set of meanings upon those under its power. But this does not arrest politics—the sovereign cannot escape the economy of violence, it cannot completely efface the meaning-creating nature of its subjects. There will always be contestation over meaning, with the sovereign as the dominant but not the sole player.

Politics is the quintessentially intersubjective form of living for persons as independent sources of meaning and value as they struggle with each other for the dominance of their own discursive positionings. As I discussed above, although Berlin himself argues that a system of maximized negative liberty does the most justice to the nature of persons as creators, he understands that there are no ultimate, objective grounds that justify his claim. If a system of negative liberty is to be pursued, it must be formed out of and maintained by a *political* process of intersubjective creation and struggle, not a scientific method of discovery and education.

As the distinctly intersubjective form of debating answers to distinctly human questions, those questions for which there are no universally objective or programmatic answers, politics is imbued with economy and aporia. Derrida contends that voluntarily circumscribing (economically, not completely) one's own creations of meaning and value in order to allow others to live out their natures as independent creative sources is the essence of justice. Nietzsche argues that we give each person, including ourselves, what is due to him, when we unashamedly live out our own natures as creators and engage in discursive struggle for dominance over others. Because they are discursive claims, these and all other formulations of justice represent the conservatism, positive libertarianism, and iterability of the legalism that denies others as independent creators of meaning and value. The discursively dominant answer to the question of justice, the law of the land, implies "in itself, a priori, in the analytic structure of its concept, the possibility of being 'enforced,' applied by force"[147] over the independent discursive positionings of others. All discursive claims directly imply their own iterability, but the law is that specific position that currently dominates an intersubjective political process of struggle over meaning and enforcement and successfully subsumed others beneath it. The law is that dominant claim which effaces the independent positionality of counter-claims through violence in whatever manifestations are necessary, from being "educated, guided, with however light a hand,"[148] to deterrence by punishment, to death. Although all competing positions have the same essential structural elements, only the law can call someone before it and force her to adhere to it under threat of punishment, treating this other as a mere phenomenal object rather than as a person capable of *épokhè* and subjecting discursive claims to an ordeal of the undecidable.

In his "boring"[149] analysis of a legal summons, Charles Yablon demonstrates this claim by showing that "the written statement 'You are hereby summoned' proves itself. If you seek to dispute it, you acknowledge its call to you, and thereby prove that you have indeed been summoned. You have been summoned, and cannot dispute it."[150] In the form of a summons, the law demands your presence before one of its instruments, and even if you do not appear as summoned you have not defied the law because this action has "already been interpreted" by the law as "a default," which is an action well within the framework of the rules.[151] There is no escape from appearing before the stated instrument of the law. Furthermore, the summons does not mention the rules under which you must appear, because if they were stated "you might read them . . . they could be opened to discussion . . . they could be interpreted."[152] By denying you access to the rules under which you are summoned, the law denies your ability to do justice to them by subjecting them to an ordeal of the undecidable and choosing whether or not to re-create and follow them. Your mechanical, legalistic obedience is simply demanded, and your potential attempt at a rejection of this authority has always already been defined under that law, as a mere default. The law thus refuses to "account for difference or for the other"[153] who stands before it because to do so would violate the principle of its own universal iterability. The law's conservation is dependent upon its lack of recognition for creative differences among persons; it is dependent upon the violent effacement of the personhood of those under its power.

Even though all law is based on the discursive positioning of particular persons in specific times and places, in order to be legitimate and effective the law must deny its own history. Derrida explains that this denial of history is necessary because "to be invested with its categorical authority, the law must be without history, genesis, or any possible derivation."[154] A law that admits to a historical genesis and change admits that it is not categorically valid, that it has been and can again be changed, an idea that reduces the law from transcendent truth to ubiquitously iterated performative act. By claiming to be without history the law hides its origins in the arché-violence of discourse and claims panoptic inevitability, the universal, eternal, and inescapable right to subsume all others beneath it. Thus for Derrida, writing about Kafka's short story by the same name, it is impossible to come "Before the Law" because the law as a foundation that analytically contains a demand for its own iteration arises as arché-violence simultaneously with discursive intersubjectivity. There *is* no "Before the Law." In our originary moment of intersubjectivity, we are all legislators. But it is also impossible to come "Before the Law," to be called before it, called into its raw presence, because when one arrives at the foundation of the law and perceives the law as it is, as ubiquitously iterated performative act, it loses its avowed transcendental character and ceases to be The Law. In a more banal sense, intimacy breeds contempt. At the moment we reach the foundation of the law, we see that is nothing but ourselves—it is neither transcendent, nor objective, nor guaranteed.

As an aside, one may argue that in most liberal theory the legitimacy of the law comes from its historical character. Both the revolutions that created new constitutions and the ongoing democratic processes of deciding upon the law are taken to be the very basis for the force and legitimacy of that law. But this historical process is not perceived as truly political, as a struggle among competing discursive creations, but rather as the scientific unfolding of great Truths that we as discoverers (not creators) are slowly bringing to light and enacting. For example, in *On Liberty*, John Stuart Mill's arguments for the freedom of speech all revolve around effectively uncovering and maintaining the Truth, not around allowing competing creations to struggle for discursive dominance. Also consider the US Declaration of Independence, perhaps the quintessential revolutionary document, which may appear to claim legitimacy because of its historical character as a rejection of certain specific acts of the British government. But the Declaration claims ultimate authorization from the pure objectivity of self-evident Truths that are closely akin to Platonic Forms: eternal, exogenous, and a-political. The American revolution is conceived of as a progressive leap towards the realization within history of the immutable natural law that exists outside history, hence the declaration's invocation of God as the guarantor of the justness of the document and its authors' actions. The French Declaration of the Rights of Man, crafted soon after the Declaration of Independence, contains similar invocations. In the Declaration of the Rights of Man, the "National Assembly recognizes and proclaims, in the presence and under the auspices of the Supreme Being,"[155] a list of natural and universal rights. The Assembly *recognizes* and *proclaims* these rights—it does not create them, it perceives them and states them, bringing these revealed trans-historical Truths into practice within history. In all these cases the law itself is without history, but progressively more discerning human lawbringers bring newly discovered statutes into the world at the particular times and places in which they were uncovered. This is not a political process—it is a technocratic process in which eternal verities are teased out of their obscurity by increasingly more advanced scientific methodologies.

Because of both its objectivization of its subjects and its denial of its historicity, the law (the discursively dominant answer to the question of justice; the present operationalization of currently dominant claims about what constitutes justice) represents positive liberty's claim to a final answer. Although all discursive positions include these elements of violence that efface the personhood of others, what we normally call the law is that claim which can, by virtue of its dominance and iteration throughout established systems of power and violence, enforce this dehumanization by summoning a massive capacity for violence to ensure its iteration throughout the realm of its effect. Just as a defendant or witness is summoned to appear before some instrument of the law, a soldier is called-up to active duty and an executioner is "just doing his job." In this process the law must not justify itself, because in doing so it would admit the possibility of an ordeal of the undecidable through which a person could choose to reject the law's iteration.

Furthermore, as a discursively dominant claim that demands its own universal conservation through depersonalizing legalistic iteration, the law must not justify itself with a "history, genesis, or any possible derivation"[156] because this would be tantamount to admitting the possibility of another law. Admitting this would allow the alternative of judging this law through a moment of *épokhè* which itself results in a choice between re-creation and revolution, rather than simply accepting the law as the "single answer to question of truth and meaning."[157] For Berlin's positive libertarian rulers, "to want necessary laws to be other than they are is to be prey to an irrational desire . . . and [to] believe these laws to be other than what they necessarily are, is to be insane."[158] Thus, those who attempt to judge the law by subjecting it to an ordeal of the undecidable must "be 'guided' or coerced by those privileged enough"[159] to have pure objective knowledge of it. Like a prisoner undergoing re-education or rehabilitation, those who do not iterate the law must be corrected by those who know it.

As the constant striving "of the spontaneous, aggressive, expansive, form-giving forces that give new interpretations and directions"[160] to the world, politics is a very Nietzschean endeavor. But Nietzsche is not so violent that he completely effaces the personhood of subjects—he remains within politics because he recognizes that persons do not discover facts, they create meaning and value based on their individual perspectives and struggle with each other through "psychology, demagogy, . . . pedagogy,"[161] and other steps along an escalating ladder of violence in an attempt to iterate their own positions over those of other persons. As Clausewitz said, war is the continuation of politics by other means. Because politics is conducted discursively among persons, it retains negative liberty and *épokhè* even in its moments of greatest legalism and decidability. By seeking to overcome the discursive positions of their opponents and force others to live according to their own creations, persons demonstrate that "liberty is . . .

[an] ontological necessity"[162] that cannot be wholly obliterated. A total lack of the negative liberty that is the recognition of the fundamental undecidability of existence and of persons' creative natures would be a pure violence that would require the complete denial of the other's similarity to oneself as a being capable of creating meaning. Inasmuch as one does not try to discursively overcome a mere phenomenal object that is devoid of the capability of positing, political struggle tacitly recognizes the personhood of the enemy as an interlocutor—as a source of meaning that must be overcome. This other is not struggled with if it is a mere mindless object, and indeed Nietzsche claims that the noble person "desires his enemy for himself,"[163] an enemy worthy of being attacked. These sought-after enemies in which there is "*very much* to honor"[164] are recognized as strong independent sources of meaning, as people worthy of a fight and capable of making victory difficult and therefore precious.

Justice is therefore not a scientific topic. It is a quintessentially political question that includes both positive and negative liberty, both law and undecidability. If we try to turn justice into pure positive liberty, the legalistic search for and iteration of one universal eternal verity, we reject the personhood of both others and ourselves as meaning and value creators. If we are slavish in the Nietzschean sense of rejecting our creative natures and, as Berlin writes, crave "the certainties of childhood or the absolute values of our primitive past,"[165] we conceive of the pursuit of justice as a scientific endeavor that terminates when pure, universal, objective fact is achieved. But "the right policy cannot be arrived at in a mechanical or deductive fashion"[166] as though it were an equation because—and this is the legalistic aspect of the aporia of justice, its definitive positive content—justice *is* the recognition of persons as meaning and value creators. Although this fact that persons are (legally, iterably, objectively) creators would seem to support the claim that policy must be formed in a mechanical way that respects this human nature, if persons are creators then there is no objective, mechanical way to do it. Persons are creators (*épokhal*, undecidable, perspectival) in a world without ethical truth, so we must struggle eternally with one another as creators to found and therefore to conserve our own answers to the content of justice as respect for our creative natures.

We thus find ourselves caught within two competing violences described by Derrida: On one side is the "decidable knowledge and certainty" that persons are creators in a world without exogenous meaning or value, "a realm that structurally remains that of the undecidable." This constitutes a "certainty of the undecidable but without decision," because our knowledge of the ultimate undecidability or non-objectivity of meaning and value leaves us undecided about which meanings and values to impose or put into play. On the other side is "decision without decidable certainty,"[167] the moment of perspectival decision that is without any ultimate objective foundation other than a *coup* of force. This is the agonistic moment of Hobbes' Leviathan (and of each of us as persons who must act within the world), who is no longer caught in the undecidability of which choice to make or which meaning to impose, but is beset by the knowledge that her choice is without guarantee. Because of the undecidability of the realm in which the decision has been made, because it is without guarantee or objective programmatic application, it may go awry or have unforeseen consequences. Whether as the lack of any firm decision, or as the agony of a decision made without ultimate justification, undecidability is present on both sides.

For Nietzsche's slavish masses and ascetic scientists, the necessity of politics as the intersubjective play of undecidability is a curse. As though caught in a version of Sartre's *No Exit*, in which "hell is other people," we can not escape the agony of living as one creator amongst others, all bound to pass violence around to each other like a commodity as we struggle to perpetuate our own meanings and reject those of others. Politics is the hateful but inevitable process of relentlessly trying to gain dominance for our own creations, always beset by the tormenting presence of other creators who simply refuse to agree with us; it is the terrible prospect of continually recognizing that we alone can justify our positions, and that natural law, the Forms, or the god of the Ten Commandments and the Declaration of Independence can not guarantee the truth, morality, or force of our claims. Just as Garcin, Inez, and Estelle can never sleep again, for us there will never be any cessation of debate or contestation. For Nietzsche's slavish near-persons, happiness is the knowable, decidable regularity of the law, without the terror of *épokhè* or the agonistic nausea of creation. For "those in whom poisonous and inimical feelings are festering," who despise or lament our creative nature and its fundamentally agonistic undecidability, who wish for the passivity of pure positive liberty at the expense of the free creativity of negative liberty, happiness is "essentially narcotic, drug, rest, peace, 'Sabbath,' slackening of tension and relaxing of limbs"[168] and minds. On the other hand, for those "creative spirit[s] whose compelling strength will not let [them] rest in any aloofness or any beyond"[169] and who embrace our creative nature, politics is a joyful pursuit of "war and festivals."[170] It is recognized as the highest manifestation of justice, the recognition and love of persons as creators, and the struggle for discursive dominance that comes from this. For these masters, undecidability and negative liberty are not curses, they are the opportunities for creation and struggle that constitute the essence of human nature.

But again, justice includes both slave and master, both positive and negative liberty, both law and *épokhè*, knowledge and undecidability, conservation and foundation. We know what we are, but what we are is precisely that which has no content—we are aporetic beings who live the political existence of discursive, creative entities within an economy of violence and respect. So, then, how do we do justice to our aporetic nature as meaning and value creators?

Jacques Derrida and Isaiah Berlin have championed peaceful approaches by advocating maintaining as much respect as possible for the personhood of the other by limiting one's own creativity to allow others as large a sphere as possible for their own independent creativity. Friedrich Nietzsche argues that the healthiest and liveliest persons are those who embrace their creative natures and respect the creativity of others by struggling for discursive dominance, which Hobbes sees as a public service. Most of us assume that if humans are value creators, we do justice by voluntarily circumscribing our own creations of meaning so as to allow others to do the same. But if humans are value creators it is also possible that the most just person promotes his/her own meanings and values as strenuously as possible, in order to do justice to his own human nature, as well as to give others what is due them, another meaning against which to struggle.

This was the beginning, which is Just as far as we can get.

Notes

1 Nietzsche, *Thus Spoke Zarathustra*, 214.

2 Derrida, "The Force of Law: The 'Mystical Foundation of Authority,'" 949.

3 Nietzsche, *The Antichrist*, 569.

4 Nietzsche, *The Gay Science*, 349.

5 Nietzsche, *Thus Spoke Zarathustra*, 168.

6 Derrida, *Writing and Difference*, 125.

7 Ibid., 128.

8 Nietzsche, *On the Genealogy of Morals*, 515.

9 Ibid., 513.

10 Ibid., 532.

11 Derrida, *Writing and Difference*, 124.

12 Ibid., 128.

13 Derrida, "The Force of Law," 1005.

14 Ibid., 997.

15 Nietzsche, *The Gay Science*, 283.

16 Nietzsche, *On the Genealogy of Morals*, 512.

17 Ibid., 481.

18 Ibid., 514.

19 Nietzsche, *Thus Spoke Zarathustra*, 226.

20 Nietzsche, *On the Genealogy of Morals*, 478-9.

21 Nietzsche, *Thus Spoke Zarathustra*, 162.

22 I use this term as Derrida does in *Writing and Difference*, taking advantage of the play of its multiple meanings. To "inaugurate" is to create anew, as well as to officially dedicate or recognize something that is already there. This duality, which follows the same general formula as that described in "Declarations of Independence," can be seen in the inauguration of a new leader. On the one hand, she only becomes The Leader after the inauguration ceremony, but on the other hand if one is having the ceremony it is because one has already been recognized as the rightful leader. But to inaugurate can also have a somewhat different meaning, derived from the root verb, to "augur," which means to predict, foretell, or serve as an omen of something to come. Thus, an inaugural being is a being whose actions simultaneously create something anew, consecrate something that is already given, and foretell something to come. These three modes of inauguration occur in reference to the same thing simultaneously. Only inaugural beings can have justice: the legal, rule-bound aspect of justice is re-dedicated or consecrated at the moment when an accepted principle is decided anew out of the ordeal of the undecidable; this same act results from a moment of *épokhè*, the aspect of justice as freedom, and is thus a new creation out of nothing; given the structure of discursive existence, this moment of creation/re-dedication is simultaneously also a claim of universal iteration, heralding its beginning (or re-beginning) as the new standard to be propagated throughout discourse.

23 Derrida, *Writing and Difference*, 117.

24 Nietzsche, *Thus Spoke Zarathustra*, 214.

25 Isaiah Berlin, "Two Concepts of Liberty," in *Liberty: Incorporating Four Essays on Liberty*, ed. Henry Hardy (Oxford: Oxford UP, 2002), 200.

26 If that is in fact his argument. Although most commentators assume that, through Socrates, Plato intends to argue for the three-class state that Socrates describes in *The Republic*, there is ample evidence that Plato does not mean this to be a serious plan for good government. There are two simple pieces of evidence from *The Republic* that throw Plato's intentions into question. First, Socrates begins describing a simple village, but Glaucon demands a luxurious state. Socrates replies that he thinks a luxurious state is bloated and feverish, and that his simple village is healthy, but Glaucon (being, of course, quite wealthy) insists on luxuries (372c). Second, the reason for constructing the theoretical state in *The Republic* is to try to discover justice, which the discussants were apparently unable to discern on the individual scale. Socrates intends to examine justice on the large state scale, then scale it back down to the individual. As his justification, Socrates uses a very suspect example. He argues that "if someone had, for example, ordered men who don't see very sharply to read little letters from afar and then someone had the thought that the same letters are somewhere else also, but bigger and in a bigger place, I suppose it would be a godsend to be able to consider the littler ones after having read these first, if, of course, they do happen to be the same (368d)." Thus, after examining the just state, they should be able to better discern justice in the individual. But whether or not the big letters are indeed the same as the little letters, whether the just state has enough in common with the just individual, is never seriously addressed.

27 Ibid., 194.

28 Bhikhu Parekh, "The Political thought of Sir Isaiah Berlin," *British Journal of Political Science* (April 1982), 217.

29 Michael Kenny, "Isaiah Berlin's Contribution to Modern Political Theory," *Political Studies* 48 (2000), 1031.

30 Berlin, "Two Concepts of Liberty," 192.

31 Robert A. Kocis, "Reason, Development, and the Conflicts of Human Ends: Sir Isaiah Berlin's Vision of Politics," *The American Political Science Review* (March 1980), 41.

32 Isaiah Berlin, "Final Retrospect," in *Liberty: Incorporating Four Essays on Liberty*, ed. Henry Hardy (Oxford: Oxford UP, 2002), 328.

33 Lao Zi, *Tao Te Ching* [*Dao De Jing*], *shuangwen* edition, trans. D. C. Lau (Hong Kong: Chinese University Press, 2001, chapter III.

34 Ibid., chapter LXV.

35 Ibid., chapter XXIII.

36 Isaiah Berlin, "Liberty," in *Liberty: Incorporating Four Essays on Liberty*, ed. Henry Hardy (Oxford: Oxford UP, 2002), 284.

37 Berlin, "Two Concepts of Liberty," 195.

38 Jean-Jacques Rousseau, *On the Social Contract*, in *Jean-Jacques Rousseau: The Basic Political Writings*, trans. Donald A. Cress (Indianapolis, IN: Hackett Publishing Company, 1987), 150.

39 Berlin, "Two Concepts of Liberty," 197.

40 Ibid., 180.

41 Ibid., 184.

42 Nietzsche, *The Gay Science*, 171.

43 Ibid., 241.

44 Hobbes, *De Corpore*, Part 2, X.8.

45 Hobbes, *Leviathan*, XXIX.6.

46 Nietzsche, *The Gay Science*, 296.

47 Ibid., 116.
48 Berlin, "Two Concepts of Liberty," 194.
49 Nietzsche, *On the Genealogy of Morals*, 512.
50 Ibid., 557.
51 Derrida, "The Force of Law," 955.
52 Berlin, "Two Concepts of Liberty," 198.
53 Ibid., 166.
54 Derrida, *Aporias*, 19.
55 Berlin, "Two Concepts of Liberty," 198.
56 Ibid., 183.
57 Ibid., 184.
58 Ibid., 216-217.
59 Ibid., 216.
60 John Gray, *Isaiah Berlin* (Princeton: Princeton UP, 1996), 74. I have italicized the word "jargon" to emphasize its use here. Gray's book is excellent—perhaps the best single piece of secondary literature on Isaiah Berlin—but I tend to find it frustrating when an otherwise fair and insightful author uses a pejorative term like "jargon" to describe someone else's way of speaking about things. This stands out with particular clarity when it occurs in the midst of a discussion of value pluralism.
61 Isaiah Berlin, "Equality," in *Concepts and Categories*, ed. Henry Hardy (New York: Penguin Books, 1978), 95.
62 Parekh, 214.
63 Isaiah Berlin, "Introduction," in *Liberty: Incorporating Four Essays on Liberty*, ed. Henry Hardy (Oxford: Oxford UP, 2002), 43.
64 Gray, *Isaiah Berlin*, 6.
65 Kenny, 1028.
66 Berlin, "Two Concepts of Liberty," 213.
67 Ibid., 169.
68 Isaiah Berlin, "From Hope and Fear Set Free," in *Concepts and Categories*, ed. Henry Hardy (New York: Penguin Books, 1978), 193.
69 Gray, 143.
70 Gerald C. McCallum, Jr., "Negative and Positive Freedom," *The Philosophical Review* (July 1967), 319.
71 Gary Frank Reed , "Berlin and the Division of Liberty," *Political Theory* (August 1980), 373.
72 Berlin, "Introduction," 36.
73 Berlin, "Two Concepts of Liberty," 204.
74 Berlin, "Introduction," 38-39.
75 Ibid., 36.
76 Kocis, 44.
77 Ibid.
78 Derrida, "The Force of Law," 965.
79 Berlin, "Two Concepts of Liberty," 217.
80 Axel Honneth, "Negative Freedom and Cultural Belonging: An Unhealthy Tension in the Political Philosophy of Isaiah Berlin," *Social Research* (Winter 1999): 1069.
81 Derrida, "The Force of Law," 1035.
82 Ibid., 1037.
83 Ibid., 1035.
84 Gray, 168.
85 Berlin, "Two Concepts of Liberty," 212.

86 Ibid., 214.

87 Ibid., 207.

88 Isaiah Berlin, "The Search for Status," in *The Power of Ideas*, ed. Henry Hardy (Princeton, NJ: Princeton University Press, 2000), 195. Of course, one may identify with a particular group for any of several reasons. Unchangeable demographic factors such as race, age, and sex are often powerful factors in group identification. Within the theme of this work, the discursive violence of indoctrination that subsumes persons beneath a system of positive liberty is also an important factor. I shall deal with this more later in this chapter.

89 Berlin, "Introduction," 49.

90 Parekh, 214.

91 Honneth, 1075.

92 Reed, 369.

93 Berlin, "Introduction," 39.

94 Berlin, "Two Concepts of Liberty," 217.

95 Berlin, "Introduction," 44.

96 Duncan Kelly, "The Political Thought of Isaiah Berlin," *British Journal of Politics and International Relations* (1 April 2002): 40.

97 Berlin, "Two Concepts of Liberty," 169.

98 John Stuart Mill, *On Liberty* (1859), http://www.utilitarianism.com/ol/two.html.

99 Ibid.

100 Berlin, "Introduction," 38.

101 Herbert Marcuse, "Repressive Tolerance," in *A Critique of Pure Tolerance*, eds. Robert Paul Wolff, Barrington Moore, Jr., and Herbert Marcuse (Boston: Beacon Press, 1969). http://grace.evergreen.edu/~arunc/texts/frankfurt/marcuse/tolerance.pdf. 11.

102 Berlin, "Introduction," 38.

103 Slavoj Žižek, *Welcome to the Desert of the Real* (London: Verso Press, 2002), 3.

104 Ibid.

105 Berlin, "Two Concepts of Liberty, " 199.

106 Nietzsche, *Thus Spoke Zarathustra*, 214.

107 Berlin, "The Origins of Israel," in *The Power of Ideas*, ed. Henry Hardy (Princeton, NJ: Princeton University Press, 2000), 157.

108 Berlin, "Two Concepts of Liberty," 173.

109 Berlin, "Equality," 85.

110 Berlin, "Two Concepts of Liberty," 212.

111 Berlin, "Introduction," 38.

112 Berlin, "Final Retrospect," 325.

113 Derrida, *Writing and Difference*, 124.

114 Michael Walzer, *Spheres of Justice* (New York: Basic Books, 1983), 314.

115 Kenny, 1035.

116 Berlin, "Equality," 82.

117 Ibid., 102.

118 Nietzsche, *Thus Spoke Zarathustra*, 211.

119 Nietzsche, *Twilight of the Idols*, 553.

120 Nietzsche, *Thus Spoke Zarathustra*, 212.

121 Derrida, "The Force of Law," 961.

122 Ibid.

123 Berlin, "Two Concepts of Liberty," 183.

124 Berlin, "The Origins of Israel," 157.

125 Derrida, "The Force of Law, "1035.

126 Parekh, 220.

127 Derrida, "The Force of Law, "1035.

128 Parekh, 215.

129 Gray, 151.

130 Kocis, 39.

131 Derrida, *Of Grammatology*, 110.

132 Derrida, *Writing and Difference*, 147.

133 Berlin, "Introduction," 21.

134 Derrida, *Writing and Difference*, 57.

135 Kenny, 1029.

136 Chung Tzu [Zhuangzi], *The Book of Chuang Tzu* [*Zhuangzi*], trans. Martin Palmer with Elizabeth Breuilly (New York: Penguin Books, 1990), 14.

137 Laozi, III.

138 Ibid., XIX.

139 One of Laozi's best quotes on this is to "block the openings; shut the doors. Blunt the sharpness; untangle the knots; soften the glare; let your wheels move only along old ruts (LVI)." Similarly, Zhuangzi says that "by the light shining out of chaos, the sage is guided; he does not make use of distinctions but is led on by the light (15)."

140 Edmund Burke, *Reflections on the Revolution in France*, ed. H.D. Mahoney (New York: Macmillan Publishing Company, [1790] 1955), 99.

141 Beverly LaHaye, *I am a Woman by God's Design* (Old Tappan, NJ: Power Books, 1980), 26.

142 Ibid., 142.

143 Chuang Tzu [Zhuangzi], 3-4.

144 Ibid., 49.

145 Kocis, 48.

146 Berlin, "Two Concepts of Liberty," 212.

147 Derrida, "The Force of Law," 925.

148 Berlin, "Two Concepts of Liberty," 203.

149 "I am a lawyer. I know many boring things. Many very, very boring things. I must be boring. I must bore. But in another sense, to bore is to dig, to probe under the surface. . .(Yablon 258)."

150 Charles M. Yablon, "Forms," in *Deconstruction and the Possibility of Justice*, ed. Drucilla Cornell (NY: Routledge, 1992), 259.

151 Ibid., 262.

152 Ibid., 260.

153 Michel Rosenfeld, "Deconstruction and Legal Interpretation: Conflict, Indeterminacy and the Temptations of the New Legal Formalism," in *Deconstruction and the Possibility of Justice*, ed. Drucilla Cornell et al (NY: Routledge, 1992), 157.

154 Derrida, "Before the Law," 191.

155 *Declaration of the Rights of Man* (1789), http://www.yale.edu/lawweb /avalon/rightsof.htm.

156 Derrida, "Before the Law," 191.

157 Kenny, 1029.

158 Berlin, "Two Concepts of Liberty," 190.

159 Parekh, 217.

160 Nietzsche, *On the Genealogy of Morals*, 515.

161 Derrida, *Writing and Difference*, 106.

162 Parekh, 222.

163 Nietzsche, *On the Genealogy of Morals*, 475.
164 Ibid.
165 Berlin, "Two Concepts of Liberty," 217.
166 Berlin, "Introduction," 47.
167 Derrida, "The Force of Law," 1035.
168 Nietzsche, *On the Genealogy of Morals*, 474.
169 Ibid., 532.
170 Nietzsche, *Thus Spoke Zarathustra*, 397.

Chapter Four
How Long Can We Remain Human?

I. Danger and Freedom—The Undecidable

Although by asking how we ought to treat persons as the creators of meaning and value in the world we may have arrived back at the beginning of this investigation, this is not the end of the story. Major themes of contemporary, that is "post-" or "in the wake of" 9/11, politics provide excellent insight into the economy of violence and justice that much of this work has been dedicated to elaborating. In turn, the inevitability of violence and the necessity of undecidability offer important lessons about the way we conduct ourselves in this world. This chapter begins with an examination of the dual nature of undecidability, through which both freedom and danger are inextricably bound to each other. It then touches upon how terrorism represents a more undecidable human threat than traditional interstate warfare, and points out how we meet this threat with nearly unprecedented attempts to impose calculability upon the human world. I also return to the idea that all positions are naturally iterative, and use it to begin developing a theory of arché-power. Finally, I discuss several ways in which our natural drive for increased security through greater calculability and reduced *épokhè* has recently become more pronounced. In our ongoing post-9/11 debates about increased security measures, we must consider not only the specific issues of balance, privacy, and the technical matters surrounding specific policies on which most commentators focus—we must also contemplate the possibility that increasing levels of calculability may nearly overwhelm our uniquely human unknowability/unpredictability. The imposition of such complete predictability would render us impervious to attack, but it would also destroy our humanity.

As has been discussed repeatedly in several guises throughout this work, humanity requires both the decidable (calculable/legalistic/conservative/positive libertarian) and the undecidable (incalculable/*épokhal*/foundational/negative libertarian). As the fundamental characteristics of the basic structure of intersubjectivity, both are inscribed in the very essence of personal existence. Also previously discussed (perhaps *ad nauseam*) is the idea that, as the drive for knowability and iteration, the calculable represents the legalistic aspect of human existence that demands the conservation of laws that yield coordination in intersubjective activities. This may be seen most clearly in Hobbes' notion, explored at some length in chapter two, that the primary function of the sovereign is to maintain a system of meanings for all matters of public import, including the definition of "public import" itself. Only under this system of coordination through the enforced knowability of law are persons free to live reasonably felicitous lives by escaping the brutality of the state of nature, in which everyone creates and attempts to enforce their own systems of meaning and value. Just as "hedges are set, not to stop travelers, but to keep them in the way,"[1] forcing otherwise independent creators to conform to one common law yields a mutual knowability or decidability among them. Because all law, from the arché-lawmaking at the origin of intersubjective discourse to the political lawmaking of states, analytically includes the necessity of its own enforcement, the drive for this imposed coordination through calculability directly implies the impetus for censorship of speech and action. Thus Hobbes writes that one of the "*diseases* of a commonwealth [is] *[t]hat every private man is judge of good and evil actions,*"[2] because when the sovereign stops effacing other persons' creative natures by censoring their creations of meaning and value in order to enforce her own positionality, the people return to the chaotic indeterminacy of multiple systems of meaning and value that characterizes the natural condition of humanity, the condition in which exists an ongoing violent struggle for the domination of discourse.

Put in less stark terms, this chaotic competition that arises out of competing systems of meaning and value is invoked by the undecidable/*épokhal* aspect of the human creative nature. Because the inevitable ordeal of the undecidable by which persons suspend the legalistic iteration of the law in a moment of distinctly human *épokhal* questioning remains in this situation an unimpeded part of intersubjective existence, the law's purely legalistic demand for its own mechanistic iteration remains unrealized. Thus this undecidability equals the human existential freedom to independently create meanings and values in the world, but it also equals the danger that arises from the lack of mutual knowability and coordination engendered when everyone legalistically iterates one system of law. In Hobbes' terms, the chaos of the state of nature is both the greatest possible realization of, and a major threat to, the human creative nature. In the state of nature, or in any condition in which persons remain uncoerced into agreement and coordination, their natural diversity of signification leads to a "war of every man against every man"[3] because their independent creations all carry with them the demand for their own universal iteration. In this situation in which "every man is his own *judge*, there properly is no judge at all; as where every man carveth out his own right, it hath the same effect, as if there were no right at all,"[4] and the preponderance of negative liberty causes liberty itself to be destroyed.

As we increase or decrease human undecidability, we increase or decrease the distinctly human capacity to step outside the legalistic and perform the unconditioned and unexpected, our ability to exceed the "the programmable application or unfolding of a calculable process,"[5] that is simultaneously freedom and danger. Freedom for the law's subjects constitutes danger for the law, which is no longer mechanistically iterated but is now subject to suspension and potential rejection through the ordeal of the undecidable. This freedom may also endanger the free subjects of the law on two counts. First and perhaps most obviously, they are in danger of increased conservative violence by the agents of the law, who themselves re-iterate the law mechanistically and demand the same of others. Second, and on the more Hobbesian note mentioned just above, the subjects of the law may also be in greater danger from themselves, their compatriots in the struggle for greater freedom, as well as others. As the strictly mechanistic iteration of the law is eroded in the name of freedom, there may slowly arise a situation in which, without the enforcement of one system of meanings and values, persons may find themselves unable to coordinate or perhaps even communicate with others. One person's freedom is a danger to another person's discursive position, which as a position that analytically demands its own iteration is itself an act of legislation, and is now open to rejection and revolution on the part of one's interlocutor. But this danger represented by freedom is also the possibility of justice. If we were able to completely remove the danger and freedom of the undecidable, we would be left with pure inhuman deterministic legalism/decidability/knowability. All our actions would be the programmable applications of calculable processes, and there would be no "decision, no responsibility, no event,"[6] and absolutely no justice. There would only be the peace and safety of mere inhuman mechanistic phenomenality.

The freedom that allows even experimental suspension of the law invites the destruction of that law because it invites independent foundational violence by the law's subjects. Law that demands freedom goes one step further—it practically insists upon its own annihilation. Thus on 7 December 2001, US Attorney General John Ashcroft could say "to those who scare peace-loving people with phantoms of lost liberty, my message is this: your tactics only aid terrorists."[7] The liberty of which Ashcroft speaks is negative liberty, the ability to be an independent source of meaning and value in the world, to experience *épokhè* and undecidability and to found. Ashcroft's characteristically Hobbesian statement points to the unity of danger and freedom. By Ashcroft's account, "it belongeth . . . to him that hath the sovereign power to be judge . . . of opinions and doctrines, as a thing necessary to peace, thereby to prevent discord and civil war,"[8] because the freedom to create one's own opinions and doctrines that may deviate from the law is what causes the conditions for terrorism. The freedom to reject the sovereign's promulgated meanings and values is surely a danger to the existence of the law itself, but more importantly it is a danger to the peace engendered by the enforcement of one single unified system of meanings. Without the strict enforcement of one system of significations, persons are free to "mete good and evil by diverse measures,"[9] which brings about that situation of creative anarchy that Hobbes calls the state of nature. That is why worrying about lost liberty aids terrorists: those who are trying to maintain the *épokhal* suspension of the law in the name of liberty inevitably also do so in the name of terrorism. The conditions for freedom—the acceptance of *épokhè*, of undecidability, of the ability to reject and act outside the law—are the same as those for terrorism because terrorism is one manifestation of freedom. Loosening the positive libertarian hold of the law opens the possibility of the negative libertarian *épokhè* that invites any leap beyond mechanistic conformity, including acts of terrorism.

Terrorism itself represents a more undecidable threat than the interstate warfare states and populations are more used to confronting. Philip Heymann, one widely read commentator, puts it succinctly: "One of the critical, defining characteristics of the situation we now face is its very uncertainty. A large part of our problem is how to prepare intelligently despite our uncertainty about the terrorist's motivations, organization, resources, and plans."[10] Whereas in interstate conflicts, the identity, strategies, tactics, weapons, and goals of the enemy are generally known, the very thing that makes terrorism so terrifying is that one never knows precisely who will attack, who will *be* attacked, or when, where, or how the attack will be conducted. The Cold War, in which infinitely more destructive capacity was deployed than is currently at issue with global terrorism, was far more programmatic and calculable than is the terrorist threat, "for there is no longer a duel or standoff between two powerful states . . . involved in a [rational; calculable] game theory in which both states are capable of neutralizing the other's nuclear power through a reciprocal and organized evaluation of the respective risks."[11] The very undecidability of terrorism, and our subsequent inability to calculate its programs and parameters, is what makes it so frightening. That anyone, not just uniformed military personnel deployed in a theater of combat, may be targeted at any time by any method, from being stabbed with a sharpened stick to incinerated by a smuggled nuclear weapon, is the most incalculable human threat we can face.

But it is not simply the unknowability or randomness of the tactics and targets of terrorism that make it frightening. Of all types of violence, terrorism is among the most afformative. Whereas performative violence (like a performative speech act) is foundational in that it does or creates something new, afformative violence "does not posit, it 'deposes.'"[12] Purely afformative violence would be absolutely anti-foundational and *épokhal*. It would neither found nor conserve—it would only depose, negate, destroy, or deface. On an interpersonal level, afformative violence would be the pure denial of the personhood of the other, without a simultaneous attempt to impose one's own positionality upon that other. Raised to the level of the political, afformative violence may be approached by pure genocide: war as simple negation, without the intention of conquest or imposition. But as with all interstate conflict, even genocide seeks some particular, positive, generally overt policy goals. Whether they be the mundane capture of a plot of land or the comparatively grotesque annihilation of a race, the goals of common interstate violence are significantly more performative than the violence of terrorism. Interstate conflict is violence with specific, known, public policy goals—it is violence that seeks to accomplish calculable ends through the use of calculable means. Terrorism, on the other hand, approaches afformative violence. As violence that tends only to negate, tear down, or efface, terrorism approaches pure *époklhè* without any decidability or foundation of a new law. The goal of terrorism is not the invasion of a country and the subsequent perpetration of a determinable discursive violence by replacing one legal code with another, nor is it the wish to rule over a specific plot of land. Although some groups do sometimes speak about instituting Islamic Law in states that do not currently use it, invasions or insurgencies to establish Islamic Law would not be strictly identifiable as terrorism by the account given here, even if they were conducted by groups using unconventional weapons and tactics. The goal of terrorism as such is simply terror, "to overturn but not take over, to destabilize the current situation,"[13] which is accomplished by presenting one's opponents with incalculable tactics in pursuit of a goal that does not found anything legalistic, determinable, or positive. Thus the attacks of 11 September 2001 are archetypes of the afformativity of terrorism. In these attacks nothing was imposed, nothing was conquered, and nothing except an environment of fear and anger, was directly created. They deposed and defaced, but did not found or enforce.

By this point it is obvious that violence can be neither purely performative nor entirely afformative. The mutual contamination of the performative and the afformative restates that between foundational and conservative violence. "Afformative . . . violence, is a 'condition' for any instrumental, performative violence"[14] because, in Nietzsche's words, "if a temple is to be erected *a temple must be destroyed.*"[15] Any foundational performative necessarily involves a suspension of existent positions, and even if this new performative reiterates the given law, it does so on its own basis, as its own foundational act. Similarly, no violence can be completely afformative. Even a violence that successfully defaces all other positions posits and successfully founds total nothingness, which, although a dim shadow of the great lawmaking projects of states and Enlightenment philosophers, nevertheless retains an element of foundation that maintains a performative element to the violence. Thus, violence can only be *economically* afformative or performative, not completely so on either count. Although terrorism therefore contains an element of the performative or foundational, its relative afformativity is, as much as the unpredictability of its weapons and tactics, a source of the terror that it invokes.

II. Enforced Calculability

The terror provoked by the afformativity of terrorism lends further credence to the truism that persons tend to want to render the undecidable decidable, the incalculable calculable, the unknowable knowable, and the *épokhal* legalistic. This normal desire is reflected is nearly everything persons do, from NASA's Near Earth Object Program, which tracks asteroids and comets that pass close to Earth,[16] to the comfort a traveler feels when he sees a familiar restaurant in a very foreign land. At the base of all such events may be a craving for legalistic predictability that Hobbes argues is a result of the universal "*fear* of power[s] invisible."[17] Fear, or terror, may simply describe the realm of unknowability or *épokhè*, the set of undecidable, nonprogrammatic possibilities that waylay (relatively) ordered society's best laid plans. But not surprisingly, Nietzsche retorts that terror in the face of the unknown is only a characteristic of the slavish, whose excitement at some new enforcement of knowledge or calculability is "the jubilation over the restoration of a sense of security . . . of something strange [being] reduced to something *familiar*."[18] But this constant drive for the achievement of calculability in the world, especially the human world that exceeds clear mathematical determination, is embedded even deeper in the nature of human existence.

Perhaps obviously, persons do not want just any knowability or predictability—they want to remove others' undecidability by forcing them to conform legalistically to one's own promulgated positions. This violence, this rejection of the other as an independent creator of meaning and value, is embedded in the very structure of discursive existence. As examined at length in chapter one, the originary moment of intersubjectivity is constituted by the arché-violent promulgation of positions that demand their universal iteration over the counter-positions of others. Each person creates his or her own system of meanings and values, and each act of creation, as an act of legislation, carries within itself a demand for this enforcement that would deface the other and force that other to reject himself as an independent creator and simply re-iterate the law given to him. Being reduced to a mere node of the law, an embodiment of the predictable, knowable, and decidable, the other would thus cease to be a person. He would instead be a purely phenomenal object, incapable of the *épokhè*, the leap out of simple mechanism and through the ordeal of the undecidable, that composes the distinctly human ability to step outside the programmatic or deterministic and *create*.

"This attempt to enforce institutionalized rules . . . [is] therefore profoundly *anti*-political, because it forecloses the possibility that the other be a legislator, and that possibility," the possibility of continuously trading would-be answers among *épokhal* persons to the unanswerable human questions, "is the possibility of the political as such."[19] Each act of discursive positioning, from the arché-lawmaking at the origin of intersubjectivity to the more overtly statutory lawmaking of a state, as an act of violence that "call[s] for self-conserving repetition,"[20] carries within it a rejection of politics because it contains a rejection of the other as an independent creator of meaning and value. By rejecting the other's personhood, one also rejects the possibility of an intersubjective play of meanings and values with that other, a play that is the substance of politics. This is the origin of the decidability, knowability, and positive liberty sought by all persons—it resides within the very structure of intersubjectivity, which is itself predicated upon this arché-violence of imposition. Even so, each act of discursive positioning also preserves the possibility of politics because it opens a relationship with an other through the respect that the other is capable of legislation.

As has been brought into high relief after 9/11, persons' responses to terrorism are no exception to this natural structure of discursive intersubjectivity, by which individual persons (or groups of persons) try to remove the danger represented by both incalculability and by others' abilities to reject one's own promulgated positions. In fact, our responses to terrorism epitomize this trend. But, as above, the undecidability or incalculability that exemplifies terrorism is not only the possibility of danger, it is also the opportunity for freedom, which is the opportunity for humanity. This is certainly not to say that terrorism is the epitome of humanity. Rather, the afformativity of terrorism's goals and the incalculability of its methods can only exist within a realm of *épokhè* outside the purely programmatic application of legalism. But this same realm of *épokhè* is what constitutes human existential freedom. As our ability to choose and to create anew, the freedom of our *épokhal* nature composes the ability for incalculability, which may take the form of terrorism. Terrorism is therefore the dark side of freedom, and the former will exist as long as the latter.

In order to overcome as much as possible the inevitable human unknowability that characterizes all freedom to suspend the law, including the freedom of terrorism, we are attempting to achieve a pseudo-Foucauldian panopticism and strict disciplinary control that would minimize incalculability. If successful, our panoptic disciplinarity would foreclose any possibility of stepping outside of or even suspending the law in order to reinstitute it in an act of justice—it would impose a strict legalistic conformity that would finally overcome terrorism, but with it, all other manifestations of our human *épokhal* nature.

Most succinctly, discipline is a set of procedures for

> distributing individuals, fixing them in space, classifying them, extracting from them the maximum in time and resources, training their bodies, coding their continuous behavior, maintaining them in perfect visibility, forming around them an apparatus and observation, registration and recording, constituting on them a body of knowledge that is accumulated and centralized.[21]

According to Foucault, discipline uses three broad procedures: hierarchical observation, normalizing judgment, and examination, each of which I shall discuss briefly in turn. The goal of this omnipresent system of training is to induce in persons complete docility to the given law, and to create a body of perfect knowledge about their thoughts and actions that can be used to calculate and thereby control them. Discipline immerses persons "in a little world of signals to each of which is attached a single, obligatory response: it is a technique of training"[22] individuals to iterate without *épokhè* every microscopic detail of an all-encompassing system of signification and regulation. Unknowability is removed both because a body of knowledge about each individual is produced, and because each person has been trained to re-iterate the training to which he or she has been subjected. In fact, this trained docility itself constitutes a body of knowledge—when the training is perfect, one knows exactly what another will do in a given situation. One's actions are no longer agonistic choices suffused with undecidability; they are the predictable, mechanistic response to stimuli. To examine this process more closely, consider a few recent anti-terrorism, anti-undecidability initiatives.

Elements of the Defense Advanced Research Projects Agency's (DARPA's) Terrorist Information Awareness (formerly the too-Orwellian Total Information Awareness, complete with the insignia of a giant eye staring out from a pyramid) program provide good examples of the disciplinary technique of hierarchical observation. For instance, their Next-Generation Face Technology and related programs aim to read what a person is doing (such as lying or using false identification) or even thinking of doing (such as running through airport security or stealing a car) by examining that person's face and body language. Such technology aims not simply to biometrically denude persons of the anonymity they think they have in a crowd—an anonymity long-since removed by video cameras that map facial features and match them to photographic files—but to observe even their thoughts simply by watching their presence.

Consider also Section 215 of the USA Patriot Act, which allows the FBI to "make an application for an order requiring the production of any tangible things (including books, records, papers, documents, and other items) for an investigation to protect against international terrorism or clandestine intelligence activities." Although for US citizens this investigation may not be conducted *solely* based upon a person's exercise of her First Amendment rights, no such protection is included for non-US citizens.[23] Those who carry out this activity on the FBI's behalf, including librarians, apartment building superintendents, or others who may be required to assist in gathering the materials demanded, are prohibited from disclosing to the subject of the investigation that it ever occurred.

These two programs obviously exemplify the disciplinary strategy of hierarchical observation. As in Foucault's famous discussion of Bentham's Panopticon, this observation is conducted invasively upon individuals through mechanisms that "remain invisible . . . like a faceless gaze"[24] that remains transparent to its scrutinized subjects. Like the infuriating non-presence of a shadowy Kafkaesque interlocutor, there is no particular entity upon which these subjects can focus their resentment or anger. Hierarchical observation thus represents "a perpetual victory that avoids any physical confrontation"[25] not only because it watches, but because as it watches it predicts, and *because* its subjects know it is watching, and are helpless to avoid it because they must assume it is everywhere, its gaze creates a predictable conformity. The major effect of the increasing ubiquity and propinquity of such observations is to "induce in the [subject] a state of conscious and permanent visibility that assures the automatic"[26] iteration of the law, without *épokhal* suspension or experimental deviation. Thus this observation works to reduce incalculability in two ways: First, observation creates knowledge about individuals' pasts and presents, and increasing predictability about their futures, that diminishes their unknowns and makes their moves more foreseeable. Second, when persons know that their every move, and perhaps even every intention, is being read, their behavior is made more legalistic and automatically iterative because they fear the consequences of their non-legal thoughts and even petty nonconformities. "The secret thoughts of a man," Hobbes reminds us, "run over all things, holy, profane, clean, obscene, grave and light," but "in public, or before persons unknown, or whom we ought to reverence, there is no jingling of words that will not be accounted folly."[27] When we are always before persons unknown, when we can never be sure that anything from our library records to even our most inner thoughts will remain unobserved, we will self-consciously reduce the scope of our ideas and remain more clearly within the bounds of conservation and reiteration.

The US Transportation Security Administration's (TSA's) cancelled CAPPS II system presents another good example of attempts to defeat the incalculability of terrorism by imposing a disciplinary regime that increases predictability and knowability. CAPPS II, a comprehensive commercial airline passenger profiling system designed to ensure that terrorists are denied access to commercial air travel, was the TSA's attempt to remove the unpredictability or unknowability of the identities and behavior of airline passengers. Under CAPPS II's data-mining regime, anyone purchasing an airline ticket would be subject to a detailed (some might say invasive) background and behavior check: both public and private databases, from law enforcement records to credit card statements, would be scoured, and other behavioral variables, such as the purchase of a one-way ticket or payment in cash, would be factored in. Using an algorithm that compiles all this information (the exact procedures remain secret), CAPPS II would determine one's threat rating and require one to undergo increased security checks or even refer a case to law enforcement officers if deemed necessary by the purely legalistic workings of the computer program.

The CAPPS II system exemplifies the technique of discipline that Foucault calls "examination." "*The examination, surrounded by all its documentary techniques, makes each individual a 'case':* a case which at one and the same time constitutes an object for a branch of knowledge and a hold for a branch of power."[28] Examination combines the "deployment of force and the establishment of truth" to establish "over individuals a visibility through which one differentiates them and judges them."[29] CAPPS II is essentially an examination that uses all the documentary evidence of individuals' lives to predict the likelihood that they are engaged in abnormal (that is, dangerously or at least suspiciously *épokhal*) behavior. It establishes the "truth" about persons' flight-related merit and uses these conclusions to deploy precisely varying levels of force against them, from allowing them to board an aircraft to detaining them indefinitely without access to legal counsel. Thus CAPPS II seeks to remove the unknowability associated with commercial air passengers through a system of examination and judgment.

But the disciplinary regimes of observation, examination, and judgment are growing far more pervasive than this. Several major cities, such as Washington, D.C., New York, Atlanta, and others are constructing major networks of surveillance cameras that will surpass even London's venerable system (which was itself constructed in response to IRA terrorism), and which may be equipped with biometric technologies to recognize and track individuals. At least as significantly, "all daily tasks—working, driving, shopping, tending to health—now create retrievable records"[30] that can be aggregated, mined, and analyzed to create detailed pictures of the lives of groups and individuals. "Each new type of surveillance forms part of an emerging, society-wide system"[31] that performs "a narrowing and impoverishment of human possibilities."[32] "It creates consumers with predictable tastes, borrowers who repay their debts, and personality structures acclimated to cooperation with authority,"[33] rather than *épokhal* persons who leap outside the calculable and undergo the ordeal of the undecidable. A regime like this, which is growing in response to the incalculable dangers of terrorism, "increases the forces of the body (in economic terms of utility) and diminishes these same forces (in political terms of obedience)"[34]—it enhances public safety by increasing predictability and legalism and reducing *épokhè*, unknowability, and negative liberty. It increases safety by removing danger/freedom.

But this is nothing new. In fact, it is simply the basic structure of discursive existence raised to the level of the governmental. All discursive positions, including (archetypically) what is commonly called Law, contain their own calls to universal iteration, which implies the deployment of violence upon counter-positions. The utterance of the Law analytically includes within itself all attempts to force others to conform to it legalistically, and our currently increasing disciplinary regime that seeks to render persons more predictable and less *épokhal* is simply a manifestation of that. In the Law's fight against the relatively afformative enemy of terrorism, decidability in itself becomes the law, the ultimate enforced demand. Growing anti-terror (anti-unknowability) regimes may appear particularly insidious to many commentators, and increasing capacities may indeed give these technologies unsettling new abilities, but they do not represent a paradigmatic shift in the nature of human political existence. They are simply new and greater attempts to perform the same task that lies at the very base of intersubjectivity—the promulgation of one's own creations of meaning and value, of one's system of signification (as I referred to it in chapter two), over the counter-positions of others. In the fight against the relatively afformative and unpredictable promulgations of terrorism, the enforcement of decidability through disciplinary technologies becomes the goal of the law.

III. An Aside: Toward a Theory of Arché-Power

Several times throughout this work, from chapter one's examination of the violence fundamental to discursive intersubjectivity, to chapter two's discussion of the slow, forceful expansion of sovereign power by superior over inferior persons, reference has been made to either the fact or process of one person's creative nature being subsumed beneath another's. For example, in chapter two I described how Hobbes' would-be sovereigns, using the enhanced reason they possess as a result of their superior language abilities, gain control over inferior persons by deploying whatever level of violence may be necessary. This purposeful violence that results in commonwealths—groups of individuals whose personhoods have been subsumed beneath those of their respective sovereigns—is the only way to escape the chaotic brutality of the state of nature. The war of all against all that results from the continuation of the natural condition, in which each person creates his own system of signification and naturally tries to impose it upon others, is overcome only by the agreement and coordination created when one sovereign forces her own system of meanings and values upon all others and denies them the ability to promulgate their own laws.

But this was not in itself the most fundamental manifestation of the drive to subsume others' personhoods beneath one's own. Violence is inevitable. Built into the implied iteration of all positionality, which resides as much in the very nature of discursive intersubjectivity as it does in ordinary lawmaking, is the act of rejecting the other as an independent creator of meaning and value and the attempt to impose one's own creations upon this other. At this point in this chapter, this forced subsumption of the other's personhood beneath one's own systems of meaning and value is represented by our growing disciplinary technologies, which seek "to supervise the individual, to neutralize his dangerous state of mind, to alter his criminal tendencies, and to continue even when this change has been achieved."[35] In previous sections, this same subsumption was represented by the philosopher-kings' demand that all persons live according to their definition of the good life (chapter three), the sovereigns' struggle to impose agreement on signification (chapter two), and life as the will to power (chapter one). I have already both suggested and implied that all these manifestations of violence, of rejecting the other as an independent creator of meaning and value, are derived from what Derrida calls arché-violence.

Based on this concept of arché-violence, the originary or foundational violence at the core of human intersubjectivity, it may be possible to construct a parallel theory of arché-power. Although the full development of this theory is well outside the bounds of this work, it may be useful to present the outlines of this approach to power. Although Derrida does not himself use his theory of arché-violence to generate a theory of arché-power, the latter may be directly implied by the former. In fact, arché-violence and arché-power may be effectively or phenomenally identical: the possession or performance of arché-violence may necessarily also be the possession or performance of arché-power. Just as arché-violence constitutes the core structure of all subsequent manifestations of violence, so would arché-power be the fundamental nature of all power. This arché of power, its original and sovereign form, would consist, as implied by the definition of violence, in one person being a primary term in another person's system of signification, such that the relatively powerful person is one of the poles around which the relatively powerless person organizes his universe of meaning and value. Although there are a great many ways of achieving this arché-power, just as there are many different manifestations of it, all subsequent forms of power may proceed from, and appeal to, this primordial feature.

If it were possible, this pure arché-power would consist in the dominant person's discursive positionality completely dominating the other, such that the other's potential for independent creativity would be totally effaced. The independent personhood of the other would be utterly destroyed by an act of violence, replaced by a pure iteration of the personhood of the power holder. But as complete arché-violence is impossible due to the paradoxes of the economy of violence, the total arché-power that would proceed from it is also impossible. Arché-power here escapes the would-be dominator because total arché-violence would utterly remove any vestige of personhood from the other, and one can not be a primary term in the system of signification of a merely phenomenal object. Simple empirical objects like lamps or water towers or dead bodies do not have systems of signification at all. The other must maintain some kernel of personhood, of discursivity, if he is to remain capable of having any system of signification, dominated or otherwise. Based on the complete effacement of the other through an (impossible) act of pure violence, the possession of pure power over an other would utterly destroy the otherness of the other. The other would cease to be other, and neither violence nor peacefulness, nor power nor submission, would be possible.

The upper limit of arché-violence is therefore, as with Hobbes' sovereign Leviathan, the simple recognition of the personhood of the other as the justification for undertaking great violence against this person. One would seek to violently overcome as completely as possible the personhood of the other, substituting one's own positionality for the other's precisely because one recognizes that this other is a person capable of independent creation and iteration. It is precisely because this other is recognized as a threat that violence is perpetrated against him for the purpose of achieving power over him. If the other were merely a phenomenal object, if the violence against him were total, the other would not be capable of challenging the independent personhood of oneself, so one would not seek power over him by violently iterating one's personhood over his own. Besides, one could not achieve power over the completely effaced other because, again, that other would have no system of signification to dominate.

This idea that a bare but peaceful recognition of the personhood of the other remains as the extreme limit of arché-power is easily at evidence in the theories of both Nietzsche and Hobbes. According to Nietzsche, an other is not struggled with and overcome if it is a mere mindless phenomenal object, and indeed he claims that the noble person "desires his enemy for himself"[36] as a rival worthy of being attacked and subsumed. These sought after enemies, in which there is "*very much* to honor,"[37] are recognized as strong independent sources of meaning, as people worthy of a fight and capable of making victory difficult and therefore precious. In fact, Nietzsche argues that "one's best enemy"[38] is one's best friend. Creators seek companionship in fellow creators, "not corpses, not herds and believers,"[39] because creators want to "strive against one another like gods"[40] and live out the principle of life as will to power. The very dominance for which Nietzsche argues requires the recognition and the companionship of strong others. If only one ego existed, the arché-power that Nietzsche posits as the goal of life would not be possible.

Similarly, Hobbes contends that superior persons must recognize that certain creatures are capable of the creation of meaning and value, that they are in fact persons, before they will attempt to do violence to them in the creation of a commonwealth. He declares that "no man can compact with him who doth not declare his acceptance; and therefore we cannot compact with beasts, neither can we give, or take from them any manner of right, by reason of their want of speech and understanding."[41] "The self-centered attitude of an agent bent at absorbing everything within his power is due not," to reiterate the words of Piotr

Hoffman, "to a lack of clear awareness of other people's independent standing in the world; rather, it is a way in which the agent responds to the very real and very acute knowledge of the others as power centers representing a constant threat to him."[42] Only upon appreciating that he is surrounded by others who are also capable of violence (discursive or otherwise) does a person perpetrate arché-violence against them in an attempt to force them to adhere to his own system of meanings.

A Nietzschean master, a Hobbesian Leviathan, or any other person may be extremely successful in dominating certain aspects of another's universe of meaning (by any of several methods of varying levels of empirical violence), effacing the other's independent creativity in this area and subordinating it to one's own. This is what happens, for instance, when a celebrity's ubiquity causes her to be reified as a model for young womanhood. She begins to govern this area of many persons' systems of signification, such that she becomes a primary definitional influence that restructures the meanings and relationships among meanings within these systems. Another example to be developed might be Richard Neustadt's classic idea that prestige is a president's most significant power. The person of the president holds such a primary place in our systems of signification, having such an extraordinarily high ability to define vocabulary (like "terrorism," "threat," etc.), set the terms and parameters of debates, and generally structure the way we think about political life, that his raw arché-power may well exceed his specifically constitutionally prescribed powers. This notion of arché-power may also provide a useful window onto such mundane events as a young man playing loud music in his car. By playing loud music, the driver is doing his best to dominate and define any situation into which he drives. One may think one is sitting at a stoplight, thinking about one's grocery list, but when the driver with the loud music arrives he exercises arché-power through arché-violence by rejecting the independent personhoods of all others within earshot and imposing his own positionality upon them. He becomes the conceptual center of the situation as all others are forced to respond to his violent presence. Some may enjoy his music and some may detest it, but either way, he has effaced the independence of the others and has become the pole around which that situation now revolves. In each of these cases, the power-holder's positionality within a certain sphere (the bounds of which are themselves discursive accomplishments) is iterated over others' relevant systems of signification—discursive violence has necessarily yielded discursive power.

At the theoretical but asymptotic extreme, it is not one or more of a person's specific definitions, or the relationships among meanings within certain subject areas, that are iterated upon the other. Rather, it is one's complete personhood that is written upon his mind and body. The other's independence is completely subsumed beneath the dominant person, such that the latter is oneself the absolutely primary term for the former. The former person is completely subsumed beneath the latter because the latter is, as an entity, the central organizing factor in the former's universe of signification. Of course, as already discussed to some extent, this complete subsumption would be a paradox because the complete dominance of the personhood of an other would remove that other's personhood, so there would be nothing left to dominate. It would be like killing someone in order to force him to agree with oneself: at the moment of total dominance, this dominance escapes one's grasp because one can not hold any sort of power, including arché-power, over a phenomenal object. But one can come close to such complete dominance, such as when a charismatic religious leader gains (again, by whatever means) identity with concepts like justice, goodness, and righteousness within the minds of others, so that whatever this leader does is defined as just, good, or right within the minds of his followers. At this point the religious leader has become the pole around which these definitions orbit.

This is also the type of subjectivity that military training attempts to infuse into trainees, as may be inferred from chapter one's example of the military's attempt to construct a purely legalistic entity. The military training of new recruits attempts to subsume as much of their pre-existing systems of signification beneath the dictates of their commanders, so that they reify these commanders' meanings and values without question. At this level of arché-power, the person who holds power would be venerated as the ultimate source of all righteousness and correctness, and any order or unspoken suggestion would receive purely legalistic compliance, without the interpolation of one's own independent positionality or the ordeal of the undecidable. The power-holder's life would be accepted as the paradigm of perfection, and he would be emulated in everything from ethical code to mode of dress. Witness, for instance, the popularity of the small Hitleresque moustache among members of "his" SA.[43]

Just as the economy of violence and peacefulness forecloses the possibility of pure violence, the total rejection of arché-violence is also an impossibility, itself conditioned by the impossibility of total communion with the fullness of the other's being. It follows that the complete elimination of arché-power is an equal impossibility conditioned by the inability of a person's discursive positionality to *not* analytically include the necessity of its own imposition over the personhood of another. The total eradication of one's arché-power would necessitate purging one's discursive positionality of all violence, but this can never be done. Arché-violence, inherent within the very nature of intersubjective existence, is minimally nothing more than Nietzsche's "sacred 'No,'"[44] a rejection of the absolute dominance of another's personhood in order to maintain one's own. This minimal level of arché-violence yields a basic level of arché-power, which is simply the demand that an other recognize oneself as a person, as an "independent source of human activity, as an entity with a will of its own, intending to act in accordance with it."[45] The demand for basic recognition still leaves one with a minor but important position within the other's system of signification—one is a person, a co-creator. One may not be as wealthy, intelligent, or attractive as the other, but one is still entitled to a level of treatment over and above that of mere phenomenal objects. One maintains some pride of place within the other's system of signification because one demands recognition as fundamentally similar to the other. One will not simply follow the inertia created by the other; one is entitled to a certain level of respect, and may demand certain rights against actions of the other that infringe upon him.

Another effect of this potential theory of arché-power that I am sketching here proceeds from the second meaning of "economy" in Derrida's use of the phrase "economy of violence." In chapter one, I explained how Derrida deploys a duality in the meaning of "economy": whereas the first meaning implies impurity or mere practicability, the second invokes the idea of a system of trade and distribution, in which the objects of the economy are exchanged from person to person. By this second meaning, violence, and thus power, is economical because it consists of persons, each of whom acts with economic (that is, partial, impure) amounts of violence and power, trading these commodities back and forth in economic levels as they conduct discourse with each other. Arché-violences are not dyadic—rather, each moment of discursive positionality does violence to all other relevant but differing positions. Certainly, the violence against specific individuals varies as greatly by degree as it does by effect, but structurally each act of positioning is economically violent to all others. Arché-power would therefore exceed the simple dyadic relationships spoken of by many theories of power. Each new position carries with it, as it expands out into the discursive universe, a minimal demand for the recognition of the personhood of the originator of that position and a maximal demand for the total effacement of the independent positionality of the audience. As author of the position, its promulgator gains arché-power over others to the degree that this position is successfully violent. By this account, persons therefore exist within overlapping webs of traded violences and powers. Each person, being partially dominant and partially subsumed, has various levels of power in relation to various others. For instance, a particularly effective CPA may find people lining up to receive financial advice from her, but she probably will not exercise any significant dominance over her clients' gender identities. Similarly, a crippled, homeless man is certainly powerless in most arenas, but he no doubt maintains a greater arché-power than most other persons we might see in the course of a given day—his image sticks with us, shaping our feelings and behavior in ways that other random strangers do not.

One further characteristic of arché-power might be that it need not be intentional. One can hold arché-power and be unaware of it, as when a singer influences how others speak without specifically intending to, or when a teacher is idolized by a student the teacher does not recall. In fact, a person can even hold arché-power over another through that other's obsession with rejecting or overcoming the person. This is easily seen in the 2004 presidential election, in which thousands of activists organized their entire lives around a rejection of incumbent US President George W. Bush's administration. Although they despised him and sought to remove him from office, he dominated their lives—he was a primary term in their systems of signification—nonetheless. Arché-power is not something that one need actively pursue, because it is inherent within the very structure of discourse. Every time one's discursive positionality is iterated over the counter-positions of others, every time one attains some primacy within another's system of signification, every time one successfully practices arché-violence, one gains arché-power. Thus, no person would be utterly devoid of arché-power, just as no person is entirely without arché-violence. Even the most relatively powerless person still imposes upon others that kernel of recognition that forces them to acknowledge his personhood and treat him accordingly. Similarly, even the most powerful person's subjectivity does not completely dominate the minds of all she encounters, such that she becomes the unique pole around which all other persons organize their lives. For most persons, arché-violence, and hence arché-power, would experience constant ebbs and flows along several fronts.

Obviously, this is simply an outline of some of the issues surrounding a development of a theory of arché-power out of Derrida's concept of arché-violence. But as this work concludes, it may be useful to consider the conceptual place and practice of arché-power in a world of ever-increasing legalism and predictability.

IV. Totalitarian Dreams

According to the fundamental structure of the law, the state must theoretically deny "all right to the individuals' decision and, instead, ascrib[e] the sole right to its own decision, the law of the State, so that he who transgresses the State's commandment is looked upon as if he were acting against God's commandment."[46] Given the inevitability of the economy of violence, this is impossible, but it nonetheless remains the goal of all lawmaking entities, from individuals at the origin of intersubjectivity to states in the course of politics. Early in the twenty-first century, it is beginning to look as though governments are able to draw closer than ever dreamed to the enforcement of complete calculability/knowability upon all persons. This is an ethically ambiguous goal, motivated by the desire for safety but entailing the dehumanization of the subjects of this security. The closer we come to achieving safety through calculability, the more we circumscribe the personhood of all persons, who become increasingly knowable, predictable, legalistic entities that lack or reject the *épokhal*, negative libertarian aspect of their existence. We might achieve total safety through complete calculability, but we would lose our humanity in the process.

There are at least four broad trends that are today decreasing *épokhè* and increasing calculability among persons. The specific programs used as examples earlier in this chapter belong to these developments, which are slowly narrowing the range of human possibility and eroding what Berlin called negative liberty. When "we are faced with choices between ends equally ultimate, and claims equally absolute,"[47] we undergo that agonistic process of the ordeal of the undecidable, of "decision without decidable certainty,"[48] the moment of purely perspectival decision that is without any ultimate objective foundation other than a *coup* of force. Yet increasingly, this agonism is being denied to persons in the name of safety, compatibility, coordination, or other advantages of predictability.

The first way in which this escalating predictability is being brought about is through increasingly high levels of disciplinary technologies of the sort discussed earlier, technologies that "are central to this making of modern man"[49] by rendering him docile and predictable. Perhaps the single best example of contemporary disciplinary technology is the Terrorist Information Awareness program, also mentioned above, which is being developed to "aggregate vast amounts of data on citizens and noncitizens alike, from sources including federal, state, and local records, credit card transactions, airline reservations, telephone and Internet service provider (ISP) records, consumer information from health, financial, and retail companies, and live surveillance-camera feeds, such as from those at airports . . . to enable the government to engage in data 'mining' that will allow it to identify suspicious terrorist activity in its early stages."[50] TIA's goal is not simply to discover who is currently engaged in terrorist activities, but to discern who might, in the future, become a terrorist—the mostly unspoken implication being that law enforcement agencies could act preemptively, before a crime has been committed, to neutralize the suspected suspect. The three tools of hierarchical observation, normalizing judgment, and constant examination are deployed here in archetypically disciplinary fashion to cause persons to police themselves, to act and think only in ways they are certain will meet with the approval of the conservative forces of the law, because they assume they are always being watched and judged. The existence of TIA causes persons to internalize the gaze of TIA and "become the principle of [their] own subjection"[51] by rejecting their own capacity for *épokhè* and self-limiting their own activities to those well within the bounds of the normal and conservative so as to avoid prompting any further investigation.

But massive governmental programs like TIA are not the only source of this increasingly ubiquitous disciplinary regime. Small local programs, like Wilmington, Delaware's recent database of individuals authorities there suspected may break the law at some point in the future, are also part of the emerging web of disciplinary calculability. Outside the arena of government, a recent survey indicated that "55 percent [of companies] review employees' e-mail messages, up from about 47 percent in 2001,"[52] and a growing number of companies, such as several Ontario nursing homes, have begun using systems that enable real-time tracking of their employees' whereabouts.[53] In the quest for ever-greater efficiency, some corporations are now using detailed electronic monitoring of their employees' specific physical actions to determine every possible point of reduced effectiveness. The goal is to surveil and regulate even the most minute details of employees' work, creating a "new digital Taylorism where every motion is watched, timed, and controlled by the boss,"[54] and where human undecidability/negative liberty is minimized in favor of profitable rote mechanism.

Cars and cellphones, for teenagers as much as for the rest of us two of the most important symbols of freedom, are themselves being converted into tools of panoptic disciplinary control. More and more private cars, to say nothing of rental and fleet vehicles, are coming equipped with systems that provide real-time data on the location and speed of the vehicle. An Australian inventor recently began marketing a dashboard-mounted digital video camera and data recorder that begins recording when it identifies risky driving, which is being installed in thousands of automobiles in the US.[55] Several companies have begun testing or marketing software and hardware that allows GPS tracking of cellphones. Verizon Wireless and Sprint PCS both now offer GPS-equipped phones.

Companies like Networks in Motion, Inc., and Microsoft now offer compatible software, marketed to both parents and businesses, that allows them to use an online map to track their children or employees via these phones. As this web of surveillance expands, it slowly encroaches upon the negative liberty that demarcates our ability to exceed the legalistic and the conservative.

But perhaps no program of enforced calculability is more rigorous than "the Bush administration's assertion of power to hold any American in detention forever, without a trial and without access to counsel, simply by declaring him to be an enemy combatant,"[56] a claim that has been the subject of much public debate and several federal court cases. This is a project of enforced calculability through near pure legalism: A person whom the executive has deemed may be a danger now or at some point in the future, is physically confined so that his every move is controlled. One may also be kept communicatively isolated, silencing and in effect defacing his ability to be an independent creator and promulgator of meaning and value. Like judicial prisoners in maximum security penitentiaries, this prionser's life approaches near total calculability. No significant action—from sleeping to eating, exercising to watching TV—goes uncontrolled. This calculability is instituted with great legalism because the confinement occurs without a trial in which the pure execution of law, which is itself the role of the execute-ive, would be confronted by the *épokhal* humanity required by justice in an ordeal of the undecidable. The executive, charged with the imposition of mechanistic conformity, is unwilling to risk the unpredictability of a trial, in which the *épokhal* undecidability of judges, jurors, lawyers, and the adversarial process are all deployed in a process fraught with unknowns, so the executive simply circumvents this circus of unknowability by incarcerating persons in an administrative, rather than judicial, fashion. In this way, the executive demonstrates the deterministic force of its constitutional obligation to "take Care that the Laws be faithfully executed."[57] The law demands that its executor pursue not justice, which includes both law and *épokhè*, but the pure legalistic enforcement of conservative violence. In a theoretical sense, it is not the executive's role to judge the law or to allow it to be judged, as may happen in a court or in public opinion—the executive's primary task is to carry out, to iterate, the law. It is a role ideally without *épokhè*, and one that appears relatively boldly with the extra-judicial detention of persons who the executive deems may present a threat to its primary task of mechanistically iterating the given law.

Increasing legalism, at the expense of the negative liberty inaugurated by the personal, is a growing trend that constitutes the second broad development of decreased *épokhè* and increased calculability. The existence of law (in the specifically banal sense of governmental legislation) or of the legalistic (in the broader philosophical sense that has been used throughout this work) itself is growing to unprecedented levels in areas that had not previously experienced the imposition of any great legality. The world is slowly being deprived of an outside to the law, of places of unpredictability.

Wars of the past have stereotypically been attempts to impose one law, one regime of decidability, upon another. They were simply militarized manifestations of the arché-violent structure of intersubjectivity. But for the contemporary first world, terrorism, which, as above, represents a more afformative, unpredictable, *épokhal* threat to law than does another law, is perceived to be the primary threat. Thus, as if to complete this contemporary symmetry, the US and other militaries are currently fighting to impose their law not upon other systems of law, but upon such "ungoverned spaces" as "the tri-border intersection of Brazil, Argentina and Paraguay, . . . parts of southern Panama,"[58] the "Colombia-Ecuador-Peru border region,"[59] parts of Afghanistan,[60] Iraq,[61] and Pakistan.[62] These lawless regions, home to smugglers, terrorists, and others who wish to exist outside the law (as well as many who do not), are the geographical manifestation of the afformative threat presented by terrorism, which is why "the emerging U.S. military strategy for ungoverned space seeks to assert control through armed force."[63] Predictability must be imposed upon these areas in order to quash the ever-present threat of the unpredictable, which is represented most clearly by terrorism. Although conquering these regions and imposing legality upon them will not defeat terrorism, it will deprive those who crave undecidability of areas of refuge beyond the subjection to positive libertarian legalism. It will tame those areas that, geographically as well as conceptually, border the law by bringing them within the geographic and conceptual realm of the determinable. The primary enemy is no longer an opposing system of signification, an opposing law—it is the absence of law, of the positive liberty or imposed predictability that would arrest the terrifying possibility of afformativity that resides within the *épokhal*.

Consider also the expansion of law onto the high seas, long feared and celebrated by poets and explorers as an unpredictable world of simultaneous danger and freedom. The United Nations Convention on the Law of the Sea of 10 December 1982, which entered into effect on 16 November 1994, is one legal document that changes all that. Under this treaty, every ship at sea must fly the flag of a specific state, and that ship remains under the jurisdiction of that state, even when it is in the middle of the ocean, far from the borders of any state at all.[64] States have also agreed to "cooperate in the suppression of unauthorized broadcasting from the high seas," such that "any State where the transmission can be received" may "arrest any person or ship engaged in unauthorized broadcasting."[65] This provision represents the wish of states to nullify the invasion of the *épokhal* or unregulated, here in the form of "unauthorized broadcasting," from outside the carefully normalized realm of the state. But perhaps the most interesting provision of this treaty holds that "a warship which encounters on the high seas a foreign ship" may board that ship if "(d) the ship is without nationality; or (e) though flying a foreign flag or refusing to show its flag, the ship is, in reality, of the same nationality as the warship."[66]

Simply put, all ships at sea must submit to the law of a particular state, and if they do not submit to any particular state they may be invaded by an agent of any state at all. "You may wish to have your refusal" to submit to the law of a state, even far from its shores, "as an act of defiance, of resistance to the rules, a grand gesture of protest. But it has already been interpreted," pursuant to article 110, subparagraph (e), above, "as merely a default, a failure to make a service . . . You have not resisted. You have not protested. You have merely defaulted.

. . . You are not free to resist"[67] being subjugated to the law of a state. You may choose, within the bounds contemplated by article 91, paragraph 1, which state you want to rule you, but you can not free yourself from law, even when surrounded by thousands of miles of fluidity. If you try to free yourself from the law, you will be invaded, and your rightful allegiance determined, no matter how much you protest that, out on the high seas, you are autonomous and free from the enforced positive liberty of legal restraint.

Not even in space can one escape from the law. Although according to what is commonly known as the Outer Space Treaty, which entered into force in October of 1967, "outer space, including the moon and other celestial bodies, is not subject to national appropriation,"[68] this does not mean that the law has renounced its hold there. Rather, under this treaty, states "bear international responsibility for national activities in outer space" even if these activities are carried out by "non-governmental entities [i.e., private corporations, non-state actors, individuals, etc.]," and all such activities "require authorization and continuing supervision" by the state in which the private enterprise is based.[69] Furthermore, "a State Party to the Treaty on whose registry an object launched into outer space is carried shall retain jurisdiction and control over such object, and over any personnel thereof, while in outer space or on a celestial body."[70] If someone tries to flee the insurmountable positive libertarianism of the law by fleeing the Earth, on which there is virtually no unclaimed territory, and founding a new law on some celestial body, the law still comprehends this act. The colony must be authorized by the state, it must satisfy this authorizing state that it adheres to the provisions of the Outer Space Treaty, and everything that occurs within that colony remains subject to the laws of the state from which the project was launched. If any of these three conditions are broken, the state will cognize a crime that it must prosecute. Again, the law has expanded its demands for its own iteration; there is no escape from the law.

After considering both the examples of the new disciplinary technologies presented earlier in this chapter and the broader trends discussed here, it seems clear that the world is slowly being deprived of places outside law and legalism, of places of unpredictability or incalculability to which one can flee if one wishes. It may be asked exactly *why* this might be considered negative, why one would want to escape the predictability and safety of the law. Why would one volunteer to forego relatively inexpensive (in a governmental budget sense) technologies that can determine if the person standing to one's left is a wanted criminal, if he has a bomb concealed beneath his coat, and if he is even now deciding whether or not to detonate it? Why would one possibly choose to set out onto the vast ocean in a tiny boat without ensuring that one remains well within the comforting blanket of legal protection, should something go wrong?[71] Why should one prefer a world in which the powers that be willingly forego the expansion of law and legalism, of predictability and accountability, that, like Hobbes' legal hedgerows, may free us from the terror of the undecidable and the agonism of negative liberty?

The real danger comes not simply from the possibility that our laws and our disciplinary apparatuses may become so detailed and effective that disobedience is no longer a practical option, but that it will no longer be a cognitive possibility. The spread of the law and the growing enforcement of the legalism (the decidability, the predictability, the discipline) that makes that law effective grow ever closer to denying us not only a place to flee, should we choose, but also to denying us the possibility of choosing to flee. In the words of Oscar Wilde, "disobedience . . . is man's original virtue. It is through disobedience that progress has been made, through disobedience and through rebellion."[72] Disobedience—the rejection of the mechanistic interation of the law, in favor of undergoing an ordeal of the undecidable that opens the possibility of the foundation and iteration of a new law—is the original virtue of humanity, born at the core of the economy of violence and justice that arises simultaneously with discursive intersubjectivity. The possibility of disobedience is the opportunity to utter Nietzsche's "sacred 'No,'" which is "the creation of freedom for oneself for new creation."[73] It is thus also Derrida's "strategy of rupture" that "assumes the right to contest"[74] the law through an ordeal of the undecidable and do justice to it by choosing it anew, or by choosing to efface it and iterate a new law of one's own. Therefore, the possibility of disobedience is also the maintenance of Berlin's negative liberty, typified by a "number of paths down which a man can walk, whether or not he chooses to do so."[75] If even the opportunity for disobedience to the law is removed, if to simply consider breaking the law or to be deemed likely to consider breaking it at some point in the future is itself knowable and thus preventable and perhaps even criminal, if in fact our methods of training become so effective that we can train the *épokhè* itself out of humanity and leave it with pure obedience, we are left with only legalism, positive liberty, and mere phenomenal mechanism.

This hypothetical pure legalism, which would be constituted by the absence of any *épokhal* "anxiety-ridden moment of suspense"[76] in which a person steps beyond the merely phenomenal "deployment of a norm or program,"[77] embraces her nature as a creator of meaning and value, and *decides*, would be a totalitarianism. Totalitarianism is that form of rule which, as described by Hannah Arendt, "claims to transform the human species into an active and unfailing carrier of the law . . . the embodiment of the law."[78] "As the attempted re-in-*corpor*-ation or re-*organ*-ization of the body politic into a transparent, homogenous unity without any remainder or transcendence,"[79] without anything in excess of the calculably legalistic, totalitarian rule seeks to reduce person-ality to mere phenomenal objecthood.

This objectification of personhood—achieved when persons are so known and so controlled that they cease to be creators of meaning and value and instead simply re-iterate whatever law they are given, be it state legislation, ethical doctrine, or consumer fad—would be a complete rejection of the human essence constituted by our ability to become "human beings who are new, unique, incomparable, who give themselves laws, who create themselves."[80] It would be the acceptance of a purely programmatic, legalistic life consisting entirely of the positive liberty that "assumes that there is one and only one true way of living a good life,"[81] which has been gifted to the ignorant, uncouth, or otherwise imperfect masses by the local (political, ethical, commercial) philosopher king.

Not even Nietzsche, sometimes considered a philosophical forefather of totalitarianism, goes this far. He, with Derrida, recognizes that "there is war only after the opening of discourse, and war dies out only at the end of discourse."[82] As discussed in chapter one, Nietzsche rejects "any final and exclusive authority, natural or supernatural, and of the accompanying compulsion and censorship"[83] that would signal the end of the discursive conflict generated by healthy living that embraces life as will to power. Peace comes only with the silencing of conflicting discursive positions, the silence imposed by Hobbes' Leviathan upon those lesser persons who are forced to accept her system of meanings and values for the sake of peace and safety. According to Nietzsche, one who truly embraces the inevitability of violence inherent within all interpersonal relationships does not seek to completely subsume others' personhoods beneath her own. Instead, she "desires [her] enemy for [her]self, as [her] mark of distinction"[84] and agrees with Zarathustra that we should "strive against one another like gods."[85] Such a person may seek to conquer the chaos of a 'lawless' region to impose her will upon it, but she would not do it for the slavish wish to rid the world of *épokhè*. She would find "altogether hateful and nauseating . . . those who never offer resistance"[86] because their *épokhal* negative liberty has been obliterated and replaced with complete knowability and lawfulness. Because she would seek "companions . . . not corpses, not herds and believers," she would revel in those lawless persons "who write new values on new tablets,"[87] who are the enemies of the iterating state rather than its subhumanly mechanistic embodiment.

In our laudable search for public safety in the face of the (faceless) afformativity of terrorism, we are developing new technologies of discipline that may close the gap with this hypothetical pure calculability of totalitarianism. The content of this totalitarianism is less important than its structure. That is, it does not matter what content the law is given by the local philosopher-kings—be it liberal democracy or kingship by divine right; whether abortion is determined to be "the killing an unborn child" or "a woman's voluntary ending of her pregnancy"; whether an economy is controlled centrally or given free reign; or whether or not rap is considered "music." As the highest achievement of positive libertarianism, totalitarianism of any content is ultimately constituted by the fervent belief that "a state of conflict [is] the sign of a vice, or a defect, or a malfunctioning"[88] that must be silenced by disciplining the creativity out of persons, by eliminating what Arendt calls the "very source of freedom which is given with the fact of the birth of man and resides in his capacity to make a new beginning."[89]

V. There is No Conclusion

Of course, no matter how close we may come to this totalitarianism of complete predictability, "where there is life is there . . . will to power."[90] The *épokhè* can not be completely squeezed out of personhood any more than there can be pure violence (the "reduction of the other to a real moment of my life, its reduction to the state of [absolute] empirical alter-ego")[91] or uncontaminated peacefuless (a complete "'letting-be' of an existent [other] as something existing outside me in the essence of what it is").[92] The economy of violence and justice always remains at the core of discursive intersubjectivity. As with Hobbes' story of the chaotic state of nature and imposition of agreement on meaning and value, totalitarian ambitions to remove unpredictability and illegality by cutting off the *épokhal* are the result of a core recognition of the other as an independent creator of meaning and value in the world. Thus even within this violence a fundamental peacefulness remains.

The dream of escaping from the nausea of terrorism's incalculability and afformativity by instituting disciplined legalism is another manifestation of the slavish dream of escaping from politics, which I discussed at the end of chapter three. As perfect predictability, perfect safety is achievable only by completely excising the *épokhal*, which, as the distinctly human capacity to act beyond mere phenomenal mechanics, is the very quintessence of politics. Politics is that inevitably human way of life by which we, as the creators of meaning and value in the world, struggle with each other to iterate our own answers to those questions that have no answers. At any given time, the politically "dominant power is the one that manages to impose and, thus, to legitimate, indeed to legalize . . . the terminology and thus the interpretation that best suits it in a given situation."[93]

But, as with Hobbes' Leviathan, the answers imposed by this dominant power are not universally true in any objective Platonic sense, for "there are no authentical doctrines concerning right and wrong,"[94] and "*good* and *evil* are [simply] names that signify our appetites and aversions."[95] Even so, in order to achieve its promise of safety through predictability, totalitarianism "destroys the plurality of men and makes out of many the One who unfailingly will act as though he himself were"[96] simply a node of the law, rather than a person who can exceed the merely legalistic and leap through the *épokhal*.

Of course, persons are not entirely *épokhal* beings. As already discussed at some length, in complete persons "*creature* and *creator* are united: in man there is material, fragment, excess, clay, dirt, nonsense, chaos; but in man there is also creator, form-giver, hammer hardness, spectator divinity, and seventh day."[97] This is why persons can pursue justice, which itself paradoxically requires (again, as already discussed at length) both *épokhè* and legalism, both undecidability and calculability. The *épokhal* aspect of justice, that facet by which one must render a "fresh judgement," "as if ultimately nothing previously existed of the law,"[98] is only possible for persons, who themselves can exceed the merely calculable. The pure calculability of simple phenomenal objects renders them incapable of stepping outside the purely programmatic, the legalistic aspect of justice, by which all things must without possibility of exception "follow a law or a prescription, a rule."[99]

As beings that exist both calculably and *épokhally*, persons require both the legal and the unknowable. In the terms of Berlin's position, as discussed in chapter three, persons require both negative and positive liberty. "We must preserve a minimum area of [negative liberty] if we are not to 'degrade or deny our nature'" as *épokhal* beings in excess of mere phenomenality, but "we cannot remain absolutely free, and must give up some of our [negative] liberty to preserve the rest."[100] Persons require some level of predictability and the safety it imposes at the expense of complete personal freedom—otherwise we would find ourselves in a chaos of nonlegality resembling Hobbes' state of nature, in which the sovereign's inflicted coordination does not yet exist to stifle persons' naturally diverse creativity with his hedgerow-like laws. "But total self-surrender" to calculability or positive liberty "is self-defeating. What then must the minimum be? That which a man cannot give up without offending against the essence of his human nature."[101]

And thus we arrive back at the question that ended chapter three; a question without an answer. What is, in fact, the amount of *épokhè*, of unknowability or unpredictability or negative liberty, that a person may give up without transgressing her essence as a person, without being effaced and becoming too much a phenomenal object and not enough a free being who exceeds this world of bare cause and effect? There *is*, of course, no Answer to this question. Our yearning for a final answer is a yearning for the end of politics. It is a yearning for the end of our nature as creators of meaning and value and "a craving for the certainties of childhood or the absolute values of our primitive past,"[102] and for the comfortable but subhuman safety announced by the impossibility of choice outside the bounds of the law.

Notes

1 Hobbes, *Leviathan*, XXX.21.

2 Ibid., XXIX.6.

3 Hobbes, *Leviathan*, XIII.13.

4 Hobbes, *Elements*, IV.6.

5 Derrida, "The Force of Law," 963.

6 Derrida, as quoted in Giovanna Borradori, *Philosophy in a Time of Terror: Dialogues with Jurgen Habermas and Jacques Derrida* (Chicago: The University of Chicago Press, 2003), 118.

7 CNN, "Ashcroft: Critics of new terror measures undermine effort," 7 December 2001, http://archives.cnn.com/2001/US/12/06/inv.ashcroft.hearing/.

8 Hobbes, *Leviathan*, XVIII.9.

9 Hobbes, *Rudiments*, III.31.

10 Philip B. Heymann, *Terrorism, Freedom, and Security: Winning Without War* (Cambridge, MA: MIT Press, 2003), 27.

11 Derrida, as quoted in Borradori, 98.

12 Hamacher, 1138.

13 Borradori, 112.

14 Hamacher, 1139n12..

15 Nietzsche, *On the Genealogy of Morals*, II.24.

16 The Near Earth Object Program's website is http://neo.jpl.nasa.gov/. It is a fascinating program that, to date, tracks 102 sizable NEOs and calculates the likelihood that each one has of striking the Earth in the foreseeable future.

17 Hobbes, *Leviathan*, VI.17.

18 Nietzsche, *The Gay Science*, 355.

19 Geoffrey Bennington, *Legislations: The Politics of Deconstruction (*New York: Verso, 1994), 4.

20 Derrida, "The Force of Law," 997.

21 Michel Foucault, *Discipline and Punish: The Birth of the Prison*, 2nd ed., trans. Alan Sheridan (New York: Vintage Books, 1977), 231.

22 Ibid., 166.

23 At this point there has been (to my knowledge) no judicial precedent directly construing exactly what evidence, in addition to activities protected by the first amendment, must be present in order to justify such a search.

24 Foucault, *Discipline and Punish*, 214.

25 Ibid., 203.

26 Ibid., 201.

27 Hobbes, *Leviathan*, VIII.10.

28 Foucault, *Discipline and Punish*, 191.

29 Ibid., 184.

30 Christian Parenti, *The Soft Cage: Surveillance in America* (NY: Basic Books, 2003), 2.

31 Ibid., 7.

32 James Bernauer and Michael Mahon, "The Ethics of Michel Foucault," in *The Cambridge Companion to Foucault*, ed. Gary Gutting (Cambridge: Cambridge University Press, 1994), 143.

33 Parenti, 92.

34 Foucault, *Discipline and Punish*, 138.

35 Ibid., 18.

36 Nietzsche, *On the Genealogy of Morals*, 475.

37 Ibid.

38 Nietzsche, *Thus Spoke Zarathustra*, 168.

39 Ibid., 136.

40 Ibid., 214.

41 Hobbes, *Rudiments*, II.12.

42 Hoffman, 8.

43 Leni Riefsnstahl, Triumph des Willens [*Triumph of the Will*], 114 min., 1935, is likely the best place to view large numbers of SA and SS close enough to see that many of them have emulated Hitler's famous and distinctive moustache.

44 Nietzsche, *Thus Spoke Zarathustra*, 139.

45 Berlin, "Two Concepts of Liberty," 203.

46 Max Stirner, Max, "The State and the Sacred," in *The Anarchist Reader*, ed. George Woodcock (Atlantic Highlands, NY: The Harvester Press Limited, 1977), 89.

47 Berlin, "Two Concepts of Liberty," 213.

48 Derrida, "The Force of Law," 1035.

49 Roger Alan Deacon, *Fabricating Foucault: Rationalising the Management of Individuals* (Milwaukee, WI: Marquette University Press, 2003), 145.

50 Kathleen Sullivan, "Under a Watchful Eye: Incursions on Personal Privacy," in *The War on our Preedoms: Civil Liberties in an Age of Terrorism*, eds. Richard C. Leone and Greg Anrig, Jr. (New York: The Century Foundation, 2003), 130.

51 Foucault, *Discipline and Punish*, 203.

52 Andrea Coombes, "Employers tracking e-mail, Web use; Surveys show more companies are monitoring their workers," *The Houston Chronicle*, 25 June 2005, 2.

53 Tyler Hamilton, "Employees fear culture of electronic surveillance," *Toronto Star*, 2 May 2005, D01.

54 Parenti, 132.

55 Jessica Lawrence, "Look out, the boss is watching—Tracking Devices spy on company vehicles," *Sunday Mail* (Queensland, Australia), 3 April 2005, 21. One may be left to wonder how this device—or rather, the device's programmer—defines risky driving.

56 Anthony Lewis, "Security and Liberty: Preserving the Values of Freedom," in *The War on our Preedoms: Civil Liberties in an Age of Terrorism*, eds. Richard C. Leone and Greg Anrig, Jr. (New York: The Century Foundation, 2003), 51.

57 US Constitution, Art. II, Sec. 3.

58 Bruce Finley, "High noon in Latin America: U.S. targets lawless areas," *The Denver Post*, 5 December 2004, A-01.

59 Ibid.

60 See, for instance, Martin Bentham, "British to assault Taliban stronghold," *The Observer* (London), 29 May 2005, 21.

61 See, for instance, Patrick Quinn, "The wild frontier; Rebels face desert showdown," *Sunday Mail* (South Australia), 19 June 2005, 45.

62 See, for instance, Ahmed Rashid, "A wild, cruel, and merciless country outside the law," *The Daily Telegraph* (London), 20 March 2004, 4. It is interesting to note that, although all four of these articles use descriptions such as "lawless," "wild," or "outside the law" to describe the regions in question, they still label the regions by the states to which they seemingly belong. Even though these areas are recognized to be outside the rule of states, they are attributed to states.

63 Finley.

64 United Nations Convention on the Law of the Sea. 10 December 1982. Arts. 91, 94, 97.

65 Ibid., Art. 109.

66 Ibid., Art. 110.

67 Yablon, 262.

68 Treaty of Principles Governing the Activities of States in the Exploration and Use of Outer Space, including the Moon and Other Celestial Bodies, Art. II, 27 January 1967, http://www.state.gov/t/ac/trt/5181.htm.

69 Ibid., Art. VI.

70 Ibid., Art. VIII.

71 The classic answer to this question is Blondie Hasler's. Hasler, who founded the OSTAR, the first single-handed trans-Atlantic sailboat race, was once asked about the race's lack of rules requiring radios and other safety gear. Hasler responded that, rather than calling for help, it would be "more seemly to drown like a gentleman."

72 Oscar Wilde, "Disobedience: Man's Original Virtue," in *The Anarchist Reader*, ed. George Woodcock (Atlantic Highlands, NY: The Harvester Press Limited, 1977), 72.

73 Nietzsche, *Thus Spoke Zarathustra*, 139.

74 Derrida, "The Force of Law," 997.

75 Berlin, "Final Retrospect," 326.

76 Derrida, "The Force of Law," 955.

77 Derrida, and quoted in Borradori, 133.

78 Hannah Arendt, From *The Origins of Totalitarianism*, in *Princeton Readings in Political Thought*, eds. Mitchell Cohen and Nicole Fermon (Princeton, NJ: Princeton University Press, 1996), 580.

79 Simon Critchley, *The Ethics of Deconstruction*: *Derrida and Levinas* (West Lafayette, Indiana: Purdue University Press, 1999), 207.

80 Nietzsche, *The Gay Science*, p. 335.

81 Parekh, 217.

82 Derrida, *Writing and Difference*, 117.
83 Stuart Hampshire, *Justice is Conflict* (Princeton, NJ: Princeton University Press, 2000), 35.
84 Nietzsche, *On the Genealogy of Morals*, I.10.
85 Nietzsche, *Thus Spoke Zarathustra*, 214.
86 Ibid., 302.
87 Ibid., 136.
88 Hampshire, 33.
89 Arendt, 582.
90 Nietzsche, *Thus Spoke Zarathustra*, p. 227.
91 Derrida, *Writing and Difference*, p. 128.
92 Ibid., 138.
93 Derrida, as quoted in Borradori, p. 105.
94 Hobbes, *Rudiments*, Preface xiii.
95 Hobbes, *Leviathan*, XV.40.
96 Arendt, 582.
97 Nietzsche, *Beyond Good and Evil*, 344.
98 Derrida, "The Force of Law," 961.
99 Ibid.
100 Berlin, "Two Concepts of Liberty," 173.
101 Ibid.
102 Ibid., 217.

Bibliography

Arendt, Hannah. From *The Origins of Totalitarianism.* In *Princeton Readings in Political Thought.* Eds. Mitchell Cohen and Nicole Fermon. Princeton, NJ: Princeton University Press, 1996.

Aristotle. *Nichomachean Ethics.* Translated by Terence Irwin. Cambridge: Hackett Publishing Company, 1985.

Audi, Robert. "On the Meaning and Justification of Violence." In *Violence.* Edited by Jerome Shaffer. New York: David McKay Company, Inc., 1971.

Austin, J.L., *How To Do Things With Words*, (Cambridge, MA: Harvard University Press, 1975).

Beardsworth, Richard. *Derrida and the Political.* London: Routledge, 1996.

Bennington, Geoffrey. *Legislations: The Politics of Deconstruction.* New York: Verso, 1994.

Bentham, Martin. "British to assault Taliban stronghold." *The Observer* (London), 29 May 2005: 21.

Berlin, Isaiah. "Equality." In *Concepts and Categories.* Edited by Henry Hardy. New York: Penguin Books, 1978.

———. "Final Retrospect." In *Liberty: Incorporating Four Essays on Liberty.* Edited by Henry Hardy. Oxford: Oxford University Press, 2002.

———. "From Hope and Fear Set Free." In *Concepts and Categories.* Edited by Henry Hardy. New York: Penguin Books, 1978.

———. "Introduction." In *Liberty: Incorporating Four Essays on Liberty.* Edited by Henry Hardy. Oxford: Oxford University Press, 2002.

———. "Liberty." In *Liberty: Incorporating Four Essays on Liberty.* Edited by Henry Hardy. Oxford: Oxford University Press, 2002.

———. "The Origins of Israel." In *The Power of Ideas.* Edited by Henry Hardy. Princeton, NJ: Princeton University Press, 2000.

———. "The Search for Status." In *The Power of Ideas.* Edited by Henry Hardy. Princeton, NJ: Princeton University Press, 2000.

———. "Two Concepts of Liberty." In *Liberty: Incorporating Four Essays on Liberty.* Edited by Henry Hardy. Oxford: Oxford University Press, 2002.

Bernauer, James, and Michael Mahon. "The Ethics of Michel Foucault." In *The Cambridge Companion to Foucault.* Edited by Gary Gutting. Cambridge: Cambridge University Press, 1994.

Best, Steven, and Douglas Kellner. *The Postmodern Turn.* New York: The Guilford Press, 1997.

Borradori, Giovanna. *Philosophy in a Time of Terror: Dialogues with Jurgen Habermas and Jacques Derrida.* Chicago: The University of Chicago Press, 2003.

Bufacchi, Vittorio. "Why is Violence Bad?" *American Philosophical Quarterly* 41, 2 (April 2004): 169-181.

Buonamano, Roberto. *The Economy of Violence: Derrida on Law and Justice.* Oxford: Blackwell Publishers, 1998.

Burke, Edmund. *Reflections on the Revolution in France.* Edited by H.D. Mahoney. 1790. Reprint, New York: Macmillan Publishing Company, 1955.

Cahoone, Lawrence, ed. *From Modernism to Postmodernism.* Oxford: Blackwell, 2003.

Caputo, John D. *Deconstruction in a Nutshell.* New York: Fordham University Press, 1997.

Chung Tzu [Zhuangzi]. *The Book of Chuang Tzu.* Translated by Martin Palmer, with Elizabeth Breuilly. New York: Penguin Books, 1990.

CNN. "Ashcroft: Critics of new terror measures undermine effort." 7 December 2001, http://archives.cnn.com/2001/US/12/06/inv.ashcroft.hearing/.

Coombes, Andrea. "Employers tracking e-mail, Web use; Surveys show more companies are monitoring their workers." The Houston Chronicle, 25 June 2005: 2.

Cornell, Drucilla. "The Violence of the Masquerade: Law Dressed Up as Justice." In *Working Through Derrida.* Edited by Gary B. Madison. Evanston, Ill.: Northwestern University Press, 1993.

Critchley, Simon. *The Ethics of Deconstruction: Derrida and Levinas.* West Lafayette, Indiana: Purdue University Press, 1999.

Culler, Jonathan. *On Deconstruction.* Ithaca: Cornell University Press, 1982.

Deacon, Roger Alan. *Fabricating Foucault: Rationalising the Management of Individuals.* Milwaukee, WI: Marquette University Press, 2003.

Derrida, Jacques. "A Discussion with Jacques Derrida." *Theory and Event* 5, no.1, (2001).

———. *Aporias.* Translated by Thomas Dutoit. Stanford, CA: Stanford UP, 1993.

———. "Before the Law." In *Acts of Literature.* Edited by Derek Attridge. Routledge, NY, 1992.

———. "Declarations of Independence." *New Political Science* 15 (Summer 1986): 7-15.

———. *Of Grammatology.* Corrected Edition. Translated by Gayatri Spivak. Baltimore: Johns Hopkins University Press, 1997.

———. *The Ear of the Other: Otobiography, Transference, Translation.* Translated by Avital Ronell. London: University of Nebraska Press, 1985.

———. "The Force of Law: The 'Mystical Foundation of Authority.'" *Cardozo Law Review* 11 (November 1990): 919-1045.

———. *Writing and Difference.* Translated by Alan Bass. Chicago: University of Chicago Press, 1978.

Dietz, Mary G. "Hobbes's Subject as Citizen." In *Thomas Hobbes and Political Theory.* Edited by Mary Dietz. Lawrence. KS: University of Kansas Press, 1990.

Dumm, Thomas L. "The Politics of Post-Modern Aesthetics: Habermas Contra Foucault." *Political Theory* (May 1988): 209-228.

Finley, Bruce. "High noon in Latin America: U.S. targets lawless areas." *The Denver Post*, 5 December 2004: A-01.

Flathman, Richard E. *Thomas Hobbes: Skepticism, Individuality, and Chastened Politics.* London: Sage Publications, 1993.

Foucault, Michel. *Discipline and Punish: The Birth of the Prison.* 2nd Edition. Translated by Alan Sheridan. New York: Vintage Books, 1977.

France. *Declaration of the Rights of Man.* 1789. http://www.yale.edu/lawweb/avalon/rightsof.htm.

Gauthier, David. "Hobbes's Social Contract." In *Perspectives on Thomas Hobbes.* Edited by Rogers and Ryan. Oxford: Oxford UP, 1988.

Gracyk, Theodore A. "Pornography as Representation: Aesthetic Considerations." In *Pornography: Private Right or Public Menace?* Edited by Robert M. Baird and Stuart E. Rosenblum. Buffalo, NY: Prometheus, 1991.

Gray, John. *Isaiah Berlin.* Princeton: Princeton UP, 1996.

Gubar, Susan. "Representing Pornography." In *For Adult Use Only: The Dilemmas of Violent Pornography.* Edited by Susan Gubar and Joan Huff. Bloomington: Indiana University Press, 1989.

Hamacher, Werner. "Afformative, Strike." *Cardozo Law Review* 13 (December 1991): 1133-1157.

Hamilton, Tyler. "Employees fear culture of electronic surveillance." Toronto Star, 2 May 2005: D01.

Hampshire, Stuart. *Justice is Conflict*. Princeton, NJ: Princeton University Press, 2000.

Harris, John. *Violence and Responsibility*. London: Routledge and Kegan Paul, Ltd., 1980.

Harvey, David. *The Condition of Postmodernity: An Enquiry into the Origins of Cultural Change*. Oxford: Blackwell, 1990.

Herbert, Gary B. *The Unity of Scientific and Moral Wisdom*. Vancouver, Canada: University of British Columbia Press, 1989.

Heymann, Philip B. *Terrorism, Freedom, and Security: Winning Without War*. Cambridge, MA: MIT Press, 2003.

Hobbes, Thomas. *Human Nature, or the Fundamental Elements of Policy*. 1640. In *The English Works of Thomas Hobbes of Malmesbury*. Ed. Sir William Molesworth. London: John Bohn, 1839-1845.

———. *Leviathan*. 1651. Edited Edwin Curley. Indianapolis, IN: Hackett Publishing Company, Inc., 1994.

———. *On the Human [*De Homine*]*. In *Man and Citizen*. Edited by Bernard Gert. Atlantic Highlands, NJ: Humanities Press, 1972.

———. *Philosophical Rudiments Concerning Government and Society [*De Cive*]*. 1651. In *The English Works of Thomas Hobbes of Malmesbury*. Ed. Sir William Molesworth. London: John Bohn, 1839-1845.

———. *The Elements of Law, Moral and Politic [*De Corpore*]*. 1650. In *The English Works of Thomas Hobbes of Malmesbury*. Ed. Sir William Molesworth. London: John Bohn, 1839-1845.

———. *The Questions Concerning Liberty, Necessity, and Chance*. 1656. In *The English Works of Thomas Hobbes of Malmesbury*. Ed. Sir William Molesworth. Vol. 5. London: John Bohn, 1839-1845.

Hoffman, Piotr. *The Quest for Power: Hobbes, Descartes, and the Emergence of Modernity*. New Jersey: Humanities Press, 1996.

———. *Violence in Modern Philosophy*. Chicago: University of Chicago Press, 1989.

Honderich, Ted. *Political Violence*. Ithaca, NY: Cornell University Press, 1976.

Honneth, Axel. "Negative Freedom and Cultural Belonging: An Unhealthy Tension in the Political Philosophy of Isaiah Berlin." *Social Research* (Winter 1999): 1063-1077.

International Military Tribunal. *Charter of the International Military Tribunal*. http://www.yale.edu/lawweb/avalon/imt/proc/imtconst.htm.

Johnson, Paul J. "Hobbes and the Wolf-Man." In *Thomas Hobbes: His View of Man*. Editwed by J.G. van der Bend. Amsterdam: Rodopi, 1982.

Kant, Immanuel. *Critique of Practical Reason*. 1788. 3rd edition. Translated by Lewis White Beck. Upper Saddle River, NJ: Prentice-Hall, Inc., 1993.

———. *Groundwork of the Metaphysics of Morals*. 1785. Translated by H.J. Paton. New York: Harper and Row, 1964.

———. *The Metaphysics of Morals*. 1797. In *Kant: Political Writings*. 2nd Edition. Translated by H. B. Nisbet, Edited by Hans Reiss. Cambridge: Cambridge UP, 1970.

Kelly, Duncan. "The Political Thought of Isaiah Berlin." *British Journal of Politics and International Relations* (1 April 2002): 25-48.

Kenny, Michael. "Isaiah Berlin's Contribution to Modern Political Theory." *Political Studies* 48 (2000): 1026-1039.

Kocis, Robert A. "Reason, Development, and the Conflicts of Human Ends: Sir Isaiah Berlin's Vision of Politics." *The American Political Science Review* (March 1980): 38-52.

Kramer, Matthew H. *Hobbes and the Paradoxes of Political Origins*. New York: St. Martin's Press, Inc., 1997.

LaHaye, Beverly. *I am a Woman by God's Design*. Old Tappan, NJ: Power Books, 1980.

Lao Zi. *Tao Te Ching* [*Dao De Jing*]. *Shuangwen* edition. Translated by D. C. Lau. Hong Kong: Chinese University Press, 2001.

Lawrence, Jessica. "Look out, the boss is watching—Tracking Devices spy on company vehicles." *Sunday Mail* (Queensland, Australia), 3 April 2005, 21.

LeCercle, Jean-Jacques. *The Violence of Language*. London: Routledge, 1990.

Lewis, Anthony. "Security and Liberty: Preserving the Values of Freedom." In *The War on our Freedoms: Civil Liberties in an Age of Terrorism*. Edited by Richard C. Leon and Greg Anrig, Jr. New York: The Century Foundation, 2003.

Manual for Courts-Martial United States. 2000. http://usmilitary.about.com/library/pdf/mcm2000.pdf.

Marcuse, Herbert. "Repressive Tolerance." In *A Critique of Pure Tolerance*. Eds. Robert Paul Wolff, Barrington Moore, Jr., and Herbert Marcuse. Boston: Beacon Press, 1969). http://grace.evergreen.edu/~arunc/texts/frankfurt/marcuse/tolerance.pdf.

May, Brian. "J. M. Coetzee and the Question of the Body." *Modern Fiction Studies* 47.2 (2001): 391-420.

McCallum, Gerald C., Jr. "Negative and Positive Freedom." *The Philosophical Review* (July 1967): 312-334.

Mill, John Stuart. *On Liberty*. 1859. http://www.utilitarianism.com/ol/two.html.

Miller, Ronald B. "Violence, Force, and Coercion." In *Violence*. Edited by Jerome Shaffer. New York: David McKay Company, Inc., 1971.

National Aeronautics and Space Administration. *Near Earth Object Program*. http://neo.jpl.nasa.gov/.

Nietzsche, Friedrich. *Beyond Good and Evil*. 1886. In *Basic Writings of Nietzsche*. 4th Edition. Translated and edited by Walter Kaufmann. New York: The Modern Library, 1992.

———. *On the Advantage and Disadvantage of History for Life*. 1874. Translated by Peter Preuss. New York: Hackett Publishing Company, 1980.

———. *On the Genealogy of Morals*. 1887. In *Basic Writings of Nietzsche*. Trans. 4th Edition. Walter Kaufmann. New York: The Modern Library, 1992.

———. *The Antichrist*. 1888. In *The Portable Nietzsche*. Translated by Walter Kaufmann. New York: Penguin Books, 1982.

———. *The Gay Science*. 1887. Translated by Walter Kaufmann. New York: Vintage Books, 1974.

———. *Thus Spoke Zarathustra*. 1892. In *The Portable Nietzsche*. Translated by Walter Kaufmann. New York: Penguin Books, 1982.

———. *Twilight of the Idols*. 1888. In *The Portable Nietzsche*. Translated by Walter Kaufmann. New York: Penguin Books, 1982.

Norris, Christopher. *Deconstruction*. London: Routledge, 1991.

Parekh, Bhikhu. "The Political thought of Sir Isaiah Berlin." *British Journal of Political Science* (April 1982): 201-226.

Parenti, Christian. *The Soft Cage: Surveillance in America*. NY: Basic Books, 2003.

Plato. *The Republic*. 2nd Edition. Translated by Allan Bloom. Basic Books: 1968.

Pontara, Giuliano. "The Concept of Violence." *Journal of Peace Research* 15, no.1 (1978): 19-32.

Powell, Jim. *Derrida for Beginners*. New York: Writers and Readers Publishing, Inc., 1997.

Quinn, Patrick. "The wild frontier; Rebels face desert showdown." *Sunday Mail* (South Australia), 19 June 2005: 45.

Rashid, Ahmed. "A wild, cruel, and merciless country outside the law." *The Daily Telegraph* (London), 20 March 2004: 4.

Reed, Gary Frank. "Berlin and the Division of Liberty." *Political Theory* (August 1980): 365-380.

Richardson, John. "Nietzsche's Power Ontology." In *Nietzsche*. Edited by John Richardson and Brian Leiter. Oxford: Oxford University Press, 2001.

Riefenstahl, Leni. Triumph des Willens [*Triumph of the Will*]. 114 minutes. 1935.

Rosenfeld, Michel. "Deconstruction and Legal Interpretation: Conflict, Indeterminacy and the Temptations of the New Legal Formalism." In *Deconstruction and the Possibility of Justice*. Edited by Drucilla Cornell. NY: Routledge, 1992.

Rousseau, Jean-Jacques. *On the Social Contract*. 1762. In *Jean-Jacques Rousseau: The Basic Political Writings*. Translated by Donald A. Cress. Indianapolis, IN: Hackett Publishing Company, 1987.

Ryan, Alan. "Hobbes and Individualism." In *Perspectives on Thomas Hobbes*. Edited by Rogers and Ryan. Oxford: Oxford UP, 1988.

Sarte, Jean-Paul. *Being and Nothingness*. 1943. Translated by Hazel E. Barnes. New York: Washington Square Press, 1992.

Sartre, Jean-Paul. *No Exit*. 1943. In *No Exit and Three Other Plays*. NY: Vintage International, 1976.

Slomp, Gabriella. *Thomas Hobbes and the Political Philosophy of Glory*. New York: Macmillian Press, Ltd., 2000.

Smith, Gregory Bruce. *Nietzsche, Heidegger, and the Transition to Postmodernity*. Chicago: University of Chicago Press, 1996.

Soble, Alan. *Sexual Investigations*. New York: New York University Press, 1996.

Spector, Jack J. *The Aesthetics of Freud*. New York: McGraw-Hill, 1972.

Stirner, Max. "The State and the Sacred." In *The Anarchist Reader*. Edited by George Woodcock. Atlantic Highlands, NY: The Harvester Press Limited, 1977.

Sullivan, Kathleen. "Under a Watchful Eye: Incursions on Personal Privacy." In *The War on our Preedoms: Civil Liberties in an Age of Terrorism*. Edited by Richard C. Leone and Greg Anrig, Jr. New York: The Century Foundation, 2003.

Treaty of Principles Governing the Activities of States in the Exploration and Use of Outer Space, including the Moon and Other Celestial Bodies. 27 January 1967. http://www.state.gov/t/ac/trt/5181.htm.

Tuck, Richard. *Hobbes*. New York: Oxford University Press, 1989.

United Nations Convention on the Law of the Sea. 10 December 1982. http://www.un.org/Depts/los/convention_agreements/texts/unclos/closindx.htm.

United States Army. "Oaths of Enlistment and Oaths of Office." Last Updated 27 July 2004. http://www.army.mil/cmh-pg/faq/oaths.htm.

United States Constitution. http://www.house.gov/Constitution/Constitution.html.

USA Patriot Act of 2001. http://thomas.loc.gov/cgi-bin/query/D?c107:4:./temp/~c107ej5p39::.

Walter, E.V. "Power and Violence." *American Political Science Review* (June 1964): 350-360.

Walzer, Michael. *Spheres of Justice*. New York: Basic Books, 1983.

Wilde, Oscar. "Disobedience: Man's Original Virtue." In *The Anarchist Reader*. Edited by George Woodcock. Atlantic Highlands, NY: The Harvester Press Limited, 1977.

Williams, Linda. *Nietzsche's Mirror: The World as Will to Power*. Lanham, Maryland: Rowman and Littlefield, 2001.

Williams, Michael. "Hobbes and International Relations: A Reconsideration." *International Organization* (Spring 1996): 213-236.

Yablon, Charles M. "Forms." In *Deconstruction and the Possibility of Justice.* Edited by Drucilla Cornell. NY: Routledge, 1992.

Žižek, Slavoj. *Welcome to the Desert of the Real*. London: Verso Press, 2002.

Index

About the Author

Rick Parrish is an Assistant Professor of Political Science at West Texas A&M University in Canyon, Texas. He received his Ph.D. from the University of Wisconsin-Madison in 2004, while teaching at Loyola University New Orleans. Rick's research focuses on questions of violence and justice in contemporary and comparative political thought, as well as on the philosophy of Thomas Hobbes. His next project compares themes of language, law, and power in Hobbes and Confucius.